2-11-16

AUG   2015

CYCLE OF FEAR

LEON T. GOLDSMITH

Cycle of Fear

Syria's Alawites in War and Peace

HURST & COMPANY, LONDON

First published in the United Kingdom in 2015 by
C. Hurst & Co. (Publishers) Ltd.,
41 Great Russell Street, London, WC1B 3PL
© Leon T. Goldsmith, 2015
All rights reserved.
Printed in India

Distributed in the United States, Canada and Latin America by
Oxford University Press, 198 Madison Avenue, New York, NY 10016,
United States of America

A Cataloguing-in-Publication data record for this book is
available from the British Library.

9781849044684 *hardback*

This book is printed using paper from registered sustainable
and managed sources.

www.hurstpublishers.com

We are all Syrians

نحن كلنا سوريون *

For S.K.G.

CONTENTS

CONTENTS

LIST OF FIGURES

Map 1. Syria (Northern Bilad al-Sham)

Source: Andrew Lonie, 2011.

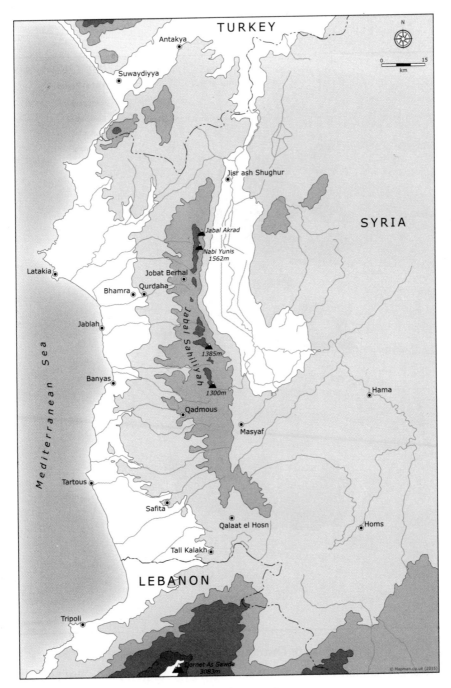

Map 2. North West Syria

Source: Andrew Lonie, 2011.

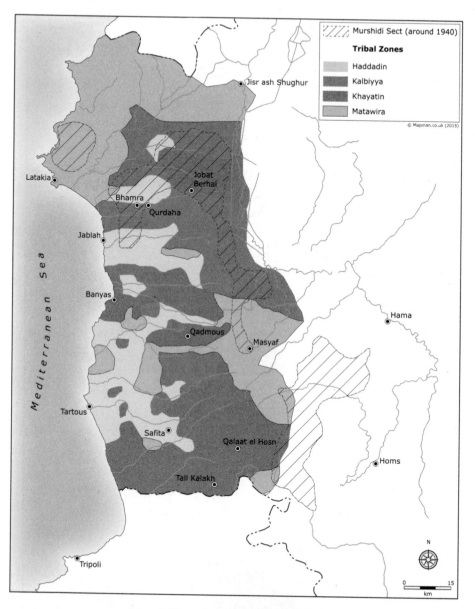

Map 3: Distribution of Alawite Tribes
Sources: De Planhol, 1997, p. 87; Weulersse, 1940, Andrew Lonie, 2011.

ACKNOWLEDGEMENTS

I started studying Syria's Alawites in 2007 as a postgraduate student at the University of Otago's Politics Department in New Zealand. For four years I strove to understand one of the world's most unknown communities and an equally opaque regime; this book is the end result. I hope it sheds some much-needed light on the subject. It was a privilege to get to know something of the Syrian people, whom I admire greatly. Syrians are a gracious, hospitable and courageous people whose potential has long been caged by fear and insecurity. I extend my sincere gratitude to all those in Syria, Lebanon and Turkey who assisted my research in some way but who, for now, must remain anonymous for security reasons. I am totally indebted to Professor William Harris for his wise mentoring, tireless efforts in securing funding, connecting me with valuable contacts and his infectious enthusiasm for the politics of the Levant. Many thanks must also go to Jean-Luc Payan for giving up so much of his precious time in helping me with my Arabic language.

Many people helped along the way but special thanks are due to the following people who made the book possible: Dr Amer Chaikouni and Ferdinand Payan for their extensive translation work, Andrew Lonie for creating the fantastic maps, Chris Rudd, Nigel Parsons, James Headley and Bernard Reich for wise advice and feedback. Margaret Goldsmith for patiently editing earlier drafts, Caroline and Dermot Byrne for their endless assistance with child minding, Mr Issa Ibrahim and Mr Hiedar al-Hassan for valuable information and feedback on the content of the final drafts, and Murat and Mehmet who facilitated my research in Anatakya.

ACKNOWLEDGEMENTS

Many thanks are due to Abdul Halim Khaddam, Detlev Mehlis, Elie Salem, Nasir Eskiocak, Ali Yeral and Muhammad Boz for giving their time to talk with me. In the publication and editing stages I am grateful to Michael Dwyer at Hurst for pushing the book along and Tim Page for his meticulous editing and feedback. The College of Economics and Political Science of Sultan Qaboos University has been a highly supportive and positive environment in which to complete the book. Financially, the research that led to this book was made possible by a University of Otago Postgraduate Scholarship, with additional funding from the New Zealand Vice-Chancellor's Committee, New Zealand Postgraduate Study Abroad Award, and the University of Otago Humanities Division and Politics Department. Last, but certainly not least, I must thank Sarah Kate Goldsmith, Cian and Madeline for their patience, support and daily inspiration.

Leon Goldsmith   Muscat, August 2014

INTRODUCTION

In the early afternoon of 25 March 2011, anti-government demonstrations broke out in the city of Latakia in coastal north-west Syria, the heartland of the Alawite sect.[1] In the city's main boulevard, protesters hurled projectiles at a towering bronze statue of a man with outstretched hands. The statue, a symbol of political supremacy in Syria, was an image of Hafiz al-Asad, an Alawite who rose from humble, rural origins to rule over Syria for thirty years before passing power to his son, Bashar, in 2000. I was near the boulevard with an Alawite acquaintance from a village in the mountains behind the city. As we moved quickly away from the crowd and the security personnel who were rapidly being deployed, I observed a look of shock and dread in my companion, who had tears pouring down his face. I knew that he, like most Syrians in 2011, was very hard pressed economically and did not benefit greatly from the political system that was being challenged by the protesters. So what was the source of my companion's distress? Was it genuine fondness for the Asad regime, ingrained communal solidarity or sectarian insecurity and fear? Exploring this question is vital for understanding the nature of Alawite politics and their contemporary dilemmas.

Shortly after arriving in Turkey from Latakia in March 2011, I discussed the anti-regime protests in Syria with prominent members of Antakya's Arab-Alawite community.[2] One religious community leader (shaykh) clearly demonstrated Alawite anxieties about the nature of the protests and the intentions of Syria's Sunni Muslim majority:

For us there is no difference between Sunni, Shi'a, Alawite and Jews. There is no difference—it's the will of God ... for us there is no problem. But for the Sunnis there

1

are problems … The Sunnis don't like the Alawites … the Sunni only like the Sunni. You tell them this one is Alawite and they will tell you he is not a Muslim. [Now] the people of the Sunna profess that [Bashar al-Asad] does not treat everyone the same way and because he is Alawite they don't want him.[3]

This perspective clearly showed the insecurity of Alawites with regard to the Sunni community and implied that the uprising was about religion and perceptions of sectarianism. Another Alawite shaykh demonstrated a different interpretation of the protests as a non-sectarian push for democratic political change, which nonetheless carried grave risks:

[The crisis in Syria] is not between communities but people want liberty and freedom [and] a decent life. We [the Alawites] hope from God the merciful that there is neither danger for the Alawites or for the Sunnis … we pray from God that the Arab people move toward freedom and democracy without killing each other and without spilling blood. [There is] need for rapprochement, for dialogue, entente and discussion, not fighting and misunderstanding.[4]

Whether or not the political upheaval in 2011 could be translated into a new pluralist political trajectory, advantageous to the diverse demographic make-up of the Syrian state and possibly the wider Levant, was in the balance. Fear was a critical variable in the equation, in particular the insecurity of religious minorities regarding the Sunni Muslim majority who had historically dominated state and society in Syria before the rise of the Ba'th regime in 1963.

Fear is a basic element of human nature and a fundamental factor governing our constant return to conflict, whether at the level of individuals or states. Sometimes, though, people awaken to the way that fear controls them and their potential to reach better futures. In the first months of the Syrian uprising, which began in the southern city of Dera'a in mid-March 2011, peaceful protesters throughout the country challenged the 'wall of fear' composed of a powerful state security apparatus and the unresolved insecurities and suspicions between ethno-religious communities. The common protest chant in 2011, 'wahid, wahid wahid, al sha'ab al Suri wahid' (one, one, one, the Syrian people are one) invoked a diverse unity and sought to counter the centrifugal forces of ethno-religious insecurity and efforts to exploit it for political ends.[5] The community most vital to this outreach were the Alawites. As the largest of the country's religious minorities and the most influential community in the state security apparatus, the question of the Alawites' ongoing loyalty to the regime was a significant factor in where the events of early 2011 would lead.

By mid-2014 the crisis in Syria had reached levels of human tragedy comparable to some of the worst horrors of the twentieth century. Over 190,000 people had been killed, millions were displaced, the Syrian economy and state infrastructure were in disarray and the country was locked in a vicious civil war that threatened to divide Syrian society around ethnic and religious identities. Despite the dire situation it is important to consider the Syrian revolution as an opportunity to break a long-standing cycle of fear between religious communities that holds back the emergence of genuine political pluralism in Syria.

For many Alawites, the Asad regime symbolised their rise to equality in Syrian society after centuries of marginalisation and periodic persecution, usually by Sunni Muslim powers. The inauguration of Bashar al-Asad's father, Hafiz al-Asad, as Syrian president on 12 March 1971 indeed marked an extraordinary rise for an Alawite, long one of the most disadvantaged minorities in the Middle East. For the following four decades Syria was ruled by the Asad family dynasty, which Bashar al-Asad inherited in June 2000. The Alawite community formed a key pillar of Asad rule through its heavy involvement in the state institutions and security apparatus. Yet despite a period of improvement under Hafiz al-Asad, ultimately, the Asad regime has not delivered significant advances in the social status or living standards of the great majority of Syrian Alawites who are subject to the same political repression and socio-economic challenges as most Syrians. Furthermore, the radically secular Ba'th regime tried to strip Alawites of much of their unique religious identity, which they had preserved against the odds for centuries. Why then did the Alawites assist in the establishment and maintenance of the Asad dynasty? And why do many Alawites defend it fiercely as the Syrian uprising, ever more tragically, continues in 2014?

The purpose of this book is to follow the path of Alawite history to that pivotal moment at the start of the Syrian revolution in early 2011 and to give a deeper perspective of the dilemmas facing the community at that juncture. It seeks to illustrate an important example of how fear affects the political behaviour of ethno-religious minorities, influences their support for authoritarian regimes and leads to recurring conflict and social dislocation.

For the North African thinker Ibn Khaldun (1332–1406 CE), history appeared to be cyclical with recurring patterns of war and peace, and rising and collapsing states and dynasties.[6] On 10 January 1401, Ibn Khaldun met the great Mongol conqueror Timurlane before the gates of Damascus, the city that would become the seat of the Asad dynasty.[7] The meeting was a defining moment for Ibn Khaldun, who saw in Timurlane and his warriors the embodiment of his theory for the rise and fall of dynasties based on their command of 'group feeling'.[8] The Arabic term Ibn Khaldun used for this type of solidarity was 'asabiyya, which was the key element in his theory that only rural tribes with high levels of solidarity have the potential to capture or create states or dynasties.[9] According to Khaldun, once a dynasty is established the supporting group's 'asabiyya erodes as urbanisation, luxury and corruption gradually lead to the dynasty becoming detached from its group, a process that accelerates as the dynasty moves into subsequent generations.[10]

Ibn Khaldun's experience of Syria was mainly restricted to the long-settled urban centres of Jerusalem, Damascus and Aleppo. It is understandable, therefore, why he wrote that tribes capable of strong 'asabiyya no longer existed in Syria.[11] Fewer than 200 kilometres to the north of where Khaldun and Timurlane were meeting, however, the Alawites resided in the coastal mountains of north-western Syria, with a distinct religion and a strong, albeit unruly, tribal structure.

A critical moment in the development of the Alawites' group feeling occurred in 1305, when they were designated as heretics and enemies of Islam by the well-known Sunni jurist Ahmed ibn Taymiyya (1263–1328), a figure whose memory is cursed by Alawites to this day. Described by one Alawite religious leader as 'corrupted, a liar and a miscreant',[12] it was largely due to Ibn Taymiyya's negative categorisation of the Alawites that they suffered periodic persecution and social marginalisation throughout much of Mamluk and Ottoman imperial rule (1250–1918 CE). This legacy of repression firmed Alawite self-reliance and particularism, in a way that fits Ibn Khaldun's definition of 'asabiyya, except, for the Alawites, it was a sectarian rather than a tribal or social ʿasabiyya. Hence in 1971, when an Alawite named Hafiz al-Asad captured power in Damascus and founded an 'unlikely'[13] dynasty in modern Syria, it was with the help of his community's sectarian ʿasabiyya.

In Chapter 3 of his famous book *Al-Muqaddimah* (Introduction to History) Ibn Khaldun advanced a theory about the factors that affect group solidarity and the implications for the rise and fall of states.[14] Ibn Khaldun measured the political dynamics of mainly tribal, sub-state groups in terms of their level of group feeling, group consciousness or solidarity.[15] To Ibn Khaldun, only a group with high levels of solidarity is capable of giving rise to a dynasty, but then the group feeling gradually declines and the dynasty becomes weak and vulnerable.[16] While this theory can help explain the rise of the Asad dynasty, its resilience, four years into a sustained uprising, can be better understood by also considering the role of sectarian insecurity in preventing a serious decline of Alawite support for the Asad dynasty.[17]

A central concept of this book is that adding sectarian insecurity to Ibn Khaldun's theory reveals a 'cycle of fear' that has shaped Alawite identity and political behaviour, which on balance has resulted in negative outcomes for the sect's security and integration in the Levant over the longer term. Security dilemma theory explains ethno-religious conflict as a consequence of political and security vacuums following the collapse of overarching state structures.[18] This explanation of ethno-religious conflict can also be usefully read alongside Ibn Khaldun's ideas about group solidarity. The combination of solidarity and insecurity produces the ingredients for identity-based conflict, which can help explain other contemporary trends in global politics, such as ethnic tensions undermining Ukrainian stability in 2014 or the rising phenomenon of far-right nationalist politics in Europe in the twenty-first century. Most importantly, conceptualising a cycle of fear helps explain why some groups remain loyal to political structures after the broad legitimacy of regimes appears to be beyond restoration, as seemed to be the case for the Syrian regime in 2011–14.

Sectarian solidarity and insecurity is often caused by collective memories of persecution, discrimination and prejudices due to lack of knowledge about the intentions and true character of other sects. A common effect of insecurity is that diverse states with weak institutions struggle to achieve genuine political pluralism, are prone to the consolidation of authoritarian rule and repeatedly descend into conflict. The political outlook of the Alawites was shaped, more than anything else, by a general deficit of security and periodic persecution at the hands of Sunni Muslim authorities over the course of their history. Insecurity has consequently been the defining feature of Alawite politics and was the main factor in the development of their 'group feeling'. To a large degree it was this Alawite solidarity that explains the establishment, consolidation and resilience of the Asad regime.

It has been suggested that sectarian bonds are not enough to maintain group loyalties to regimes over the long term, which 'necessarily involves selective distribution of privileges'.[19] This book proposes that political support built on sectarian insecurity is more resilient than social-patronage support structures. Very few Alawites are disproportionately privileged in Syria today, yet their loyalty to the Asad regime remains largely intact.

The Faces of the Alawite Sect

Like any religious group, Syria's Alawites should not be reduced to one-dimensional ethno-sectarian terms, while an exhaustive taxonomy for the sect's many faces is also difficult. To be 'Alawi' can mean many things to different members of the sect. Syrian Alawites have multiple sources of overlapping and crosscutting identities as Muslims, Shi'ites, Arabs and Syrians. They are split between urbanites and rural peasants, coastal (*Sahel*) or interior (*Dakhel*) territorial identities, tribal loyalties and socio-economic and religious/class divisions.

Demographically, Syria's Alawites are part of the broader Arab Alawite community of approximately 4 million people[20] who mostly live in the north-eastern arc of the Mediterranean littoral, between northern Lebanon and the Cilician Plain in Turkey. The Syrian Alawites are easily the largest of the Alawite populations, comprising 12 to 15 per cent of the Syrian population, or approximately 3 million people.[21] The Alawites are concentrated in north-western Syria, with major populations in Latakia and Tartous. There are also significant Alawite populations in Damascus, Homs and Hama. Much of the Alawite community, however, remains resident in numerous small villages in and around the Jabal al-Sahiliyah (coastal mountains).

The Syrian Alawite community is divided among four main tribal confederations, the Khayatin, Matawira, Haddadin and the Kalbiyya to which the Asad family belongs. Each of these confederations contains several sub-tribes. The Khayatin tribes are concentrated in the south of the Jabal al-Sahiliyah and around the Kabir River that follows the Lebanese border. The Matawira are numerous to the north and east of Latakia, extending to the Turkish border in the north and in the south around Masyaf. The Haddadin, traditionally the most influential of the tribal confederations before the rise of the Asads, are predominant in the coastal regions around Tartous, Banyas, Jablah and Latakia. Finally, the Kalbiyya tribes centre on the Asad hometown of Qurdaha and the Jablah, Haffa and Latakia districts.[22] Another branch of the Alawite sect is the Murshidiyya, who branched off as a sub-sect in the 1920s.[23] The largest proportion of the sect, however, has no tribal or sub-sectarian affiliation, a feature that is likely to have increased into the modern era where up to a third of the sect has no particular tribal sub-identity (see Table 1).

Table 1: Tribal Demography of Syria's Alawites

Confederation	Pop. 1930 ~	1959	1970	2011
Kalbiyya	50,700	79,156	108,800 ~	480,000 ~
Khayatin	42,700	79,113	108,800 ~	480,000 ~
Haddadin	49,600	91,962	125,800 ~	560,000 ~
Matawira	46,200	94,421	129,200 ~	570,000 ~
No tribe/unknown	24,670	150,348	204,000 ~	900,000 ~
Total	213,870	495,000 (1960)	680,000	3,000,000 ~

Sources: Gubser, 1979; Winckler, 2009; EJ Brill, 1927 (~ denotes estimate).

The Alawites are often considered an extremist (*ghulat*) break-away group from Shi'a Islam;[24] however, they consider themselves a legitimate school within Twelver Shi'a Islam.[25] Their principal point of difference from the Twelver Shi'a is their elevation of the fourth caliph, 'Ali ibn Abi Talib, and his descendants, the Imams of *Ahl al-Bayt* (People of the House of the Prophet Muhammad), to near divine status.[26] This aspect of Alawite religion is the main reason they have been accused of heresy by orthodox Sunnis and extremism (*ghulaw*) by orthodox Twelver Shi'a Muslims.[27] In general, Alawite religious beliefs are highly syncretistic, containing elements from Christianity and paganism along with a belief in metempsychosis (transmigration of the soul after death).[28] Alawites are relatively liberal in interpreting the role of religion in their daily lives. Alcohol is permitted and Alawite women are not required to wear headscarves and can associate freely in public. Alawites have traditionally not been required to pray in mosques, believing that expression of faith is a personal act. Instead, shrines of Alawite 'saints' and holy men act as focal points for Alawite religious devotion.[29]

The religious structure of the sect is divided between a class of 'shaykhs' and a class of 'commons'. This class system differs from other class structures that distinguish between superiors and inferiors in society, and instead relates to different functions within Alawite society for dealing with religious or secular matters. Historically, shaykhs tend to derive from specific families; however, talented individuals from among the commons are occasionally elevated into the shaykhly class in acknowledgment of their exemplary knowledge and faith. Ideally, an Alawite shaykh should be fluent in the Arabic language, know the Quran by heart and be knowledgeable about its many interpretations, especially those regarding the line of Shi'a Imams, from Ali ibn Abi Talib and his descendants up to the Twelfth Imam. Alawite shaykhs should also be cultured in poetry, literature and ancient philosophy.

A primary problem for the Alawites for most of their history has been the outward mysteriousness of their religious identity. This ambiguity has confused observers and produced suspicion among political authorities for centuries. As a consequence, the academic literature on the religion of the Alawites remains limited[30] and often polemic.[31] Alawites are understandably sensitive about how their religion is portrayed. When I asked the Alawite Shaykh Muhammad Boz for permission to publish the contents of an interview with him, he agreed but urged me to emphasise that 'the Alawites love God, we love all the prophets: Muhammad, Jesus, Moses, all are the same, [we make] no discrimination between Sunnis, Christians, or

Jews'.[32] This book does not claim to resolve theological questions around the Alawite religion;[33] nonetheless, the fact that confusion has long existed about the nature of Alawite religious identity is an important factor in understanding their sectarian insecurity.

The social structure of the Alawite community has been influenced most by their political and religious marginalisation in the Muslim world, which excluded them from urban areas. Since the end of the eleventh century the sect was predominantly rural and poor. The main division in the community up to the twentieth century was between the peasants of the coastal and inland plains[34] and the mountaineers of the Jabal al-Sahiliyah.[35] The former were mostly indentured labour to Sunni landlords, whereas the Alawite mountaineers were strongly tribalistic and fiercely independent.[36] Overall, the community was essentially egalitarian with little vertical class stratification. Some opportunistic Alawites did rise up socio-economically to become notables or feudal-style lords (*muqaddams*). They often became rich by collecting taxes on behalf of the political authorities of the time, became private landowners and pragmatically switched allegiances according to prevailing power structures.

Traditionally, Alawites tend to keep a level of separation between religion, politics and society. This can be traced to the basic nature of the Alawite religious doctrine which applies Gnostic reason and philosophy as a path to faith. In addition, the rural nature of Alawite society depended on the equal participation of men and women in cultivation and farming. The agricultural occupations of Alawites before the modern period also meant that most ordinary Alawites, apart from shaykhs, were not well educated.

However, for a long time the Alawite community was deeply divided by strong loyalties to localised tribal groups, which kept the community fragmented and incoherent. The diffuse structure of the community is shown by their erratic tribal distribution, which was a result of the precipitous and discontinuous topography of the Jabal al-Sahiliyah. Tribal groupings were often more related to strategic alliances and personal interests than simple blood relations. This explains why the heads of two different tribes may have originally been brothers or cousins. Despite the tribal divisions, each tribe's traditional shaykhs and religious leaders would usually share a basic commonality of habits, customs and faith.

New educational opportunities from the early twentieth century onwards meant that a new class of educated Alawites emerged who went on to join the Syrian middle class as skilled workers and professionals. This class began to engage in politics and participated in various political and ideological movements during the period of Syria's emergence as an independent state in the first half of the twentieth century. The Alawite community's traditionally poor rural condition, egalitarian social structure and history of religious discrimination meant that many Alawites' ideological inclination was towards Arab nationalism, secularism and socialism.[37] This explains the popularity of the Ba'th Party among Alawites from the mid-1950s.

The emergence of Hafiz al-Asad's regime in the 1970s brought the first signs of major class division in the community as his Kalbiyya tribe benefited disproportionately to other tribes. Although only a general rule, Alawite elites have tended to belong to the Asads' Kalbiyya tribe or the Haddadin tribe of Hafiz al-Asad's wife, Anisa. Alawite urbanisation accelerated greatly in the 1970s, although most maintained a dual existence between the metropolitan centres and their home villages. Therefore, for most Alawites, any social/ideological impact of urbanisation was offset by the retention of strong rural ties.

From the 1990s, and particularly after 2000 with Bashar al-Asad's ascension to the presidency, the Alawite community started to become more stratified in terms of class and ideology. Many of the children of the Alawite political elite grew up in a privileged urban environment, were educated abroad and lost touch with the rural, socialist and egalitarian character of the rest of the community.[38] Bashar al-Asad himself typified this new generation of elite Alawites and began implementing neoliberal economic reforms, which had the effect of enlarging social/class division within the Alawite community.

While specific knowledge of their religion may have dwindled among many Alawites, from the 1970s sectarian affiliation became the strongest source of commonality for Alawites who had previously been divided along tribal lines.[39] So while disparities in ideology, wealth and status undoubtedly emerged over time among the Alawite community, the Asad regime, as Alawites, remained connected to the rest of their community who look to the regime to provide their security.

INTRODUCTION

The 2011 Syrian revolution threatened to bring down the political system that had brought the Alawites out of social and political marginalisation and allowed some of them to rise to the peak of power. Many Alawites feared a return to second-class status, or worse a violent retribution by a revanchist Sunni Muslim majority. It seemed as though the cycle of history had once more turned for the Alawites who had experienced persecution many times over throughout their 1,100-year history. But was the Syrian revolution the latest and gravest threat to the Alawites? Or was it in fact an historic opportunity to break their cycle of fear and achieve secure coexistence in the diverse social mosaic of the Levant? In order to understand how the Syrian Alawites arrived at this critical juncture the following chapters examine the course of Alawite political history. Using Ibn Khaldun's ideas around group solidarity and a cyclical history as reference points, the book follows a chronological structure from the origins of the sect to the start of the Syrian revolution in 2011.

1

ORIGINS

From its very beginning Alawite history contained episodes of persecution by political and religious authorities that shaped the community's identity of particularism, self-reliance and insecurity. But there were also long periods when the sect enjoyed relative security and interaction with wider society. Somehow these periods always gave way to renewed conflict and persecution. This regular return to conflict can be viewed as a result of mutual negative perceptions by both hegemonic powers and the Alawites. The Mamluks and the Ottomans, especially, were highly suspicious of Alawite loyalty to their empires and, equally, the Alawites never felt secure enough to seek genuine integration or to reveal their real beliefs and identity.

During the millennium from their beginnings in ninth-century Abbasid Iraq to the start of the Ottoman decline in Syria from the 1830s, the Alawites evolved from a small, urban-based religious sect in Iraq to an isolated tribal society in the mountains of north-west Syria. Other factors in the Alawite political evolution were their transformation from a diffuse minority to a compact minority,[1] limited economic opportunities caused by the inhospitable physical environment in their mountain refuge and social factors such as legal and religious discrimination.

Between 850 and 1070, the Alawites developed into a unique off-shoot of Shi'a Islam and were present in the main cities of Iraq and, from the tenth century, Syria. During this period the religious doctrines of the Alawites were formulated by the central figures of Alawite tradition,

Muhammad ibn Nusayr (d. 873 or 883), Husayn ibn Hamdan al-Khasībī (d. 956–57 or 969) and Abu Qasim al-Tabarani (d. 1034/5). The followers of these individuals were largely drawn from the middle class, and included theologians and intellectuals from the urban areas of the Middle East.

The broad political context of this early period was chaotic. The Abbasids were struggling to maintain their authority,[2] Islam was fragmenting into distinct sects with political overtones and the caliphate was under pressure from a resurgent Byzantium in the north. In this environment the Alawites received political support from influential Shi'a benefactors, first in Iraq and then in Syria. The resurgence of Sunni orthodox power, with the arrival of the Sunni Seljuk Turks towards the end of the eleventh century, left the Alawites without political support in the interior of the Levant, and they were forced to relocate. The community found refuge in the 'no-man's land' that existed until the 1080s, between Byzantine forces on the Levantine coast and the Sunni Seljuk forces in the interior.

The process of relocation, which saw the sect transform from an urban community to a rural, tribally structured peasantry with little political relevance or support, was largely complete by the end of the eleventh century. Thereafter the Alawites, after merging with existing rural populations, were limited to the mountainous region of north-western Syria. The geopolitical division of the Levant caused by the arrival of the Crusaders allowed the Alawites the chance to consolidate in their new territory. This 'breathing space' helped them to survive when Sunni hegemony resumed over the Levant after the Crusader withdrawal in the late thirteenth century.

For seven centuries the Alawites merely survived, developing a unique social and religious identity in their inhospitable mountain refuge. The Alawites remained marginalised until Sunni imperial rule in the Levant finally began to wane in the nineteenth century. Ironically, it was perhaps their downtrodden state and political irrelevance that was a major reason for their survival.[3]

Foundations of the Sect

Early Alawite history is difficult to portray accurately as it is necessary to distinguish factual, mythical and misleading accounts of events. Most of the credible work on the early history of the Alawites has focused on theology and pays little attention to the political characteristics of the early community.[4]

It is generally accepted that the history of the Alawites began with the career of the eponym of the sect, Muhammad Ibn Nusayr (d.883 or 873) in Iraq in the middle of the ninth century.[5] Ibn Nusayr's activities can be viewed as a part of the Iraqi Ghulat (literally exaggerators) movement that began in eighth-century Kufa in Iraq.[6] At its most basic level the Ghulat represented a movement that deified the fourth caliph 'Ali ibn Abi Talib and his descendants.[7] This movement is considered extreme by the Shi'a and often heretical by orthodox Sunnis.

The Ghulat movement occurred within the context of the political fragmentation of Islam in the seventh century. The Prophet Muhammad had predicted that his community would splinter into seventy-two (or seventy-three) sects.[8] The main branch of Islam that the Ghulat extended from was the Shi'a, or partisans of 'Ali, who began crystallising into a distinct religio-political movement from the time of Caliph Uthman (r.644–56).[9] The separation between the two main branches of Islam, the Shi'a and the Sunnis, was mostly a political separation based on a disagreement over how the leaders of the Muslim community should be chosen. The Shi'a believed that the leader should come from the family of the Prophet (ahl al-bayt), whereas the Sunnis believed in the appointment of a 'rightly guided' successor (caliph). The Ghulat took this separation to another level with their elevation to near divinity of Prophet Muhammad's first cousin and son-in-law, 'Ali ibn Abi Talib. The individual attributed with instigating this movement is Ibn Sa'ba, a Jewish Yemeni convert to Islam who publicly declared 'Ali as 'divine' during the caliphate of 'Ali ibn Abi Talib (r.656–61).[10]

The Ghulat interpretation of Islam would have been problematic for the political and religious authorities of this time as it challenged the authority of the temporal caliphate. The Ghulat were not, however, universally considered radical in their early years, as they were representative of the syncretism of the new ideas of Islam with established traditions, and were relatively well tolerated.[11] It was only from the beginning of the Abbasid caliphate (750) that the Ghulat began practising taqiyya (dissimulation) and kept their beliefs secret in order to avoid persecution.[12] This tradition of religious dissimulation continued throughout Alawite history up to the present. While this approach was important for the survival of the sect in its early stages, over time it would add to the lack of understanding about the group, which would contribute to the pattern of recurring conflict with major powers and other religious groups.

The founder of the sect, Muhammad ibn Nusayr, was a charismatic theologian and mystical figure in the mid-ninth century. He was a member of the Shi'a Banū Numayr tribe, settled near the Euphrates in Iraq and allied to the Banū Taghlib tribe, who would form the core of the Hamdanid dynasty (c.890–c.1005) of northern Syria in the tenth century.[13] Ibn Nusayr rose to prominence when he declared himself the *Bab* (door) to the divinity of the Shi'a Imams around 850. Alawite adherence to Ibn Nusayr's claim was confirmed by the Alawite Shaykh Nasīr Eskiocak who said, 'Muhammad Ibn Nusayr is in Alawite belief, the *Bab* (door) and helper of the eleventh Imam of *Ahl al-Bayt*, Al-Hasan al-'Askarī …'[14]

It was a combination of Nusayr's colourful personality and his tribal affiliations that gained him a following in Iraq in the mid-ninth century. To his supporters he was 'a charismatic leader with supernatural powers'.[15] It was also probably Nusayr's personal qualities that allowed him to achieve close contacts with the tenth and eleventh Shi'a Imams, 'Ali al-Hādī (d.868) and Hasan al-'Askarī (d.873).[16]

An Alawite tradition regarding Nusayr's relations with the eleventh Imam al-'Askarī gives an insight into his purported association with the Shi'a Imams and also the mystique that Ibn Nusayr cultivated:

A delegation of Persian horsemen paid a visit to Hasan al-'Askarī, they found him dressed all in green, surrounded by green mats and pillows, and next to him Ibn Nusayr, also clad in green … the Imam then ordered them to present their requests and to set forth what they had with them. Each took out a dinar and offered it to the Imam. The Imam then directed Ibn Nusayr to sign the coins and return them to their owners … And behold, on one side of each coin was written: 'There is no God but Hasan al-'Askarī, his *ism* [name] Muhammad and his *bab* [door] Abu Shu'ayb Muhammad b. Nusayr b. Bakri al-Numayri, whoever says otherwise is lying.'[17]

This narrative places early Alawite tradition alongside the key figures of Shi'a Islam. It also signals their views regarding the divinity of the descendants of 'Ali and that the *bab*, Ibn Nusayr, was the gateway to this divinity.

It is unclear exactly what influence Nusayr exerted over the Shi'a Imams, but as the Imams were given only limited symbolic religious and political authority by the Abbasids, any influence could only have been minimal. For example, a meeting is reported to have occurred between Ibn Nusayr and the Imam al-Hādī around 850 concerning the excavation of the sacred site of Imam Husayn at Karbala by the Abbasids.[18] The subsequent destruction of the site by the Caliph al-Mutawakkil (r.847–861),[19] despite the Imam's efforts, illustrates Ibn Nusayr and al-Hādī's lack of influence. It seems that Ibn Nusayr's links with the Shi'a Imams mainly lent him rhetorical opportunities. Nonetheless, he exploited these opportunities to create a mystical image of himself that he used to attract a following.

The community that built up around Ibn Nusayr numbered ten direct disciples. These were most likely the leaders of a larger community that was based within the tribal group, the Banū Numayr, and it was this association that provides an explanation for the sect's survival within a hostile environment.[20] The basis of the Banū Numayr's support for Nusayr and his followers is uncertain. It may have been based on support for his religious revelations. It is more likely, however, that it was based on tribal solidarity. The fact that the Banū Numayr's close allies, the Banū Taghlib (later the Hamdanids), retained a strict adherence to orthodox Imami Shi'ism would support this conclusion.

The very first manifestation of the modern Alawites was contained within this marginal community. It was arguably brought into existence by the sheer fact of Ibn Nusayr's personality; its survival was ensured by the support of Nusayr's powerful tribal links and by an association with the last living Shi'a Imams. Yet Ibn Nusayr was a controversial figure who made enemies among both the Shi'a and Sunni religious establishments. He was subsequently discredited and 'cursed' by some of the Shi'a leadership for his claim to mystical links with the Imams and was accused of 'immoral behaviour', which led to his condemnation and exclusion from the Shi'a community.[21] In Alawite belief, the discrediting of Ibn Nusayr deprived him of his rightful place in the Shi'a religious tradition. According to the Shaykh Nasīr Eskiocak, 'There was a group of people who attacked the Lord Muhammad ibn Nusayr. They attacked him to lower him and to lower the future that was reserved for him. They accused him … without any foundation—lies.'[22] To the Alawites, therefore, this 'treachery' was the first example of their community's mistreatment and marginalisation in politics and religion. In Alawite thinking, the deprivation of Ibn Nusayr of his rightful status was the first act in a long history of Alawites being denied their rightful status as 'true believers'.

Ibn Nusayr played a key role in the creation of the new sect, but the group struggled to gain ground in the period following his death (873 or 883).[23] The two leaders that followed Ibn Nusayr: Ibn Jundab, about whom very little is known, and then Abu Muhammad Abdallah al-Jannan al Junbulani (849–900), kept the group alive but did not to make any clear advances. It was not until the emergence of Abū 'Abdallah al-Husayn ibn Hamdan al-Khasībī (b. 873) from Junbula in southern Iraq as the leader of the sect around 926 that the group began to flourish and to develop a distinct identity.[24] 'Al Khasibi came from a family of Shi'a scholars who had been closely connected to the Shi'a Imam Al Askari, and was himself a gifted student. It was after coming into contact with Abdallah al-Jannan that Al Khasibi took up the study of Ibn Nusaryr's mystical teachings.[25]

In the early tenth century the tenuous political situation for Ghulat groups like the Alawites in Abbasid Iraq continued. Al-Khasībī was imprisoned at some stage between 926 and 945, but he eventually escaped and fled to Syria.[26] There is a story told of how an emanation of Jesus Christ came to al-Khasībī while in prison and that this was his reason for migrating to Syria rather than Persia.[27] There is little information regarding the Iraqi branch of the Alawites after the mid-tenth century, although they possibly retained a centre up to the Mongol destruction of Baghdad in 1258.[28] From the time of al-Khasībī's migration, however, Syria was the centre of gravity for the Alawites.

The Alawites' gradual reduction to the Jabal al-Sahiliyah took place over the course of the tenth and eleventh centuries. This relocation marked an important transformation for the Alawites. In Abbasid Iraq they were a small, marginal group attached to the Shi'a branch of Islam, influenced by Persian cultural activity.[29] With the group's relocation to Syria they moved out of this sphere and into a region with a large Christian population and a fractured geopolitical environment shaped by the Muslim–Byzantine struggle.[30] Syria constituted a very different environment. In this diverse political and physical landscape there would be opportunities for the Alawites to manoeuvre between competing powers and to seek security and integration in Levantine society.

Golden Period

Alawite migration to Syria was propelled by persecution, which engendered a sense of insecurity for the Alawites and led to hostility between the community and the Sunni religious and political authorities.[31] Following Al-Khasībī's departure from Baghdad, however, the Alawite sect experienced a 'golden period' of relative security and social integration in Syria, which was split between the Shi'a Hamdanids and the Christian Byzantines. The first Alawite community established in Syria by al-Khasībī was in Harran, a city in northern Syria, now Turkey, which was populated by philosophers, astronomers and the Sabean sect.[32] Many of the pagan aspects of Alawite tradition have been attributed to the interaction with this city.[33] Politically, this city was peripheral and was more or less a last lingering remnant of antiquity in a reclusive corner of the medieval Middle East.

It was al-Khasībī's arrival in Aleppo at the Hamdanid court of Sayf al-Dawla (d. 967) that more significantly marked the group's arrival in Syria. In order to ingratiate himself with the Shi'ite Hamdanids, al-Khasībī emphasised his orthodox Imami credentials, essentially exercising a politically pragmatic taqiyya. In order to achieve political support, al-Khasībī had to maintain two distinct identities, that of Imami scholar and that of leader of the Alawite sect.[34] There is little evidence to suggest that the Hamdanids empathised with or endorsed the particular religious doctrines of the Alawites.[35] The suggestion that there was a major religious differentiation between Sayf al-Dawla and the group led by al-Khasībī is not accepted by Alawites, however. According to Shaykh Eskiocak, al-Khasībī was the leader of a legitimate 'school' of Shi'a Islam, in the same way as there are Maliki, Hanbali, Hanafi and Shafi'i schools in Sunni Islam.[36] Either way, it is clear that the period of Hamdanid rule in Aleppo (945–1005)[37] coincided with the first real period of Alawite consolidation and integration in what was a golden period for the community.

The Alawite association with the Hamdanids, and in particular with the Emir Sayf al-Dawla, was the group's first contact with political power in

Syria. The support of the Hamdanids was essentially an extension of the tribal support the Alawites received from the Banū Numayr and their allies the Banū Taghlib (now the Hamdanids) in Iraq. The Alawites at this time basically fell under the umbrella of the tribal 'asabiyya of the Hamdanids. Overall, while only a relatively small religious movement, the group was well tolerated and operated freely. These conditions meant that there was little impetus for the development of a separate sectarian 'asabiyya along Khaldunian lines.

Hamdanid support provided a window for al-Khasībī to advance the sect. He was a prolific writer and it was during his time in Aleppo that he canonised the Alawite religious doctrines that proliferated across northern Syria.[38] By the time of al-Khasībī's death in 969 the sect had branches in Aleppo, Harran, Beirut, Tiberius and Tripoli.[39]

The Hamdanid dynasty suffered setbacks in 962, the first of which occurred when Aleppo was sacked by the Byzantines, who temporarily forced Sayf al-Dawla out of the city.[40] The effect of the Byzantine resurgence on Alawite activities in Syria is not entirely clear. It is likely that the community would have been of little consequence to the Byzantines, who turned northern Syria into a tributary buffer state.[41] The lack of a strong Muslim state in northern Syria after the 960s was, however, not completely negative for the Alawites, who spent this period consolidating the body of literature compiled by al-Khasībī.[42]

It is noteworthy that the resumption of strong Muslim authority in Aleppo proved detrimental for the Alawites. According to Friedman, their activities were strongly curtailed when the Imami Mirdasids came to power in Aleppo in 1025[43] (or 1023).[44] The Alawites are reported to have 'cursed' the Mirdasids, which suggests that the new dynasty actively repressed Alawites.[45] From this point on the sect ceased to have solid political support in the interior of the Levant.

The next important figure for the Alawites was Abu Sa'id Maymun b. Qasim al-Tabarani who came from Tiberius in the late tenth century.[46] Al-Tabarani's importance lay in his standardisation of the rituals necessary for a working religion for general consumption.[47] In addition, it was most likely he who pioneered the Alawite migration into the Jabal al-Sahiliyah (literally coastal mountains), a move that possibly saved the sect from destruction. After moving to Aleppo at the age of eighteen, al-Tabarani is reported to have left again due to the turbulence of that city.[48] Exactly where al-Tabarani first migrated is uncertain, although for a long time it was generally agreed that he migrated from Aleppo to Latakia on the Mediterranean coast.[49] He can be placed in Tripoli around 1007–8[50] and it seems he moved into the rural mountainous areas inland and south of Latakia (but not to the town itself) at some stage between this time and his death in 1034–5.[51] Al-Tabarani's reasons for heading north into the far less favourable mountains of northern Syria were most likely twofold: one, the mountains behind Beirut, Tripoli and Tiberius were already well populated. The second possible reason was the support the sect retained from a local Shi'a family, the Banū Muhriz, who owned a fortress, the Balātunos, in the Jabal al-Sahiliyah near Latakia.[52] This fortress was ceded to the Byzantines around 1030,[53] and thus it might be cautiously concluded that al-Tabarani's migration actually occurred before 1030.

Al-Tabarani and his followers are likely to have been responsible for beginning a process of conversion in the rural hinterland of Latakia, which paved the way for the rest of the group. It is almost certain that the arrival of the Sunni Seljuk Turks in the Levant from 1070 proved disastrous for the remaining Alawites in Aleppo and the interior of the Levant.[54] The Seljuk defeat of the Byzantine army at Manzikert in 1071 dramatically altered the strategic balance of the Levant in favour of a new vigorous Sunni ascendency. The Seljuks sought to achieve religious unity in Bilad al-Sham, which marginalised the Alawites, most of whom fled to the refuge of the Jabal al-Sahiliyah. The survival of the group at this point can partly be attributed to fate. If the Seljuk Turks had decided to consolidate their power in northern Syria immediately rather than turning back into Anatolia,[55] then the Alawite flight into the mountains may have not been enough to save them. There was approximately a fifteen-year gap between the Seljuk conquest of the interior of the Levant and their return in the 1080s to eliminate the Byzantine presence on the Syrian coast. This small window, combined with al-Tabarani's earlier pioneering in the Jabal, gave the Alawites enough opportunity to become established in the mountain before Sunni hegemony enveloped the entire Levant.

For the Alawites, the cycle of setbacks in the face of Sunni political power continued and the group was again pushed further on to the periphery of the Islamic world. By this time Alawite enmity for Sunni Muslims had become an official part of their religious discourse. Al-Tabarani, for example, wrote about the *dawlat al-didd* (demonic rule) of the Sunnis and of the Alawites' eventual liberation from Sunni persecution.[56] The golden period was over.

With the exception of remnant communities in Harran and Iraq, the Alawite retreat to the coastal mountains of northern Syria completed their transformation from a diffuse community, with tribal links, to what French scholar Xavier de Planhol terms a 'Montagne Refugee' community.[57] This consistent regression into rural isolation and the pattern of persecution by Sunni Muslim powers planted the Alawite cultural trait of sectarian insecurity and potential for a strong 'asabiyya.

Becoming Ibna' al-Jabal (Sons of the Mountain)

In the period from the late eleventh century until the consolidation of Mamluk rule in Syria in the late fourteenth century, the Alawites carved out a new existence in their mountain refuge. While the early period saw the sect's religious identity formulated, the long period of isolation in the physically unfavourable Jabal al-Sahiliyah played the major role in the formation of the group's socio-economic and cultural identity.[58]

The Alawite mountain refuge, while deficient in economic potential, was strategically favourable and did provide reasonable defence against efforts to extinguish or subvert them.[59] Moreover, the relative insignificance of the Alawites to the major political events of the period ultimately worked in their favour. In contrast, the more assertive Ismailis' (also known as the Assassins) and Armenian attempts at political autonomy were abruptly curtailed by the major powers.[60]

The mountains of northern Syria were very sparsely populated until the eleventh century.[61] By the late eleventh century there were only two settlements of any size in the Jabal al-Sahiliyah, both Christian, located in the mountain range: in the south at Safita and Jabal Helou, and in the north at Nahr al-Kabir, both of which had been there since antiquity.[62] This lack of population may have partly been due to the relocation of Christian Mardaite mountain tribes in the late seventh century.[63] In any case, the inhospitable physical characteristics of these mountains were not attractive for settlement by any but those seeking refuge.

In general, the populations that existed in the marginal areas of north-western Syria were heterodox and dissident Christian and Shi'a groups.[64] The Christians, especially, retained a considerable presence in rural Syria despite the increased pace of Muslim conversions that occurred in the first century of Abbasid rule (750–850).[65] Batatu suggests that the bulk of Syrian peasants were Christian right up until the late thirteenth century.[66] This is particularly likely to have been the case in the inaccessible mountainous areas. The Christian populations that survived the Muslim conquests were then buoyed by the reinsertion of Byzantine power in the Levant between 963 and 1025.[67] The Christianity that persisted among the peasants of Syria was of a traditional and superstitious character, including a belief in charms, magic and miracles.[68] Rustic Christians and Shi'ites would therefore have been the kind of communities that the Alawite missionaries would have encountered as they travelled into the mountains in the eleventh century.

The establishment of the Alawites in the coastal mountains of Syria requires further research, as the mechanics of the whole process remain very unclear. The group's small numbers up to their introduction to the Jabal Sahiliyah compared with the relatively large Alawite population (approximately 4 million) in modern times means that conversion must have taken place. Although the Byzantine authorities in Antioch and Latakia would not have tolerated open missionary activity by Alawite mystics in and around the coast and Latakia, it is possible that the marginalised Nestorian Christians[69] and Shi'a peasants may have been open to Alawite conversion.[70] The urban communities of the Levantine coastal towns were already firmly established in their religious affiliation, whether Sunni Muslim or Orthodox Christian, and hence the rural peasants may have been the only available targets for conversion. In addition, the rural peasant groups could be proselytised largely out of view of the Byzantine authorities. Friedman suggests that the urban cells established by al-Khasībī in Syria surrounded rural areas deliberately targeted for conversion by the missionaries of the sect.[71] If it is assumed that some active conversion took place, then this was an important period of demographic expansion for the sect. The Alawite failure to (re)gain an urban foothold in the towns of the Syrian coast was another factor in the Alawite development as an exclusively rural community.

The intervention of the First Crusade in 1097 proved important for the fledgling mountain community. The political re-dislocation of the Levant by the Crusaders provided important breathing space for the Alawite community, now established in the Jabal al-Sahiliyah. The first contact between Europeans and the Alawites may have occurred when the Crusader army advanced south to Latakia from Antioch in May 1098.[72] The Crusader arrival revived the geopolitical dislocation in north-western Syria that had existed previously in the form of the 'Fatimid–Byzantine standoff'.[73] However, where the Byzantines had utilised the Hamdanid state as a buffer on the eastern side of the mountains flanking Antioch and Latakia, the Crusaders took direct possession of the territory surrounding the Alawites.[74] This encirclement insulated the Alawites against the Seljuks. It was within this geopolitical 'cocoon' that the Alawites developed their own society.

In the period following the death of al-Tabarani in 1034 or 1035,[75] the community, in its new mountain refuge, appears to have fractured along political and religious lines.[76] Local chiefs asserted political dominance within small compartments of the mountain, and the community began to become highly tribalistic.[77] It seems paradoxical that the previously geographically dispersed community actually lost cohesion when reduced to a compact minority in the Jabal al-Sahiliyah. Two factors explain this, the first being the lack of strong leadership after al-Tabarani. Yet, and perhaps more importantly, it was the physical characteristics of the Jabal itself that splintered the cohesion of the Alawites and inhibited the emergence of a new, unifying leadership.[78]

The Jabal al-Sahiliyah averages 1,400 metres in height, and consists of a very broken topography with poor continuity between the various parts of the range.[79] Movements of the Arabian plate between the Miocene and the Holocene epochs (between 23 and 11.7 million years ago) resulted in a process of folding, fracturing and faulting, which, combined with erosion over time, led to a very 'hummocky topography'.[80] The range is therefore highly compartmentalised, which hindered communal cohesion.[81] Another characteristic of the Jabal al-Sahiliyah that played heavily on the fate of the

Alawite refugees was the very poor quality of the soil. The ground generally consists of 'poorly cemented soils resulting from weathering of kimberlitic-peridotitic rocks'.[82] From the eleventh century the Alawite settlers and converts were therefore residing in small, disconnected and agriculturally inferior hamlets throughout the ranges.[83] This situation did not change for many centuries. Hanna Batatu noted that in 1930 the average size of Alawite villages was between 100 and 250 inhabitants.[84]

Another factor that contributed to the future underdevelopment of the group was their lack of connectivity with the coast. Alawite isolation was compounded by their exclusion from the coastal strip, 175 kilometres long and 10–20 kilometres wide, which separates the range from the coast.[85] The chance of any external interaction to the west was fully closed when the Sunni Mamluks occupied the coast in the thirteenth century. In the words of Jacque Weulersse, 'their refuge became a prison'.[86] This isolated existence in the Jabal al-Sahiliyah reinforced Alawite particularism, self-reliance and hardiness—all elements that Ibn Khaldun would include as essential for a high-level of 'asabiyya.

While the Alawites were isolated from the outside world, they were also isolated from one another. The rugged, discontinuous topography of the Jabal al-Sahiliyah contributed to the solidification of tribal divisions, and obstructed the formation of a broad sectarian 'asabiyya. Figure 1 exemplifies the hummocky terrain throughout the Jabal al-Sahiliyah.

Disconnection was a feature of the tribal federations. For instance, the Khayatin federation has sub-tribes in both the extreme south and the far north with others interspersed in-between. The other tribal federations became similarly irregular in their distribution. The most geographically compact tribes were the Kalbiyya, who came to be concentrated around Qurdaha and extended inland from Jablah and Latakia.

In general, the geographic distribution of the Alawite tribes highlights the political and social diffusion of the group in their mountain refuge. In addition, the incorporation of rural Christian and Shi'a peasants into the sect is likely to have made for a highly eclectic Alawite religious identity, especially during their early occupation of the Jabal al-Sahiliyah. Although the Alawites had developed rural tribal characteristics, as an overall group they were very fragmented. Ibn Khaldun believed that 'even if a [group]

Figure 1: Alawite Village in the Northern Jabal al-Sahiliyah, August 2009

has many houses there may exist an 'asabiyya that is stronger than all other 'asabiyyas, and in which all 'asabiyyas coalesce'.[87] Although the Alawite community at this stage showed few signs of developing this kind of broad sectarian 'asabiyya, a common feature of insecurity shaped their identity.

At the beginning of the twelfth century the Crusaders were entrenched in their newly erected principalities including and surrounding the Jabal al-Sahiliyah.[88] It does not appear that the Crusaders had a profound or direct impact on the daily lives of the Alawites. In the main the Crusaders coexisted with the various sectarian communities in the mountains of the Levant.[89] The Alawites were most likely of no real consequence to Crusader security in this early period. The Syrian chronicler Bar Hebraeus (1226–1286) recorded that the Crusaders initially killed a number of Alawites (Nusayris), but when they learnt they were not a 'truly Muslim sect, they became tolerant toward them'.[90] Some people have commented on the 'burly' and 'European' physical appearance of many Alawites as an indica-tion that they share ancestry with the Crusaders.[91] It is not altogether unlikely that some intermarriage took place, adding to the already diverse Alawite gene pool.

In the twelfth century the Alawites would have somewhat resembled the Christian population of the Jabal in appearance and, in some ways, their traditions. Interaction among ordinary people of different religions in the medieval Levant, away from the struggles of power politics, was in the main cordial and often actively cooperative. Muslims participated in Christian festivals, and vice versa, simply to be sociable and because the festivals closely followed the seasonal cycle of rural life.[92] Whether the Alawites actively presented themselves as Christians in order to avoid per-secution cannot be known for certain as there are no sources confirming this, yet given the community's previous strategy of presenting themselves as orthodox Shi'a to the Hamdanids it is possible that a similar approach would have been adopted with regard to the Crusaders. However, for the Alawites it would have been more difficult to impersonate Christians than Shi'ites, with whom they share a great deal more religious characteristics.

The Crusader period provided an important opportunity for the Alawites to consolidate their position in the Jabal al-Sahiliyah, and they did not suffer undue persecution. Alawite sectarian insecurity may there-fore have subsided somewhat in this period. In the early twelfth century, however, the Alawites came into competition in the Jabal al-Sahiliyah with another minority sect, the Nizari Shi'a Ismailis from Iran (often referred to as the Assassins).

The Ismailis succeeded in establishing an autonomous state around Qadmus and Masyaf in the southern part of the Jabal al-Sahiliyah in the early part of the twelfth century.[93] The newcomers competed with the Alawites in the mountains for over a century and a half until their demise as a power at the hands of the Mamluks in 1271–3.[94] The Ismaili state could be categorised as a religio-political dynasty founded on sectarian 'asabiyya. The small size of this group and the rigidity of their religious and political structure could also explain the limited extent of the Ismaili state.

The Alawite situation further deteriorated with the Sunni revival in the Levant, which was begun by the Seljuks but interrupted by the Crusaders.

A turning point occurred when the Emir Nūr al-Dīn Mahmūd (1118–1174) won an important battle against the Crusaders at Banyas from 23 July to 21 August 1164.[95] The Alawites were now faced with hostile Sunni forces directly adjacent to their mountain refuge. As the Sunnis were highly suspicious of the role that the heterodox Shi'ite groups played in relation to the Crusaders they monitored the Alawites very closely.[96] As a small and divided minority, faced with a powerful Sunni Muslim majority, the Alawites' situation began to deteriorate once again. The relative autonomy and religious freedom the Crusader presence had afforded the Alawites began to give way to renewed isolation and insecurity.

It is paradoxical that the factor assisting Alawite consolidation—the Crusader intervention—was also the major catalyst for their further religio-political marginalisation. The challenge of the Crusades served as a unifying force for the Muslim world in which Sunni orthodoxy emerged supreme. In addition, the re-designation of the coastal mountains of the Levant as strategically salient in the struggle with the Crusaders meant that the Alawites came into the purview of Sunni strategic calculations.[97] Nūr al-Dīn pursued a 'unified Jihad theory to support the military efforts', which included resisting not only the Crusaders but also suspect Shi'a-oriented groups such as the Alawites,[98] who were viewed as weakening Islamic unity.

The overthrow of the last major Shi'ite political power, the Fatimids in Cairo, by the Ayyubids in 1171 left Sunni Islam as the dominant force in Syria.[99] This was a sustained setback for the political fortunes of the Alawites who were not to see another Shi'a power involved in the Levant until after the 1979 Iranian revolution.[100] The only parts of the Northern Levant not under Sunni control by the end of the twelfth century were the Crusader enclaves of Tyre, Tripoli and Antioch,[101] and the Ismaili enclaves around Qadmus and Masyaf.[102] The Alawites were not without allies, however, in this challenging environment.

The Iraqi prince, Shaykh Abū Muhammad al-Hasan ibn Yūsuf al-Makzun al-Sinjārī (b.1164 or 1168), came to the aid of Alawites in the Jabal al-Sahiliyah around 1220–3.[103] Al-Makzun was a descendant of a contemporary of al-Khasībī in Iraq[104] and, according to Alawite tradition, adhered

to the Alawite religious philosophy.[105] His support to the Alawites, therefore, was a 'throwback' to the early period of Alawite history, which illustrates that this link still featured in their political calculations. According
to an account regarding Shaykh al-Makzun, published in 1972:

In … 1218, Nusayris [Alawites] from the region of Banyas and Latakia sent a letter
to al-Makzun [then the emir of Sinjar in north-west Iraq] asking for help against
their rivals, the Kurds (brought to their region by the Ayyubids and the Ismailis.) It
was a massacre of the Nusayris [Alawites] in the Sahyun fortress during their celebration of Nawrūz that persuaded al-Makzun to intervene. He came from Sinjar with
25,000 of his warriors to fight the Kurds … But he returned to Sinjar in order to
double his forces, and brought 50,000 warriors in 619/1222 … He continued his
battles until the Kurds and the Ismailis fled from the Jabal.[106]

The figures provided in this account are unreliable and unrealistic, which
Friedman admits is due to the lack of original medieval sources.[107]
However, there is documentary evidence to suggest that a migration did
occur from Iraq to Syria around this time. A copy of an Alawite manuscript written in Iraq twenty years before the Mongol invasion in 1258
appeared in Syria around the same time as al-Makzun.[108] This transfer
supports the conclusion that there was a relocation of Alawite sympathisers
from Iraq to Syria in the first half of the thirteenth century.

Al-Makzun was an important figure for the Alawites in the thirteenth
century; his victories buttressed the group against Sunni repression and
other groups such as the Ismailis. Exactly how many of al-Makzun's army
remained in Syria is uncertain; it has been suggested that around 1,000
relocated to the Jablah region, which constituted a major demographic
boost for the sect.[109] Matti Moosa suggests that the Haddadin, Matawira,
Muhaliba, Darawisa, Numaylatiyya and the Banū ʿAli tribes, and sub-
tribes, are all descendants of Makzun's army and followers.[110]

Al-Makzun was important for another reason. According to Friedman, he
arranged a theological debate against the Alawite rivals, the Ishaqiyya (a
dissenting group who were more extreme in their interpretation of the nature
of the divinity of ʿAli ibn Abi Talib), whereupon he 'massacred them and
burned their books'.[111] Thus al-Makzun somewhat ruthlessly succeeded in
eliminating a potential schism in the Alawite community.

Overall, the timing and effect of al-Makzun's intervention was fortunate for the Alawites, and possibly for the followers of al-Makzun. The Mongol 'atom bomb' that hit Baghdad and Iraq shortly afterwards in 1258 would most likely have eliminated any chance of reinforcement for the Alawites from this direction. Although Shaykh al-Makzun was a very important leader for the Alawites and is even credited with mystical religious qualities,[112] he failed to mobilise Alawite 'asabiyya to form a state or dynasty. The lack of cohesion among the Alawites across the Jabal al-Sahiliyah can possibly explain this. The wider geopolitical environment was not conducive to an Alawite dynasty either. There were far more powerful forces with higher 'asabiyya, such as the Mongols. Shaykh al-Makzun al-Sinjari died near Hama on his way back to northern Iraq in 1240.[113]

The famous Mamluk victory at 'Ayn Jālūt in northern Palestine in 1260, against a relatively small Mongol contingent, meant the Mamluks 'inherited' Syria from the Ayyubids, whose rule had been exterminated by the Mongols.[114] The Mamluks were ethnic Turkish slave soldiers from north of the Black Sea, who had established their rule in Cairo from the 1250s. Like the Ayyubids, the Mamluks were devout Sunni Muslims and viewed groups such as the Alawites with suspicion, mostly because of their Shi'a tendencies and acquiescence of the Crusaders. Thus they waged punitive expeditions against the Alawites, as well as the Druze and the Twelver Shi'ites, in the late thirteenth and early fourteenth centuries.[115]

It was the Ismailis, however, that suffered the most severe setbacks. Their main strongholds at Masyaf and Qadmus fell to the Mamluk Sultan Baybars between 1271 and 1273.[116] The Ismailis were effectively paying for their assertiveness, which included an assassination attempt on Salah al-din,[117] openly allying with the Crusaders (at the battle of Inab the Ismailis sided with Raymond of Antioch),[118] and generally trying to maintain their autonomy in the southern reaches of the Jabal al-Sahiliyah. The demise of Ismaili power would have been a boost for the Alawites, who from this time forward were the dominant community based in the Syrian coastal mountains.

It is clear, by way of comparison with the Ismailis, that the Alawites' political future was in fact assisted by their low profile, their less organised structure, their religious ambiguity and their general receptivity to new members.[119] In the meantime, the Alawite sect grew demographically, and firmly established themselves throughout the Jabal al-Sahiliyah.

By the end of the thirteenth century a clear pattern was becoming evident in Alawite history, involving periods of social and political advancement punctuated by episodes of persecution and intolerance, usually by Sunni Muslim powers. The early advances of Muhammad ibn Nusayr and al-Khasībī in Iraq were thwarted by the Abbasid authorities. The consolidation and dissemination of the sect across northern Syria was ended by the Seljuks. The relative autonomy and security enjoyed by the Alawites in the Crusader period was diminished by the Ayyubid victories in the Levant. Moreover, the momentary military protection of Shaykh al-Makzun al-Sinjari was followed by the arrival of the Mamluks. Each time the Alawites were persecuted they were pushed further into the geographic and social periphery of the Muslim world. Each episode of persecution firmed Alawite insecurity, especially with regard to Sunni Muslims. At the outset of Mamluk rule in Syria the option of further retreat and migration was closed. For better or worse, the Alawite community had become *Ibna' al Jabal* (sons of the mountain), and it was here where they would have to survive as a community.[120]

Fatwas and Officialdom

The departure of the Crusaders after 1291 left the Mamluks in control of the Levant, although they continued to face threats from the Mongols to the east of the Euphrates and their Armenian allies to the north.[121] Thus, heterodox groups like the Alawites residing near the northern front remained strategically important to the Mamluks. Following the Mongol capture of Damascus in 1299, the Mamluks looked to shore up their position regarding the 'suspect' mountain communities.[122] They implemented policies such as the resettling of loyal Turcoman soldiers on the coast adjacent to the Jabal al-Sahiliyah in order to monitor the 'threat' posed by the Alawites.[123] The preferred strategy of the Mamluk sultanate, however, was to bolster the economic and social conditions of their border territories.[124] This was fortuitous for the Alawites because, on the Mongol side of the border, the city of Harran previously inhabited by Alawites was completely decimated by the 1270s.[125]

The Mamluks did present a significant challenge to Alawite interests as a military power and an efficient political bureaucracy. *Rawk* (cadastral surveys) were carried out between 1313 and 1325 throughout the Mamluks' Syrian territories to ascertain the nature of the populations.[126] The district of Tripoli, including the Alawites of Jabal al-Sahiliyah, was surveyed in 1317.[127] Subsequently, in November 1317, the Mamluk Sultan al-Nāsir issued an order regarding the Alawites which read:

we outlaw the Nusayrīs' *khitāb*. After the issue of this order they may not perform any kind of *khitāb*. The influentials (*akābir*) and village shaykhs among them should bear witness not to restore their *khitāb*. Those who dare to do it will be punished severely.[128]

The *khitāb* in this context referred to the initiation rites of the Alawite faith.[129] Thus the Mamluk authorities sought to steer the Alawites on to the 'correct' religious path. The Mamluk Sultan Baybars had already ordered the construction of mosques among the Alawite villages and hamlets, which, according to Ibn Battuta, the Alawites used for sheltering live-stock.[130] This order was reasserted following the survey of 1317.[131] For the Alawites, successful implementation of these policies, especially the prohi-bition of the *khitāb*, would effectively mean the termination of their par-ticular community, which had been developing now for nearly five centu-ries. Overall, the Mamluk edicts of 1317 constituted a bureaucratic attack on the existence of the Alawite creed.[132]

Shortly afterwards, on 20 February 1318, an Alawite revolt occurred in the Jablah district.[133] The revolt centred on an individual who assumed the name Muhammad b. al-Hasan al-Mahdi, which in Shi'a terminology refers to the hidden Imam. 'Al-Mahdi', whose real name is not known, came from the village of Qirtiyāwus, somewhere behind Jablah.[134] Al-Mahdi claimed to have received divine guidance/intervention in the form of a white dove.[135] He subsequently gathered 3,000 Alawite peasants, declared the Mamluk sultan in Cairo dead and proceeded to attack the town of Jablah on the coast.[136] Al-Mahdi then proclaimed the Alawites sovereign over the Jablah area.[137] Al-Mahdi is supposed to have declared, 'There remains neither renown (*dhikr*) nor state (*dawla*) among the Muslims. We should therefore rule over the whole land (*bilād*).' In any event, the revolt was easily crushed in five days by 1,000 Mamluk cavalrymen dispatched by the governor of Tripoli. Six hundred of the Alawite insurgents, includ-ing al-Mahdi, were killed in putting down the rebellion.[138]

The causes of this rebellion can be attributed to three factors. First, the land allocation to Turcoman soldier-settlers would have been negative for the Alawites, restricting their access to fertile land. Secondly, the rebels were possibly reacting 'emotionally' against the challenge to the Alawite creed represented by the decrees of the Mamluk sultan.[139] It is very possible that the followers of al-Mahdi genuinely believed that he was the returning Mahdi (the hidden Imam) and followed him for religious reasons.

Taking into account the history of the Alawites to this point, the 'Mahdi' uprising was a departure from the group's previous strategies. Either migration or the judicious application of taqiyya had been the course of action when the group was at risk. The former option was no longer available as they were now territorially restricted in their refuge, yet it is unclear why the Alawites of Jablah did not apply taqiyya and outwardly accept the Mamluk edicts to avoid persecution. Friedman proposes that because the Alawites in the Jablah region were the descendants of Makzun's army, their military tradition contributed to their taking up arms.[140] This hypothesis has some credibility; however, the ease with which 1,000 Mamluk troops defeated 3,000 Alawite insurgents suggests that these descendants of Makzun's army displayed little real military talent or, perhaps, they were simply ill equipped.

The uprising was a localised event that did not garner broader Alawite support. There was no general rising in support of the revolt by Alawites from other parts of the Jabal, although the high number of participants (3,000) in the revolt suggests that it did incorporate a significant proportion of the local Alawites around Jablah. Alawite 'asabiyya was insufficient at this point to achieve a military victory against the powerful Mamluk state, although the subsequent Mamluk response would further increase Alawite insecurity.

The wider Alawite clans were punished for the revolt. According to Ibn Battuta, a punitive attack was carried out by the emir of Tripoli that killed 20,000 Alawites.[141] Battuta's figure is most likely an exaggeration. It is illustrative that it was actually the emir of Tripoli who interceded on behalf of the Alawites when the Mamluk sultan in Cairo ordered their elimination in the wake of the rebellion. The emir transmitted to the sultan that the 'Nusayris [Alawites] were working for the Muslims by ploughing the land, and if they were killed it would weaken the Muslims.'[142] The sultan subsequently spared their lives. This explanation of events fits with the general Mamluk policy of strengthening the communities in its border areas—the Mamluk-Mongol peace treaty was signed in 1323.[143] For their part, the leaders of the Alawite tribes pleaded with the Mamluk authorities to be included with the *ahl al-Kitab* (people of the book—i.e. the tolerated communities of Christians and Jews) and offered to pay the poll tax levied on such groups.[144]

Overall, the 'Mahdi' rebellion of 1318 was the first attempt by the Alawites to assert themselves militarily against a Sunni power. Their complete failure illustrated the futility of attempting such an approach, a conclusion that no doubt influenced the (outwardly) passive conduct of the Alawite tribes in the centuries that followed. The rebellion was an anomaly in Alawite political history to this point, and the Mamluks did not feel compelled to eliminate them. On balance, it seems Alawite economic value outweighed any strategic threat to the Mamluk Sultanate.

Pragmatic Mamluk political and strategic approaches to minority groups were often contradicted by the Sunni religious establishment. By the early fourteenth century, the accumulation of the Crusader and Mongol threats inflamed Sunni religious chauvinism. Another factor in rising religious intolerance was the 'Little Ice Age' of the late thirteenth century, which destroyed harvests and caused famine in both Europe and the Middle East.[145] The Sunni jurist, Taqil-din Ahmad Ibn Taymiyya (d.1328), was the most famous proponent of intolerance for religious heterodoxy.[146] Ibn Taymiyya, who would have a profound impact on the future of the Alawites, came to the Levant from Harran as a refugee from the Mongol campaigns in the 1270s.[147] His flight before the 'godless' Mongols may have played a part in his religious extremism, which even the Mamluk authorities considered problematic.[148] Nevertheless, his three religious rulings, or fatwas, concerning the Alawites played a major part in their future socio-political standing. Ibn Taymiyya delivered his fatwas between 1305 and 1318. The first, sometime around 1305, endorsed Mamluk military expeditions to the Kisrawan region (Lebanon), which killed many Alawites and saw the survivors fleeing north to the Jabal al-Sahiliyah.[149] The timing of the second fatwa is uncertain, but the third occurred in the wake of the Mahdi revolt of 1318.[150]

Fatwas are generally structured as an *istiftā* (question) and a decision (*fatwā*).[151] The opening part of Ibn Taymiyya's first fatwa reveals the main tenets of his theological attack on the Alawites.

Q: What is the view of the noble scholars, the religious leaders, may God help them to reveal the truth about the Nusayriyya that allow drinking wine, believe in metempsychosis, the antiquity of the world, deny the revival, heaven and hell ... according to them God who created the world is Ali ibn Abi Talib ... they have their own initiation ceremony ... Is mixed marriage between them and the Muslims allowed, is it allowed to eat from their slaughter ... may they be buried in the Muslim graveyards or not ... are we allowed to kill them and confiscate their money or not ... is fighting them considered more important than fighting the Tatar [Mongols]?

A: 'Praise be to God the Lord of the Worlds, those people called Nusayris, they and the other kinds of the Batiniyya Qaramita, are more heretical than the Jews and the Christians and even more heretical than many of the polytheists and their harm to Muhammad's community is greater than the harm of the infidel fighters such as the Mongols, the Crusaders, and others. They pretend to be Sh'ia and support *ahl al-Bayt* [family of the Prophet] while in truth they do not believe in God, or in his messenger [i.e. Muhammad] or in his book [i.e. the Quran] ... there are many famous incidents that show their enmity towards Islam and the Muslims ... they killed the pilgrims and threw them in the well of Zamzam, and they once took the Black Stone ... they conquered the land of Egypt and ruled it for two hundred years ... The religious leaders have agreed that intermarriage with them is forbidden and their slaughter [butchered meat product] is not allowed ... it is forbidden to bury them in the Muslim graveyards.[152]

Ibn Taymiyya's fatwa demonstrated Sunni apprehension about weakening Islamic solidarity in the face of the Crusaders and the Mongols, which led to suspicion about the loyalty of heterodox sects. It also indicated a lack of specific knowledge about the Alawites as he lumps them together with other 'deviating' Muslim groups.[153] Moreover, as Friedman has argued, the text of the fatwa suggests that Ibn Taymiyya may actually have the Alawites confused with the Ismailis.[154] The question of whether Ibn Taymiyya was accurately addressing the Alawites specifically is, from a political perspective, only a technicality. As a Sunni fundamentalist, Ibn Taymiyya put heterodox groups into one category: heretics and enemies of Islam. Politically therefore, the importance of Ibn Taymiyya's fatwas lies in the fact that the Alawites were for the first time, in an official capacity, named as outside Islam.[155]

This was a critical moment in Alawite history as it cemented Alawite religious separation and insecurity. If the importance of this event is projected forward for a moment, a considerable paradox emerges: by propelling the development of Alawite sectarian 'asabiyya, Ibn Taymiyya actually contributed to the fate of Syria's twentieth-century Sunni Muslim community, whose political status and interests would suffer relative to the more cohesive Alawites.

From the time of Ibn Taymiyya's fatwas until 1936, the Alawites were considered non-Muslims in most official Sunni jurisprudence. This had the effect of virtually eliminating any chance for Alawite upward social mobility in the religio-political environment that persisted in the Levant until the twentieth century. Even after the end of Sunni imperial rule, the effect of Ibn Taymiyya's fatwas was still felt by Alawites. In 2007 Sunni fundamentalists would cite Ibn Taymiyya and call for the 'physical annihilation' of the Alawites.[156]

The rest of the fourteenth century saw the conclusion of the Mongol–Mamluk war in 1320, and the eventual 'extinguishing' of the Armenian Kingdom to the north in 1375.[157] This consolidation of Mamluk power in the surrounding region meant that the Jabal al-Sahiliyah lost strategic salience. Lack of information regarding the Alawites after the fourteenth century is perhaps explained by this geopolitical shift.[158] Moreover, the legacy of the Mamluk reaction to the 'Mahdi' rebellion of 1318 no doubt kept the Alawites quiet beneath secure Mamluk rule and there is no evidence of any additional major Alawite dissent. The Mongols returned briefly, this time as Muslim converts. Timurlane occupied Damascus in 1401,[159] and Ibn Khaldun conducted his famous meeting with the Mongol conqueror outside the gates of Damascus.[160]

Outside this brief Mongol intervention, Mamluk rule in the Levant, including the Jabal al-Sahiliyah, continued uninterrupted until 1516. Meanwhile the Alawites continued their isolated development, becoming increasingly set in their various tribal configurations, applying taqiyya when necessary and generally trying to carve a livelihood out of their harsh territory. In their isolation the Alawites developed a common identity based around their attachment to the Jabal al-Sahiliyah. To this day Alawites like to be known as *Ibna' al-Jabal* (sons of the mountain).[161] The Alawites have an attachment to the natural features of their territory which for them is 'dense with spiritual symbols'.[162] This aspect of the Alawite creed is absent from the early period when the sect was largely an urban phenomenon that focused on intellectual explanations of religion and philosophy without any need, or opportunity, to develop a territorial identity. The Alawites, now removed from the social life of the 'Islamic cities' of the Middle East,[163] developed instead the characteristics of a community strongly imbued with Ibn Khaldun's 'asabiyya.

To the sedentary urban populations of Syria the Alawites developed a reputation as heretics, renegades and wild men, which was partly due to their detachment and mysteriousness to the bulk of medieval Syrian society. The Syrian Sunni Arab population, who were also subjugated under the Turkish-speaking Mamluk elite, regarded the Alawites with suspicion and often fear. The longer the Alawites remained separated from the rest of the population the more pronounced this alienation became.

Ottoman Rule: Continued Alawite Marginalisation

The Mamluk demise at the hands of the Ottoman Turks from Anatolia in 1516 left the Alawite situation unchanged, and they remained a marginal and despised minority.[164] The new rulers were Sunni Muslim ethnic Turks who emphasised religion as the core identity of their empire, lending legitimacy to their rule.[165] There would be no respite for the Alawites from the change in rulers and their sectarian insecurity remained high, if not heightened.

The new authority, keen to consolidate its power, sought to crack down on suspect groups, including Shi'ites and Alawites. The Ottomans were also concerned about the loyalties of these groups in relation to their major preoccupation, the war with the Shi'ite Safavid Persians.[166] Some sources claim that the Ottoman Sultan Selim I 'the Grim' (1470–1520), after obtaining a fatwa from a Syrian mufti, executed 9,400 Shi'ites in Aleppo after he took the city in August 1516.[167]

The impact of Selim's pogrom for the Alawites is unclear. How many Alawites were resident in Aleppo at this time is impossible to determine;

however, as most of them had migrated to the Jabal al-Sahiliyah in the eleventh and twelfth centuries they were probably few in number. According to Moosa, who admittedly relies on the 'problematic' account of al-Tawil, the Ottoman sultan attempted to exterminate the Alawites in their territory but was thwarted by the mountainous terrain of the Jabal al-Sahiliyah. The Alawites residing in the plains fared worse and were almost entirely displaced.[168] Another problematic report by Moosa suggests that Selim I relocated 'half a million members of Turkish tribes' to the area of the Jabal al-Sahiliyah in order to 'weaken the Nusayris'.[169] This figure is grossly unrealistic as the total population of Syria was only around 2 million at the turn of the sixteenth century.[170]

The inconsistencies in the available details concerning the Alawites at the outset of Ottoman rule in Syria make it difficult to ascertain any real change in their political environment under the new rulers. It is safe to assume that the Alawites did suffer severe setbacks in the early years of Ottoman rule. It would have taken some time for the Ottomans to assess the nature of this group who would, in the meantime, be regarded with extreme suspicion. Like the Mamluks, the Ottomans eventually took a pragmatic approach towards the Alawites.[171] From Alawite perspectives, the Ottomans were very similar to the Mamluks: Turkish-speaking Sunni Muslims who persecuted them whenever they offended Sunni Muslim sensibilities or openly challenged the authority of the state. The main Alawite policy during the Ottoman period in Syria (1516–1918) therefore remained dissimulation. The observation of British traveller Henry Maundrell in 1697 illustrates the ambiguity of Alawite identity during this period:

[The Alawites are] of a strange and singular character. For 'tis their principle to adhere to no certain religion, whatever it be, which is reflected upon them from the persons with whom they happen to converse … Nobody was ever able to discover what shape or standard their consciences are really of. All that is certain concerning them is that they make much and good wine, and are great drinkers.[172]

The combination of Alawite ambiguity, stubborn resistance and their entrenchment in rugged mountains meant that they posed a difficult, time-consuming target for complete subjugation. For both the Mamluks and the Ottomans there were usually far more pressing concerns than campaigns against the peripheral and impoverished Alawite mountain tribes. Moreover, from the mid-seventeenth century the Ottoman Empire felt the strain of maintaining their earlier gains; they faced continual wars throughout the sixteenth to nineteenth centuries with combinations of the Habsburgs, tsarist Russia, Safavid Iran, Venice and Poland. Thus for Istanbul the priority for regions like the northern Levant was peaceful and efficient tax collection.[173]

The Alawites therefore became integrated, somewhat awkwardly, into the Ottoman system of millets and the general economy of the empire.[174] Apart from some minor problems caused by rebellious Alawites in the Latakia region in 1691–2, the Alawites served some purpose and posed no real strategic threat.[175] The tobacco industry was one area where the Alawites developed a role. Despite an attempt to prohibit tobacco as un-Islamic by the Ottoman Sultan Murad IV (r. 1623–40) in 1631,[176] the crop came to be an important revenue source for the empire by the eighteenth century.[177] A manifesto of a Damascus merchant in 1728–9 includes a shipment of tobacco of the Sahilī (coastal) variety from the 'Djebel 'Alawi' region, which was by this time one of the main producers of tobacco in the empire.[178] By 1850, Frederick Walpole noted 3,000 quintals (300,000 pounds) of tobacco were exported annually from Latakia.[179]

By the eighteenth century, Alawites developed a source of revenue from the limited agricultural potential of the mountain. Yet the potential that this trade held for the Alawites to develop economically was obstructed. In 1769 the Ottoman authorities in Aleppo rejected a proposal for a port facility at Suwaydiyya to facilitate external trade. They were concerned about foreign 'privations' and the detrimental effect on the traditional land trade routes through Aleppo.[180] In addition to this obstruction of Alawite commerce, oppressive taxes levied by the Ottoman state on tobacco producers were a major burden. For example, Alawite peasants abandoned their fields in the mountains near Tripoli due to over-taxation on tobacco cultivation.[181] Jacques Weulersse also noted that the main beneficiaries of the tobacco industry in the Latakia region at the end of the nineteenth century were the Sunni merchants in the coastal towns.[182]

The tobacco trade remains important for the Alawites today. The crop is widespread and a source of revenue for many Alawite families. The Syrian government introduced new laws in 2009 restricting tobacco smoking in public places, and banned the felling of Syrian oak, a key component in the production process for Latakia tobacco, both of which harmed ordinary Alawite economics.[183] Considering the long history and importance of the tobacco industry for Alawites, it is ironic that the first anti-smoking legislation in Syria since the decree of Murad IV in 1631 came from a supposedly Alawite regime.

Alawite legal status in the Ottoman social and economic system was ambiguous and caused something of a dilemma for the Ottoman authorities.[184] In the early period of Ottoman rule, at least up to the late sixteenth century, the Alawites had to pay the *dirham al-rijāl*, which was a special head tax levied on the Alawite 'apostates' for their 'heresy'.[185] The dilemma for the Ottomans was that according to 'Islamic law' the Alawites should not have been tolerated at all, in contrast to the Christians and Jews who were acceptable as *ahl al Kitāb* (people of the book). In legal disputes also, technically according to Islamic law, Alawite testimony should not be valid, yet it appears that in most cases their testimony was at least considered.[186] It is noteworthy that the Alawites were an important source of income for the local authorities, making up 73 per cent of the rural tax farms (*muqātaʿa*) in the vicinity of the Jabal al-Sahiliyah.[187] Thus the Ottomans and local authorities often chose to turn a blind eye to the Alawites' problematic religious identity, although the Ottoman state was quick to persecute the Alawites when they transgressed.

The period of the late eighteenth and early nineteenth century was difficult for the Alawites. The Ottoman state was struggling to maintain its authority in its peripheral territories; therefore it was increasingly intolerant of any trouble in its core provinces, especially from lowly Alawite mountaineers. Ottoman contempt for the Alawites was evident in 1783 when the official view of Alawite religion was that it consisted of 'wrong thinking and shallow ideas'.[188] When the Alawite Shaykh Saqar Mahfouz, of the Shemseen clan of the Haddadin around Safita, refused (or was unable) to pay his taxes to the Ottoman authorities in 1806, 3,000 imperial troops were sent against him. The troops are reported to have 'burnt farms, harvests, everything and took innumerable amounts of money from the Nusayris'.[189]

The Alawite situation further deteriorated after the suspected murder by Alawites of a visiting French colonel in 1811. The Ottoman governor of

Tripoli, Suleyman Pasha al-'Adel, waged a five-month campaign against the Alawites, killing and beheading many in the process.[190] This disproportionate reaction no doubt caused anger among the majority of Alawites who had nothing to do with the crime against the French colonel. In 1813, when the Kalbiyya Alawites from Qurdaha protested against Ottoman repression, Suleyman Pasha responded brutally according to the Ottoman chronicles:

[1228/1813:] In this year the people from the Nusayri province of Qurdaha rebelled from their works in Latakia. Mustafa Barber proposed to the emir of Trablus [Tripoli] to send soldiers to fight them and make an example ... [Barber] marched on them and beheaded twenty-seven people and took their heads away. The heads were displayed for three days in Bab Āka, and after that he [the emir of Tripoli] sent the minister to Bab al-'Ali [the Ottoman Imperial Palace in Istanbul]. He [the sultan] gave Barber directions for the province and categorised them for slavery, forced them to return to allegiance. [Thereafter] he left them and sent the soldiers back to their barracks.[191]

It should be noted that the primary Ottoman concern was to maintain firm control and collect taxes; it was the native retainer armies (local Sunni Arabs) involved in these crackdowns, not the Turkish imperial troops, who apparently displayed the greatest religious hatred for the Alawites.[192]

It was probably the combination of these campaigns along with general economic and religious discrimination against Alawites that caused many to migrate north to the Adana province and Suwaydiyya, near Antioch, in the early nineteenth century.[193] The reported Ottoman destruction of orchards and silk trees in Alawite villages would have further propelled emigration from the Jabal al-Sahiliyah.[194] The Alawites who remained in the Jabal al-Sahiliyah, however, became further entrenched in their sectarian insecurity and hostility towards their Sunni antagonists.

The ruthless methods of the waning Ottoman Empire correspond with Ibn Khaldun's hypothesis that the emergence of 'exaggerated harshness' is a symptom of a dynasty in decline.[195] Conversely, rising Alawite 'asabiyya started to become apparent in the Jabal al-Sahiliyah. Alawite strongmen (*maqaddams*) began to achieve significant autonomy and commanded substantial armed followings. The Ottomans often found it necessary to delegate authority informally to some of these maqaddams for tax collection and law enforcement. From the early 1800s Saqar al-Mahmud assumed this role around Safita,[196] and in the late 1820s another Alawite maqaddam, Uthman Khayr from the Matawira tribal confederation, predominated over much of the southern reaches of the Jabal al-Sahiliyah. Uthman Khayr was able to 'mobilise quite formidable forces' and even claimed for himself the title of Bey, a Turkish military title.[197] Uthman's son Ismail would rise to even greater prominence in the 1850s.

Increasing Alawite assertiveness unnerved the Sunnis of Latakia and other coastal towns, sparking renewed religious chauvinism. Hence in the early 1820s the Sunni shaykh, Muhammad Nasīr al-Din al-Mugrabi (d.1827) of Latakia, issued a fatwa, the first against the Alawites since 1516, which according to Samuel Lyde, decreed 'that the lives and property of the Ansaireeh [Alawites] were at the free disposal of the Musulmans'.[198] Shortly afterwards, in 1824, a group of Ottoman soldiers attacked Alawite villages near Latakia, killing thirty to forty men and taking woman and children as slaves.[199]

These harsh reactions against the Alawites in the 1820s came within the context of Ottoman efforts to contain emerging nationalist movements within their empire. In particular, they faced a resilient Greek independence movement in their Balkan provinces. In a repeat of the early Mamluk and Ottoman periods when Alawite loyalty was doubted, the community was suspected of collusion with the Greeks. Hence, despite pragmatic toleration of Alawites during the great part of Ottoman rule, the default view of the Sultanate towards the Alawites was hostility, suspicion and contempt. This attitude is demonstrated in a communiqué to Istanbul regarding the Greek uprising:

In order to achieve the evil and contemptuous deeds which the sinister Greek nation connivingly forces upon the people of Islam, and—through the advocacy of its corrupt thought—to make comply with their principle of collusion and unity, the Druze and Nusayri sects, who have no share in the ornament of Islam and who are perhaps worse than enemy infidels.[200]

Whether the Alawites were actually cooperating with the Greek nationalists is doubtful. Persistent tribal divisions, lack of any central authority and their still negligible level of overall sectarian 'asabiyya meant they would have harboured little impulse for a nationalist struggle like the Greeks.

In Ottoman eyes, it appeared that the Alawites' status and dependability had not improved at all. In fact the Ottoman correspondence shows they still suffered the effects of Ibn Taymiyya's 1305 fatwa. This continuity of marginalisation and segregation from the social mainstream was the primary factor in the development of Alawite insecurity. So long as political authority operated along the lines of Sunni Islamic orthodoxy, the Alawites would continue to be marginalised. In the 1830s this system of rule, dominant throughout the Mamluk and Ottoman eras, would finally receive a major jolt. For the Alawites the cycle of history appeared to take a positive, albeit slow, turn.

2

INTEGRATION

For a one-and-a-half centuries from the 1830s to the 1970s the Alawites appeared to make gradual progress towards integration in wider Syrian society. This was by no means a smooth transition. Local sectarian hostility periodically flared; the Ottoman state continued with its discriminatory policies towards the Alawites, and in the period between the Ottoman collapse in 1918 and Syrian independence in 1946, the French applied strategies of divide and rule to suppress the broadening of Syrian nationalism to the religious minorities. The dynamic and often chaotic politics of independent Syria was nevertheless an environment where Alawites came to believe genuine integration was possible. Overall, the general trajectory of the modern period seemed to lead towards the end of the Alawites' long history of social and geographic isolation in and around the Jabal al-Sahiliyah.

The Alawite sect's path towards integration can be divided into four stages. The first, between 1832 and 1918, saw the decline and collapse of Sunni Ottoman authority in the Levant, which provided opportunities for Alawite assertion in politics and society on a larger scale than previously possible. The second, between 1919 and 1945, was characterised by Alawite involvement in a novel, pluralist political environment in the coastal region in the form of the French-sponsored Alawite State. This was a somewhat artificial situation, however, engineered according to French geopolitical designs in the region. Impending French withdrawal in the late 1930s led to a pragmatic decision by Alawite leaders not to oppose the sect's incorporation into the majority Sunni, independent Syrian state. Then, from 1946 to 1963, Alawites enthusiastically sought involvement in many aspects of Syrian society, including joining the national defence forces. Previously unavailable educational opportunities would also allow Alawites to participate in the political and ideological ferment that came after Syrian independence in 1946. Hence Alawites like the Arab nationalist Zaki al-Arsuzi (1899–1968) played a part in the development of political ideologies suitable for a religiously diverse state.

The final stage of Alawite integration from 1963 to 1971 coincided with the Ba'th party's rise to power, which brought a social revolution that not only benefited disadvantaged rural minorities like the Alawites but forged cross-sectarian social coalitions based on class and ideology. The culmination of this revolutionary period was the elevation to the Syrian presidency of Hafiz al-Asad, an Alawite from humble origins in rural coastal Syria. This seemed to prove to most Alawites that their quest for acceptance in Syrian society had finally succeeded. Beneath the surface, however, growing Alawite assertion began to trigger lingering, mutual suspicions of sectarianism and prejudice that could lead to a renewed cycle of fear.

First Opportunities

In the 1830s the long era of Ottoman ascendency appeared to be coming to a close. Across the empire alternative power centres challenged the central authority of Istanbul. European powers began to intervene deeply in the politics and economics of the Ottoman provinces, including the Levant. In this context of Ottoman fragmentation there was potential for greater Alawite assertion and involvement in Syrian society. The Alawites had existed on the margins for hundreds of years. If given the opportunity, would they look to integrate with wider society, or would they mobilise politically as a sect? By the early nineteenth century Alawite particularism was already very strong at a localised level and tribal 'asabiyyas had already helped Alawite maqaddams carve out semi-autonomous fiefdoms in the Jabal al-Sahiliyah.

INTEGRATION

The conquest of Syria by the viceroy of Egypt, Muhammad 'Ali, in 1832 was a major juncture in Syrian and Alawite history, breaking a 300-year monopoly of power by the Ottoman state. After a successful campaign against the sultan's forces, Muhammad 'Ali's son, Ibrahim Pasha, ruled Syria for nine years until he was finally dislodged with the help of British forces in 1841.

Ibrahim Pasha's objective was to consolidate control of Syria and establish a 'modern' state based on industrialised European models.[1] The achievement of this objective could have been beneficial for Alawites. Many Syrians from all sects, fed up with 'bad' Ottoman rule, were 'thrilled' to hear of the approaching Egyptian army, and even offered support to the invasion.[2] Alawites of the coastal and inland plains, who were mostly indentured peasants to Sunni landlords, welcomed the prospect of change.[3] It was the first secular-leaning political system to be attempted in Syria; a political shift that could have reduced the main Alawite source of insecurity: their inferior social and legal status according to Islamic law. Before long, for instance, Ibrahim Pasha equalised the tax system which had long disadvantaged Alawites.[4]

Fear and suspicion of Egyptian intentions, however, saw this opportunity turn to conflict. Alawite tribes of the Jabal exploited the division in the empire, and some became allies of the sultan, who supplied them with arms to fight the Egyptians.[5] The British naval officer Frederick Walpole, who lived among the Alawites for a time in 1850–1, was told by Alawite leaders on several occasions that their main problem with the rule of Ibrahim Pasha was the heavy-handed attempts by the Egyptians to conscript them.[6] But for this factor, Alawites may not have opposed Egyptian rule so strongly.

A good example of the potential for improved Alawite status under the rule of Ibrahim Pasha occurred when Egyptian troops, learning of the fatwa of Shaykh al-Mugrabi, tried to enslave Alawite women but were immediately ordered to free them by their officers.[7] The Egyptian commanders refused to acknowledge al-Mugrabi's classification of the Alawites as non-Muslims.[8] Admittedly, the Egyptian desire to conscript the Alawites as legitimate Muslim soldiers played a part in this.[9] Nevertheless, Egyptian revision of the sect's legal status was the first major opportunity for Alawites to improve their social status and security.

In the event, many Alawite tribes strongly resisted the Egyptian presence and were highly resistant to attempts by the Egyptian authorities to disarm, conscript them into the army and generally domesticate them within a 'Syrian–Egyptian state'.[10] Resistance peaked in 1834 when Alawite tribesmen attacked Latakia after the Egyptians tried to disarm them, and were repelled only with the assistance of troops from Lebanon under the powerful Bashir al-Shihab II (1767–1850).[11]

In the 1830s the Alawites were still very much a tribal society with loyalties only to their particular maqaddam, their tribe and their families.[12] Moreover, Alawite insecurity was such that they were disinclined to trust anyone outside their own creed. While the Egyptian intervention in Syria was the first opening in the Alawites' long history of isolation and discrimination, Alawite defiance helped ensure that the opportunity for an improvement in their social status and security was lost. This was an example of sectarian insecurity impeding the potential emergence of a more pluralist state.

Regardless of Alawite resistance, Muhammad 'Ali's Syrian project was doomed. Britain, the industrialising superpower of the time, was not prepared to let Ottoman power collapse further and intervened to defeat Ibrahim Pasha in 1840/1, reinstalling the Ottomans in Syria.[13] With the outbreak of the British–Egyptian war, Alawites, whom Ibrahim Pasha had succeeded in partially disarming, took the opportunity to rearm.

It was a weakened Ottoman state that returned to the Levant. This emboldened some Alawite maqaddams, strengthened by the weapons they had acquired during the 1830s.[14] In 1851 Frederick Walpole observed, 'The mountaineers are armed; it remains to be seen what they will do.'[15] What followed was a chaotic situation in the Jabal al-Sahiliyah as various Alawite clans fought for ascendancy. Out of this environment emerged Ismail Khayr Bey, the son of 'Uthman Khayr Bey, the first Alawite leader with the potential to mobilise Alawite 'asabiyya.

Ismail Bin 'Uthman Bin Khayr Bin Ismail Bin Kin'an Bin Haydar al-Sinjari (1822–58) came from al-Lukbah village in the district of Hama, and inherited his father's claim to the rank of Bey. His rise coincided with the start of the Crimean war between the Ottomans and tsarist Russia in 1853. The war greatly strained the capacity of the Ottomans in the Levant, which Ismail Khayr Bey took advantage of to establish dominance in the district of Safita among the Haddadin and Khayatin tribes. Powerless at that moment to restrain him, the Ottomans took the radical step of appointing the Alawite strongman governor of the Jabal al-Sahiliyah (Mushir al-Jabal).[16]

This Alawite maqaddam was now governing a population of 120,000 residents of the mountain, excluding its northern part, but including Christians and many Sunni Muslims.[17] This was an unprecedented situation in the politics of the area, which was greeted with dismay by many local Sunni Arabs who refused to accept governance by a 'heretic'. The view of the local Christians towards Ismail Khayr Bey seems to have been less hostile. Among Alawites, Ismail was an inspiration and he managed for a time to unite many of the clans under his leadership, although it is also argued he exploited his position to enrich himself and his followers by ruthlessly extracting revenue from the population under his governance.[18] Ismail Khayr was reported to have engaged in great cruelty; to punish 'rebellious subjects' he was said to have 'burned out their eyes, cut off their ears and noses, and flayed them alive'.[19]

In late 1858 the Ottomans decided to terminate Ismail Khayr's power. The American missionary Henry Jessup, who was resident in Syria for fifty-three years, said the Ottomans turned on Ismail because he was 'not a Moslem and will not pay bribes enough to the government'.[20] But it is certain that the Ottomans already knew (or thought) he was not Muslim, when they pronounced him Mushir al-Jabal. It is likely Jessup was partly correct in thinking the Ottomans turned on Ismail Khayr due to his failure to pass on taxes (or bribes, as he called them). However, the Ottomans were also concerned about increasing Alawite unity as Ismail Khayr began to establish his dominance.[21] While the Alawites fought among themselves and were divided they were no real threat to Ottoman authority. A correspondent to Henry Jessup wrote in 1858, 'It is well for the Sultan's government that these wild denizens … expend their strength in fighting each other than in rebelling against the government.'[22] However, the best explanation for the Ottoman decision to depose Ismail Khayr Bey is that by 1858 the Crimean war had been concluded positively for the Ottomans and they were in a better position to wrest back full control of the

Levantine provinces. Ismail Khayr Bey had served his purpose during a difficult period by providing a semblance of Ottoman control as their appointed Mushir al-Jabal. Now his authority needed to be extinguished.

The Ottoman methods of deposing Ismail Khayr were to arouse the local Sunni Muslims to jihad against the Alawite 'heretic', along with the dispatch of newly available imperial troops. This reminded Alawites that their religious status was at the mercy of arbitrary decisions by the Sunni authority. There were major skirmishes between the warriors of Ismail Khayr and the Ottomans but the Ottomans ultimately prevailed by exploiting Alawite divisions. Other Alawite clans, which Ismail had never fully trusted, began deserting him.[23] Ismail's demise eventually came at the hands of his maternal uncle, 'Ali al-Shila, who shot him (and his son) at the village of Ain Keroom, and handed his head over to the Ottomans.[24]

The demise of Ismail Khayr Bey ended a promising period for the Alawites, who had established some limited autonomy and greater cohesion during his short rule. The Ottomans took the opportunity to re-establish their authority by force in the Jabal and sought to break up the momentary Alawite solidarity.[25] According to another contemporary observer, Reverend Samuel Lyde, in 1859 'the government was engaged in burning villages ... and murders had been committed with the connivance of government officials ... as it is the [Alawite] population must decrease instead of increasing'.[26] For Alawites today, this dreadful period may serve as a reminder of the consequences of a resurgent Sunni power in their territory after a period of Alawite rule.

Although Ismail Khayr Bey was the first Alawite to hold official political authority on a large scale, there were some other notable examples of Alawites achieving high positions. Mehmed Pasha, an Alawite from Latakia, joined the Ottoman janissary corps in the early nineteenth century, was promoted to *agha* (commander) of the corps in 1811 and made governor of Tripoli in 1823/4.[27] The local Sunni populace reacted negatively, however, denouncing him as a tyrant and a Nusayri. He was killed, along with several of his family, in Latakia shortly after his appointment.[28] Alawites still recalled this event many years later. In 1851 Frederick Walpole was told by the Alawite shaykh, Shemseen Sultan, 'We had a Nusayri Pasha once, they thought him a Turk, but directly they knew really what he was, they killed him.'[29] Another prominent example was Kara Mehmed Pasha, ostensibly of Alawite origins, who rose to the rank of grand admiral of the Ottoman navy and then governor of Ankara and Çankırı in the nineteenth century.[30] In the case of Mehmed Pasha, it was ultimately impossible to conceal his origins in the eyes of the Sunni Arabs of his home region. Whereas these individuals are not mentioned in Alawite sources, Ismail Khayr Bey, whose rise occurred within the territory of the Alawites, is seen as an important figure.[31]

The geopolitical rupture in the Levant caused by the Egyptian intervention and then the Crimean War had provided the Alawites with a small window of opportunity to assert themselves politically, interact with other communities and to broaden their social and political horizons. The Ottomans, with the help of Western powers, firmly closed this opportunity. The ability of the Ottomans to exploit tribal divisions in the Jabal al-Sahiliyah illustrated continued Alawite political dislocation in the mid-nineteenth century. An entirely different geopolitical environment would be required for the Alawites to begin a sustained transition out of isolation.

Saving Alawite Souls

The Egyptian intervention convinced the Ottomans of the need to modernise and reform the empire; this led to the introduction of the Tanzimat (literally, reorganisation) reforms from 1839. Stefan Winter suggests that 'in the Tanzimat and especially the Hamidian periods ... the Sublime Porte [began] to perceive the Nusayris as ... citizens to be educated and as wayward believers to be reconfigured'.[32] This policy towards the Alawites resembled that of the Mamluks in the early fourteenth century. The Tanzimat reforms never really delivered any tangible benefits for Alawites, however. In fact, the years from the middle of the nineteenth century to the beginning of the French Mandate were some of the hardest years economically for the Alawites. It was during this period that Alawites supposedly began selling their daughters as servants to wealthy urban Sunnis as a means of alleviating crippling poverty.[33]

The Ottomans did not seem to be interested in changing their governance style in the Alawite territory. In the 1860s, the governor of Hama,

Kamil Pasha, noticed the popularity among the Alawites of an American missionary named Dr R.J. Dodds, who would ride his donkey unescorted in the Jabal al-Sahiliyah. In contrast, the governor commented that 'he could not go through the mountains unless attended by 100 soldiers'. This gave the governor pause and, according to Jessup, he requested the permission of the sultan to try a new governance approach towards the 'wild Nusairiyeh and win them instead of alienating them'. To this Istanbul sent instruction to 'oppress and tax them as of old'.[34] Whether or not this account is entirely accurate, history shows that the Ottomans never really changed their uncompromising approach towards the Alawites.

Another significant event for Alawite politics, related to Western Christian activity, was the conversion of the Alawite, Suleiman Effendi al-Adhani (b.1834), to Protestantism in 1862. Al-Adhani, who was already initiated in the secrets of the Alawite faith, came to the missionary Henry Jessup in Beirut and proceeded to disclose secrets of the Alawite religion, a grave offence in the eyes of their religious hierarchy. Jessup's description of al-Adhani portrays a talented yet somewhat irrational individual who was prone to drunkenness.[35] Nonetheless, many of the details that he gave on Alawite religion, all from memory, proved consistent with otherwise obtained knowledge about Alawite religious beliefs.[36]

In 1862–3 Suleiman Effendi completed and published a book on Alawite religion, entitled *al-Bakura al-sulaymaniya fi kashf asrar al-diyanat al-nusayriya,*[37] excerpts of which were translated into English under the title, 'First Ripe Fruit, Disclosing the Mysteries of the Nusairian Religion'.[38] This book was widely read in Syria as the first available exposé of Alawite religion, long a mystery to most Syrians. Among Alawites, however, the book caused great alarm and many shaykhs called for the traitor's immediate assassination.[39] This 'necessary' punishment was postponed until some years later when Suleiman Effendi visited his home region of Adana, whereupon, according to Henry Jessup, the Alawite religious leaders had him 'buried alive'. Jessup claims to have confirmed this version of events during a trip to Adana in 1888.[40]

In 1850 the British traveller James Fletcher observed that the Alawites 'cultivate in their inaccessible retreats a mysterious and unknown worship'.[41] The consequence of Suleiman Effendi's disclosures in 1862 was that

Alawite religion was no longer so 'mysterious', which limited the effectiveness of taqiyya. In short, the Alawite ability to remain outwardly 'ambiguous' in terms of their religious identity was reduced.

American Protestant missions to Syria played an important part in Alawite history in the late Ottoman Empire.[42] The American Protestant missions were the closest the Alawites came to enjoying a foreign benefactor, something that most other Levant minorities enjoyed. The Maronites, for example, were supported by the French, and the Druze enjoyed British support.[43] In contrast to other foreign missions, and perhaps to the Alawites' misfortune, the Protestant missionaries came solely with evangelising rather than political intentions.[44] Genuine evangelistic fervour was evident in Reverend William Thomson's 1835 request for a mission station to be opened at Latakia to undertake work among the Alawites:

Will not every friend of man, and more especially every true Christian, rejoice that a people so awfully sunk and degraded by ignorance and vice, have at length come up in remembrance before the church. Without any known religion, without either schools or books, intensely hated by every Christian they have seen, and trampled into the dust by their Moslem lords, literally no man caring for their souls, nor even cherishing compassion for their bodies, thus poor and miserable, hated and oppressed, ignorant and vicious, they carry as strong an appeal to the ear and the heart of the church as any people on earth.[45]

Thomson's plea presents a somewhat condescending but tragic view of Alawite conditions under Ottoman rule. It was not until 1857, however, that the American missionaries began their work among the Alawites.[46] In all, twenty-five schools were established in and around the Jabal al-Sahiliyah,[47] and a total of 153 American Protestant missionaries (including families) were sent to Syria.[48] It seems, however, that the Alawites were not particularly prone to Protestant conversion;[49] in the Kalbiyya village of B'hamra, for example, the missionary school succeeded in (temporarily) converting seven students.[50] Yet there was potential for the missionary schools to advance Alawite education, which was sadly lacking.[51] The Ottomans responded to the threat of Protestant proselytising and in 1874 shut down all twenty-five schools in the Alawite region.[52] The Ottomans clearly did not want an enlarged Christian population in their Levant provinces but more importantly remained convinced that the Alawites could be reconfigured into 'proper' Muslims.[53] They seemed unaware of the possibility that Alawites despised orthodox Sunni Islam, a sentiment accumulated over many centuries of persecution.

For the best part of forty years, the Protestant missions and the Ottomans competed to convert the Alawites to Christianity or Sunni Islam. By the 1890s neither had succeeded, either in a religious or educational sense. As Yvette Talhamy has noted, this highlighted the Alawites' 'ethno-religious particularism'.[54] While Alawite identity remained strong and resistant to conversion at the close of the nineteenth century, this did not preclude the possibility that Alawites sought greater integration and acceptance in a pluralist Syrian society.

New Horizons

The Ottoman decision to join the Central Powers in World War I was the beginning of the end for the Ottoman Empire. For the Alawites it was the prelude to the eclipse of Sunni imperial rule, almost constant since the late thirteenth century. This presented an unprecedented opportunity for the Alawites to escape from their long period of social, economic and religious marginalisation.

The first opportunity for Alawite assertion existed during the war years (1914–18). Alawite military potential evident from the exploits of Ismail Khayr Bey did not, however, materialise into any significant armed uprising against the Ottoman forces, although there may have been some small guerrilla operations.[55] It is possible that the forceful re-imposition of Ottoman control in the Jabal after 1858 had weakened some of the Alawite tribes. Yet it is more likely that Alawites, similarly to the Crusader period, chose to remain neutral and not to expose themselves unnecessarily. A pragmatic policy of 'wait and see' may have been the prevailing view in the Jabal al-Sahiliyah.

The pitiful circumstances of the Christian Maronites of Mount Lebanon, who suffered famine during the war, were not experienced to the same extent by the Alawites to the north.[56] The reasons for this are not well documented. Ottoman suspicion about Maronite allegiances partly explains their poor treatment,[57] though the reliability of the Alawites would surely have come under Ottoman scrutiny as well. The Tanzimat hope of 'reconfiguring' the Alawites as Sunni Muslims may have lingered. In contrast to 1858, the Ottoman proclamation of jihad in November 1914 was not directed against the Alawites.[58] Overall, there is no evidence of any major crackdown against the Alawites during the war years; the Ottomans possibly wished to avoid provoking any reaction from the Alawite tribes.

The Allies, on the other hand, viewed the minorities of the northern Levant coast as potential allies against the Ottomans. The French had an intelligence station on Arwad Island, near Tartous, during the war, and landed thirteen agents on the northern Levant coast at various locations in order to gather intelligence on the local populations and the Ottoman forces.[59] These sources, plus information from a Lebanese Maronite informant, Antoine Eddè, had the French Quai d'Orsay convinced that up to 148,000 local militiamen, including Christians, Shi'ites and the Alawites of the Jabal al-Sahiliyah, were ready to rise up in support of an Allied invasion.[60] As it happened, no such invasion took place on this part of the coast so it can only be speculated whether such an uprising would have occurred. Ironically, it was only after the war, when the French began penetrating the coast in 1918, that the Alawites took up arms.

The exit of Sunni imperial rule and its replacement by Western colonial rule in the Alawite territory was a pivotal moment in Alawite history. The political equation changed dramatically both in terms of the situation of the various communities and the physical parameters of the contested political space. The Sunni Arabs of the region had long been the beneficiaries of political and military support from Sunni Muslim empires in Cairo or Istanbul. In post-Ottoman Syria the Sunni Arabs remained the great majority; however, they were now forced to negotiate their interests from a far weaker position. Sunni Arabs had, on the whole, taken a passive role in military and political matters in Syria since the Abbasid caliphate. In contrast, minorities like the Alawites, Druze and Ismailis began to assert their interests.

The breakdown of the diverse Ottoman Empire led to competition among the various communities to protect their security and interests. The strong 'asabiyya of the religious minorities would eventually prove politically advantageous for individuals seeking to establish themselves in powerful positions. Of these groups, the Alawites were by far the largest. In 1914, what would become modern Syria was home to 175,000–200,000 Alawites, the Druze were approximately 50,000 and the Ismailis numbered 12,000–15,000.[61] The scaling down of the political arena to a truncated Syrian state meant the scaling up of the smaller actors in terms of their relative ability to negotiate their interests. For the Alawites, the breakdown of Sunni imperial rule essentially provided the opportunity to coalesce the 'asabiyya that they had hitherto possessed only in small pockets in the mountain.

It is difficult to imagine the mindset of the Alawite tribes as they witnessed the downfall of a geopolitical order that had been intact more or less since 1291. Beneath Sunni imperial rule Alawite goals had been simple: maintain as much autonomy as possible, preserve their identity and customs in the face of Sunni hegemony and generally seek security and subsistence within their delimited tribal groups. The situation in 1918 would, therefore, have seemed like peering into the unknown. According to the historian Keith Watenpaugh, the collapse of Ottoman rule led to a dilemma for its former subjects, 'who are we and where do we belong, or rather, of which whole do we belong?'[62] Then a novel event occurred. The Alawites were asked what their political preference was, a question they seemed unable to answer.

The US King–Crane Commission (1919) set out to canvas the Levant populations on their political wishes in the post-Ottoman era. The conclusions for Syria were: the 'Moslims' wanted American or British assistance for Arab rule from Damascus, the Druze supported a British Mandate, the Maronites and most other Christians were for France and the Ismailis were mostly in favour of a French Mandate; the Alawites, however, were 'divided'.[63] Alawite indecision illustrates three things: first they were uncertain of where their best interests lay in this new political environment; second, it showed the Alawites' lack of political cohesion compared to the Maronites, Druze and Ismailis, who had unified positions; and third, all these other communities enjoyed external support, whereas, except for the Protestant missions, the Alawites were long isolated as a community.

INTEGRATION

It is reasonable to assume that the Alawites were suspicious of the intentions of all the main parties at the outset of the transition period. The only reliable political support the sect had ever experienced was from the Shi'a; therefore both the French/Allied forces and the Sunni Arab Hashemites could have been viewed as potentially hostile to Alawite interests. Moreover, every major power shift in the Alawite region since the eleventh century had been accompanied by an initial period of repression against the Alawites.

Resistance and Receptivity

From late 1918 until 1921, the Alawite Shaykh Saleh al-'Ali (d.1950) resisted French intrusions into the Jabal al-Sahiliyah from their position on the coast.[64] There is debate about his intentions; some scholars suggest that he was a nationalist working in coordination with the Arab nationalists in Damascus;[65] others have put forward the hypothesis that his primary goal was ensuring Alawite autonomy.[66] An important, albeit contested figure in Syria's modern political history, Shaykh Saleh al-'Ali (1883–1950) hailed from the town of Al-Sheikh Badr inland from Tartous. He was well educated and was said to have learned Ottoman Turkish, Farsi and French. According to information transmitted by his grandson, Issa Ibrahim, Shaykh Saleh al-Ali, who had good contacts with the liberal nationalist Hashim Al-Atassi, was dedicated to promoting the sustainable integration of the coastal region and its communities into a secular Syrian state and opposed the external control of both the Ottoman and French powers.

At a meeting of notables and leaders of the Syrian coastal mountains hosted by Shakyh Saleh al-'Ali on 15–17 December 1918 it was agreed that the latter would lead armed resistance against the French, who planned to separate the coast from the interior. It was also discussed that the Alawites along with the other religious communities should look to forge closer strategic and political relations between the coastal region and the national government of Prince Faysal in Damascus. The Alawites were divided on this matter, however, and many were inclined to seek ties with the incoming French power as a protector against renewed Sunni hegemony after the long experience of Ottoman rule. To these parties Shaykh Saleh al-Ali used to say 'he who seeks shelter from the Ottomans to the French is similar to seeking shelter from the frying pan to the fire'.[67]

It is possible that many Alawites had very little forewarning of French intentions and only saw a powerful military and political presence encroaching on their territory. According to the Alawite Shaykh Nasīr Eskiocak (b.1940), some Alawites wanted independence and autonomy while others actively sought the protection of the French:

After the dislocation of the Ottoman Empire and the taking of these countries by France, some groups of people, families and tribes, wanted to be alone and independent. And it is in this regard that there were problems between them and the French State. But not all the Alawites were against the French. We were grateful and we agreed that France govern us and we were satisfied to be governed.[68]

Desire for French support and protection by some Alawites was evident as early as the mid-nineteenth century. In 1851 the shaykh of the Alawite village of Hinadee, in the northern reaches of the Jabal al-Sahiliyah, told Frederick Walpole that a French agent had promised 'French assistance, and that they [the Alawites] were then awaiting the order to declare for that nation.' Walpole told the shaykh, 'He had better not trust to such a rotten stick, and embroil himself or his people with the ... French.'[69] Consistent with the results of the King–Crane Commission, it seems that the Alawites remained politically divided in 1919 and lacked a unified position on the French intervention. Some Alawites felt their interests would be better served under French rule, others looked to overcome the obstacle of sectarian insecurity and fight for inclusion in an independent Syrian nation, while many suspended judgement until their position in the new environment became clearer.[70]

With Saleh al-'Ali still putting up resistance in 1920, the French asserted their claim to northern Syria as prescribed in the Sykes–Picot agreement. The French immediately applied a policy of divide and rule, or the 'Moroccan Formula'.[71] This policy sought to pit Syria's ethno-religious minorities against the Sunni majority, create divisions between rural and urban notables and to undermine the existing political class.[72] In addition, due to their aspiration for a major role in the Eastern Mediterranean,[73] the French wasted little time in separating the coastal regions off from the interior, which renewed the geopolitical situation of the Crusades.[74] The French deliberately set out to establish an artificial Alawite state that lacked the necessary elements for a viable independent state and would instead be heavily reliant on French support.[75] Hence the autonomous Alawite Territory was established on 31 August 1920.[76]

In July 1922 the French acquired international legitimacy for their colonisation of Syria with an official mandate from the new League of Nations to supervise the political education of the former Ottoman Syrian provinces.[77] The substance of the Mandate appeared to be beneficial to the Alawites. Article 8 of the Mandate document held particular relevance to the political situation of the Alawites and their security and social integration:

[Article 8] The mandatory shall ensure to all complete freedom of conscience and the free exercise of all forms of worship which are consonant with public order and morality. No discrimination of any kind shall be made between the inhabitants of Syria and Lebanon on the ground of differences in race, religion or language. The mandatory shall encourage public instruction, which shall be given through the medium of the native languages in use in the territory of Syria and the Lebanon ...[78]

The Alawites faced religious discrimination for most of their history; therefore Article 8 represented a potential advance for the group, putting them, in theory, on an equal political footing. Moreover, the educational opportunities would open doors for the Alawites. Implementation of Article 8 should have been a major step towards achieving social integration in Syria. French interests dictated, however, that exactly the opposite occurred and they divided Syria along sectarian lines. They established a Druze State, a state based around Antioch and Alexandretta, which contained a significant Turkish population, and an Alawite state in the coastal area.

Artificial Integration

The Alawite State created by the French was essentially a larger version of the governorate of Ismail Khayr Bey, including not only the full extent of the Jabal al-Sahiliyah but also the coastal plain and the main towns of Latakia, Tartous, Banyas and Jablah, an area of around 6,500 square kilometres.[79] At the end of 1933 this state had a population of 334,173, of which 64 per cent was Alawite.[80] The next largest community was the Sunnis who were an 18 per cent minority and were mainly located in Latakia. There was a significant population of Christians mostly around Qala'at al-Hosn (Krak des Chevaliers) near the Homs Gap and north of Tartous. In addition there were small communities of Ismailis at Qadmus and Masyaf (see Table 2).[81]

Table 2: Demographic Composition of the Alawite State (1933)

Sect	% of Population	Population
Alawites	64.00	213,870
Sunni Muslims	18.00	60,151
Christians (mainly Greek orthodox)	16.00	53,467
Ismailis	0.02	6,683
Total	100.00	334,173

Source: E.J. Brill, *First Encyclopaedia of Islam 1913–1936* (1927; 1993).

From 1923 the Alawite State was governed by a representative council based in Latakia with a French governor who oversaw affairs (see Table 3).[82] The council was comprised of seventeen members: ten Alawites, three Sunnis, three Christians and one Ismaili.[83] The council therefore roughly reflected the sectarian make-up of the new state, and equated to a consociational political system based on proportional representation of the different communities.[84] While this political arrangement was advantageous to Alawite security as the overwhelming majority, the sectarian formulation of the state would only serve to exacerbate inter-communal tensions. The minority Sunnis were particularly unhappy with this situation. The representative council struggled to govern effectively and, in addition, urban Sunni Muslims and Christians continued to hold most of the non-elected government positions.[85] Like the Sunni reaction to Ismail Khayr Bey's period of rule in 1854, insecurity and mutual suspicion played a part in promoting communal tensions. Ironically, the substance of Article 8 of the Mandate also protected the rights of the Sunnis who were now a minority in the Alawite State and could not be discriminated against.

Table 3: Composition of the Representative Council of the Alawite State

Sect	% of Population	% Representation	Members
Alawites	64.00	59	10
Sunni Muslims	18.00	18	3
Christians	16.00	18	3
Ismailis	0.02.00	5	1
Total	100.00	100	17

Sources: De Planhol, 1997, p. 378, Longrigg, 1958, p. 210, n. 1; E.J Brill (1927; 1993).

In addition to inter-communal rivalries, the Alawites remained susceptible to fighting among themselves, and the representative council became a forum for playing out old rivalries. Despite these shortcomings, in the context of Alawite history, the Alawite State provided a valuable opportunity for the sect to begin participating in a relatively pluralist, albeit fractious and inefficient, political arena. They could openly pursue their interests; engage in dialogue among themselves and with other communities. One notable achievement of the council was a restructuring of the tobacco industry in 1934 to the benefit of local growers.[86] Another positive development was the establishment of a profitable tourism industry in the coastal mountains for *estivants* (summer visitors).[87] All of this suggests a possible weakening of Alawite insecurity. It seems, however, that Alawite insecurity persisted. This was demonstrated by the lack of migration from the Jabal al-Sahiliyah into Latakia. In fact, as Patrick Seale has noted, Alawites were still reluctant to travel to the 'Sunni town' of Latakia even in the 1940s.[88]

The Alawite State contained a diverse population previously contained under the multi-cultural umbrella of the Ottoman Empire. However, whether it provided a true indication of the potential for social integration or communal conflict following the collapse of a multicultural state—as ethno-religious security dilemma theory examines—is not clear.[89] Essentially, the communities passed directly from Ottoman imperial authority to French colonial control. Nevertheless, the limited interaction of the various communities of the Syrian coast provided some insight into the potential for Alawite social integration on a wider Syrian level.

The three key Alawite leaders in the 'Alawite State' were Jaber al-Abbas, Ibrahim al-Kinj and Suleiman al-Murshid. Jaber al-Abbas was the leader of the Khayatin tribal confederation and president of the Representative Council until 1930. His main rival was Ibrahim al-Kinj, leader of the Haddadin tribes, who succeeded in deposing al-Abbas in the council elections of 1930.[90] Neither of these men had the same impact on Alawite politics during 1920s and 1930s, however, as a shepherd boy from the mountain top village of Jobat Berghal by the name of Suleiman al-Murshid (b.1905 as Suleiman Younis).[91] In some ways al-Murshid resembled Hasan al-Mahdi of the fourteenth century in that he began life in a low station, but after receiving 'divine revelations' he became influential as the focus of a new messianic movement.[92] Beginning in 1923, al-Murshid embarked on a religious and political career that included uniting a great portion of the Alawite territory under his influence. He played a decisive role in determining the make-up of the Representative Council and even won a position in the National Assembly in Damascus.[93]

Al-Murshid failed, however, to establish his dominance in a way that could broadly mobilise Alawite 'asabiyya. This was the result of several factors. The French, while mindful to maintain Alawite separatism at a national level, were also, much like the Ottomans, keen to keep the Alawites themselves divided and under control. Thus they monitored al-Murshid's activities and even sent him into exile on one occasion.[94] The French (and later the British) were aware of al-Murshid's value as an ally against the Arab nationalists and tried to exploit his autonomous inclinations.[95] Yet according to other accounts, al-Murshid's inclinations seemed mainly towards personal enrichment. It was his controversial profile, 'avarice in fund raising' in Alawite villages (which was especially unpopular during the depressed economic climate of the early 1930s) and dissent among his close supporters that prevented him from reaching greater heights as an Alawite leader.[96] Nevertheless, his legacy is still felt in Syria and there remains a significant community who call themselves 'Murshidis'. I visited one of their villages in 2009 and observed Suleiman al-Murshid's portrait hanging with great reverence inside the houses. According to some

Alawite religious authorities, the Murshidis are no longer Alawites and their devotion to Suleiman al-Murshid is misguided.[97]

On 14 May 1930 a decree from the French high commissioner in Beirut changed the name of the Alawite State to the 'Government of Latakia',[98] a title less offensive to the other communities.[99] More importantly, however, the French delegated full authority to the incumbent governor, M. Schoeffler, whom the council would now only assist.[100] The Representative Council was reduced therefore to 'window dressing' for direct French rule, meeting only once a year for a month, and answerable in all important matters to the French governor.[101] The Alawite period of political independence in an awkward association with the other minorities of north-west Syria was curtailed.[102]

Despite the limitations of the Alawite State during the 1920s, the experience opened up the Alawites' political horizons. Moreover, the education the younger generation was receiving according to the provisions of Article 8 was creating a new generation of Alawites who could envision a life beyond their limited territorial and religious identity. Thus on the surface the role of the French was beneficial for the Alawites. Certainly the French believed this to be true. In 1930 the former French prime minister and Nobel Prize winner Aristide Briand wrote to the League of Nations:

Not only do these [autonomous] regimes conform to the desires of the population, but they are also in accordance with their interests, since the closer co-operation of the mandatory power in their economic and social development is the greatest advantage to them.[103]

It is unclear how the French authorities came to the conclusion that the regime reflected the desires of the population. It is fair to say that the French only sought to promote their interests through the continued political division of the Syrian lands. This objective differed greatly from that sought by the League of Nations. The Mandate clearly stated: 'The mandatory shall secure the adhesion of Syria and Lebanon, so far as social, religious and other conditions permit ...'[104] In theory, the Mandate sought to achieve a broad Syrian political entity that embraced the diverse populations without discrimination.[105] The French objectives ran counter to this and they instead sought to emphasise and exploit religious divisions.

From the beginning of the Mandate, the French strategically recruited Alawites, along with other minorities, into their security forces to counter Syrian nationalists, but also as part of a general policy of pitting the various communities against each other.[106] In contrast to the Alawite reluctance to be conscripted into the army of Ibrahim Pasha in the 1830s, poverty-stricken Alawites in 1920/1 were drawn to enlist in French army units by the promise of a steady income.[107] It is significant that while Shaykh Saleh al-'Ali was still fighting the French, Alawites from other tribes were signing up for the Syrian Legion, of which Alawites comprised nearly 20 per cent by 1925.[108] This again highlights the disunity of the wider Alawite community during this period. Alawite over-representation in French colonial units continued after the renaming and enlarging of the Syrian Legion as 'Les Troupes Spéciales du Levant' from 1930.[109] It is important to note that Alawites generally made up the lower ranks in the Troupes Spéciales. Between 1921 and 1946 only sixteen Alawites graduated from military academies compared to 128 Sunni Arabs.[110]

The real legacy of the French role was to foster divisions in Syrian society so that when they eventually departed in 1946 little progress had been made in reconciling the different communities. Extending this concept forward, the emergence of an Alawite sectarian 'asabiyya in support of the Asad regime would have been less likely had the intentions of the League of Nations been pursued. Thus the Mandate period played a paradoxical role in bringing the Alawites out of isolation and providing them with educational and political opportunities previously unavailable to them on the one hand, while perpetuating deep-seated suspicions between the communities of Syria on the other.

Genuine Integration?

In the 1930s the French came under increasing pressure internationally and from Syrian nationalists in Damascus to begin winding down the Mandate.[111] In 1936 they agreed to consider the unification of a Syrian state incorporating the autonomous regions of Latakia and Jabal Druze.[112] The strong Alawite reaction to this announcement illustrated their new political consciousness, their latent insecurity, but also their continued political division. Following the release of French proposals for the annexation of the Alawite territory in February 1936, 'long queues of protesters lined up at all hours at the Latakia post office in order to dispatch telegrams to Beirut, Paris and Geneva, supporting or rejecting the idea of unity'.[113] Ninety-eight petitions were received by the League of Nations, many of which expressed 'apprehensions on the part of minorities' towards Syrian unity.[114]

According to Matti Moosa a letter was sent to the French prime minister, Leon Blum in June 1936, opposing unity with Syria and stating that 'abolition of the mandate will expose minorities in Syria to the dangers of death and annihilation'. The six Alawite notables who supposedly signed the letter included Suleiman al-Murshid and Suleiman al-Asad, the father of the future president, Hafiz al-Asad.[115] This document has been the source of some controversy and, if genuine, was a potential embarrasment to the Asad regime's Syrian nationalist credentials. It is reported to have gone missing from the French archives in the late 1980s.[116] Anxiety about being absorbed by the overwhelmingly Sunni Syrian state was also evident in Alawite appeals in 1936 for their territory to be attached to Lebanon instead.[117] The appointment in Damascus of Ata Bey al-Ayubi as prime minister by the French may, however, have played a part in convincing some Alawites that unity was an option, due to his purported (but apparently unknown to the French) Alawite origins.[118]

A historic convention took place at Tartous on 25 February 1936, which was attended by all the important Alawite leaders in what was in effect a 'referendum' on the Alawite position on Syrian unity. Despite the attempts of the French intelligence services to portray a separatist victory, the debate was vigorous and the outcome was not definitive. The Haddadin leader, Ibrahim al-Kinj, argued for separation under French protection, while Munir al-Abbas from the Khayatin tribes supported unity.[119] There were also Alawites who were prepared to fight for their autonomy with or without French assistance.[120] Overall, Alawite indecision was influenced by sectarian insecurity about recommitting the Alawites to a state dominated by their historic antagonists, the Sunni Muslims.

Meanwhile, the sect's religious leaders pragmatically worked to ensure community security within the nascent Syrian state in the event of unification. Hence in May 1936 fifteen Alawite shaykhs issued a decree stating:

Every 'Alawi was a Muslim and that every 'Alawi who denied being a Muslim and who did not admit that the holy Qur'an was his holy scripture, and that Mohammad was his Prophet, was not considered an 'Alawi in the legal sense by the Shar'ia.[121]

If this was a politically judicious exercise of taqiyya, it produced the desired result. Two months later, in July 1936, the Arab nationalist and grand mufti of Jerusalem, Muhammad Amin al-Husayni (1895–1974), issued a fatwa which, astonishingly for a Sunni cleric, strongly vouched for the Islamic credentials of the Alawites.[122]

This was a dramatic reversal from previous judgements by Sunni religious authorities such as Ibn Taymiyya. Ironically, al-Husayni's fatwa came within a similar geopolitical context as Ibn Taymiyya's 1305 fatwa. The European powers had deeply penetrated and divided the Islamic world, and the Alawites and their territory were again salient to Muslim strategic interests. But instead of alienating the Alawites and accusing them of complicity with the enemies of Islam, Amin al-Husayni took the opposite approach and looked to bring the Alawites into the Muslim fold. This was the type of approach that the governor of Hama had wanted to try in the 1860s. The timing and impact of Husayni's fatwa was effective and it helped convince the Alawites that their futures would be secure within a wider Syrian, or Arab, polity.[123] Thus in 1937, without any Alawite resistance, the coastal region was officially joined to the rest of Syria.[124] This was a critical moment in Alawite history which indicated that, despite centuries of discrimination and persecution at the hands of Sunni Muslims, Alawites were willing to attempt integration into wider, Sunni-dominated, Syrian society.

The actual attachment of the Alawite territory to Syria was delayed for another decade. War loomed in Europe and the French postponed their agreements for Syrian independence and unity. In 1939 France found justification again to detach the Alawite territory from Syria and allowed Turkey to annex Alexandretta.[125] With France's defeat and occupation in 1940, Syria was ruled by the Vichy French and formed part of the German axis.[126] This was a confusing period for the various Syrian communities, who must have found it difficult to know where their best interests lay. Once again the Alawites did not participate directly in the war although they were by now heavily enlisted in the French colonial force, the Troupes Spéciales.

An interesting event occurred in 1941 involving other Syrian minorities. Vichy-commanded Druze and Allied Circassian units faced each other on the front line in southern Syria. When ordered to attack, both units refused, stating they had no wish to attack their 'countrymen'.[127] This incident signified a burgeoning common identity among Syrian communities. It would have been interesting to observe the result had the Alawite units faced a similar situation; they were stationed in north-western Syria and were not ordered to the front.[128] The Alawites quite possibly empathised with this national impulse. Having no real wish to remain isolated, and now with a fatwa from a high-ranking Sunni mufti providing them with religious credibility, the stage was set for them to continue their transition from isolation, a trend that would diminish their insecurity.

After the conclusion of the war, the French tried to reclaim Syria but were met with strong resistance by the Syrian nationalists, now with American and British support.[129] The French were forced to withdraw for the last time. However, their aerial and artillery bombardment of Damascus on 29–30 May 1945 left an extremely negative impression of the supposedly 'liberal' Allied victors of the Second World War. This had the effect of undermining Syrian advocates of 'Western-style' political liberalism in the newly independent state.[130] According to Longrigg, the French actions were perceived with 'revulsion' even in the Alawite region.[131] This perhaps signalled that the Alawites no longer desired a French presence in Syria and were ready to begin integration with the Syrian state, a decision they had made ten years earlier.

Independent Syria and the 'Problem' of Pluralism

The political make-up of Syria in 1946, in terms of its extent and demographic composition, assumed the general form that remained in 2011. According to the 1947 census, Sunnis formed a 70 per cent majority whereas the Alawites numbered 339,466, or 11.2 per cent of the population. The Christians comprised around 10 per cent, and the Druze and Ismailis less than 5 per cent (see Table 4).[132] By ethnicity the state had a large Arab majority with Kurdish and Armenian minorities. The diversity of the Syrian state was a cause of concern for the new Syrian government.

Sunni Arab and nationalist leader, Jamil Mardam Bey, wrote at the time that minorities posed a grave threat to the Syrian state.[133]

The new Syrian government recognised the centrifugal potential of the minorities but did not seem to have a coherent policy for dealing with this problem. For instance, there were no policies aimed at reducing sectarian insecurity and promoting inclusive citizenship. Although the Alawites had taken a 'leap of faith' in acquiescing to their inclusion in the Syrian state they still maintained a high-level of latent sectarian 'asabiyya, which could prove decisive in a factional political arena. In the first years of Syrian independence, however, the minorities were busy seeking advancement within the new state and secessionist thoughts were not being entertained.[134]

Table 4: Religious Composition of the Syrian State (1947 Census)

Sect	% of Pop.	Pop.
Alawites	11.2	339,466
Sunni	70.0	2,121,662
Christians (all sects)	10.0	303,094
Ismailis and Druze	< 5.0	< 151,547
Jews	< 1.0	15,000
Total	100.0	3,030,946

Sources: Winckler, 2009, 1989; Reeva et al., 2003; Syrian Census 1947.

The only real path to a stable income for the economically disadvantaged Alawites remained the military.[135] During the French period many Alawites were enlisted in the Troupes Spéciales, a colonial force that had played the major role in suppressing nationalist dissent. As a result, the taint of collaboration hung over the Alawite community.[136] Thus the Syrian contingent of the Troupes Spéciales, which numbered 7,000 in 1946, was reduced to 2,500 by 1948.[137] Exclusively Alawite units, such as the Bataillon de Côte, were demobilised, and when the French departed Syria in 1946, 500 Alawites from the Troupes chose to go with them as *avenantaires* (mercenaries).[138] There is little reason to believe that the Alawites gained an advantage in post-independence Syria from their involvement with the Troupes Spéciales—in fact, it was more likely a disadvantage.

The remnants of the Troupes Spéciales were absorbed into the new national armies of independent Syria and Lebanon.[139] Alawites continued to be well represented in the lower ranks of the Syrian army, which in 1945 numbered no more than 10,000, rising to 12,000 by the start of the Palestinian campaign in 1948–9.[140] The Syrian military academies, which had largely been closed to poor uneducated Alawites during the Mandate,[141] became one of the few 'avenues for upward mobility'[142] for Alawite youths, and they enlisted in high numbers.[143]

In 1945 the Syrian army was in a very poor state organisationally and had little equipment, supplies or ammunition. The Syrian government requested training and supplies from the United States, the first Arab state to do so.[144] After some deliberation, the United States declined the request, not wanting to offend the French.[145] The Syrian army subsequently remained disorganised and ill equipped, and without a professional and disciplined structure it became prone to the formation of factions. It could be speculated that had the Americans sent a military mission to Syria in 1945–6 the succession of military coups that began in 1949 may have been avoided. In this scenario the role of the army in Syrian politics may have been quite different. A comparison between the Turkish and Syrian militaries could be informative in this regard.[146] The politicising effect on the Arab armies from the disastrous Palestinian war of 1948–9 must also be taken into account.[147] Ultimately, the combination of Alawite overrepresentation in a politicised Syrian army would be important in creating the conditions for the re-emergence of insecurity and the mobilisation of Alawite 'asabiyya.

In the civilian political sphere of the new Syrian state, the Sunni majority of Syria was prepared to live with the Alawites as long as they did not overstep certain bounds or threaten the unity of the state. The colourful career of Suleiman al-Murshid, for example, was abruptly ended in 1946 when he was executed in Damascus by the new Syrian government for posing a threat to Syrian unity.[148] While al-Murshid's execution was committed in the name of national unity, it had the effect of alienating the Murshidis, who would not forgive the (mostly) Sunni authorities for this blasphemous deed. Murshidi 'asabiyya was perhaps stronger at this point than other Alawite groups. This was demonstrated when al-Murshid's son, Mujib, attempted a failed Murshidi revolt in 1952.[149]

For Alawites in general, however, the Syrian political arena of the late 1940s was dynamic and exciting. Alawites began descending the Jabal al-Sahiliyah in droves seeking new opportunities and a better life, although the return option was never cut off completely.[150] A key figure for Alawites at this time was, ironically, a Sunni by the name of Akram Hawrani from Hama. Through his Arab Socialist Party (ASP) Hawrani played a major role in furthering the political goals of the peasant classes of all sects. Hence he became a focal point for Alawite social and political aspirations.[151]

A new generation of educated Alawites began to engage in national politics during the early period of independence. Turkey's absorption of the Sanjak of Alexandretta (now Hatay), which had a significant Turkish population, dismayed the Arabs of Alexandretta, including many Alawites, who found themselves cut off from the Arab nation.[152] Many moved to Syria, including an Alawite teacher named Zaki al-Arsuzi (d.1968).[153] Arsuzi was deeply affected by the loss of Alexandretta by the Arab 'nation', and felt the Arabic language and culture were under threat.[154] This moved him to establish a party named al-Ba'th al-Arabi (Arabic renaissance/resurrection) in Damascus in 1940, beginning with only five members.[155] His message was very close in substance to that of the founders of the Ba'th Party, Michel Aflaq and Salah al-Din al-Bitar,[156] who preached a message of secular Arab nationalism, or an Arab renaissance based around the Arabic language. Arsuzi later withdrew into obscurity but was subsequently rehabilitated by the regime as the party's ideologue in replacement of Aflaq and al-Bitar.[157] After Arsuzi's withdrawal from political life, another Alawite, Dr Wahib al-Ghanim, a physician from Latakia and an associate of Arsuzi, played a key role in extending the Ba'th cadres among Alawites around Latakia.[158] By this stage the two strains of the Ba'th came together.[159] In the late 1940s al-Ghanim had a strong political influence on a young and gifted Alawite student from Qardaha and the Kalbiyya tribe, by the name of Hafiz al-Asad.[160]

For young Alawites like Hafiz al-Asad the political situation seemed to be evolving in a favourable direction. Centuries of isolation and repression were seemingly left behind, and this new generation yearned for a better life than their ancestors had experienced. The naive exuberance of rural Alawites descending from the Jabal al-Sahiliyah soon began to push up against long-established traditions of urban Sunni chauvinism. There was a 'glass ceiling' in Syrian society that held back the aspirations of Alawites like Hafiz al-Asad. Overall, however, in the first years of Syrian independence there was little indication of an imminent mobilisation of Alawite 'asabiyya. Alawites descended the mountain to interact with wider Syrian society for the first time since the Hamdanid period. However, their attempts to integrate came within a context of continued Sunni prejudice; this would prove a catalyst for the unconnected Alawite tribes to start unifying as a sect.

Suspicions of Sectarianism

In the 1950s the tension between the 'raw' rural young Alawites and the established social mores of the 'Islamic cities' of Aleppo and Damascus became palpable. A Syrian army cartoon entitled 'Those Whom the People Scorn' depicts this tension in a cautionary warning to its rural recruits about their behaviour in the more 'refined' urban environment (see photo 2). The urban Sunni Arabs' condescending view of these rural émigrés in the 1950s, which included rural Sunnis as well as religious minorities, reveals a mindset which could not fathom that these rustics could pose a threat to the natural political order that saw them 'rightfully' at the top.[161] The army was long considered an occupation for lower classes and ethnic outsiders such as Turks and Kurds, who were generally Sunni and therefore had interests in maintaining the status quo in the cities as far as the urban merchant and religious classes went.

At this juncture in Syrian history, therefore, it can be said that the urban Sunni Arabs had a very low-level of 'asabiyya; they certainly possessed few of the ingredients that Ibn Khaldun lists as necessary for a strong 'asabiyya.[162]

In contrast, the Alawites, having developed high levels of 'asabiyya in their tribal groups, finally began to develop a common sectarian 'asabiyya. This occurred as a result of increased exposure to wider Syrian society, leading to a realisation of their common identity and interests.

However, it was not the Alawites who first asserted their higher 'asabiyya in the fledgling Syrian state. In the wake of the military disaster in Palestine

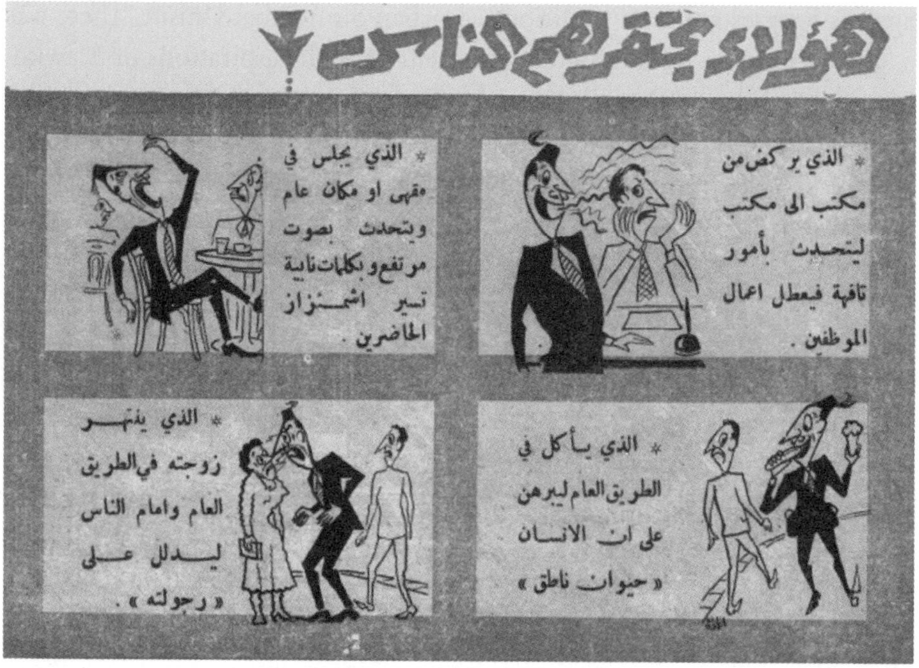

Figure 2: 'Those Whom the People Scorn'

in 1948 the civilian political leadership suffered the backlash of public anger and in 1949 a military coup installed the Kurdish colonel, Hosni Zai'm, as president.[163] According to Jordi Tejel, Zai'm attempted to mobilise an ethnic Kurdish 'asabiyya in combination with an ideology of Syrian nationalism to support his rule.[164] As non-Arabs, Kurdish political interests were best served by a Syrian rather than an Arab identity. Being mainly Sunni Muslims the Kurds had no problem associating themselves with the religious majority in Syria, but the victory of Arab nationalism would see them marginalised.

The Syrian Social Nationalist Party (SSNP) was an important political vehicle for the Kurds.[165] The Alawites (and Christians) were also drawn to the SSNP because of its secular and socialist focus and its willingness to incorporate heterogeneous groups under a single Syrian banner.[166] Moreover, the Alawites would not be as insignificant within a national identity limited to the Syrian lands, whereas Arab nationalism included a large geographical area incorporating an overwhelming majority of the Alawites' historic antagonists, the Sunni Muslims. The decline of the SSNP from around 1955 and the victory of Arab nationalism was a blow to the long-term political aspirations of the Kurds.[167] The Alawites, however, had room to manoeuvre. As ethnic Arabs, the Ba'th Party's secular vision of Arab nationalism could still include them within the Syrian mainstream. Thus, from the time of the SSNP's decline an increasing number of Alawites began to join the Ba'th Party. The Ba'th (literally renaissance or resurrection) ideology was centred on radical secularism and socialism. The basic premise of the party was that the defining source of identity for the nation should be the Arabic language, to which was ascribed almost religious significance. While secularism was to be strictly maintained, the special status of Islam was acknowledged, in particular because it encapsulated in the Quran and other Arab traditions the beauty of the Arabic language. Arab nationalism was the other defining feature of Ba'thist ideology and the political unification of all the Arabic-speaking people was the ultimate goal.[168]

Despite the radical secularism of the Ba'th, Alawites did not limit their options to secularism as a means to improve their security in Syrian society. A parallel strategy of trying to promote themselves as orthodox Muslims continued in the 1950s. In 1952 Alawite religious leaders successfully made a request to the mufti of the Syrian Republic to be recognised as part of the Twelver Shi'ite creed.[169] Then, in 1958, a historic fatwa from the al-Azhar religious school in Cairo recognised Twelver Shi'ites as 'religiously correct'.[170] The combination of these two rulings, along with the Husayni fatwa of 1936, put the Alawites nominally back inside the Muslim fold and in a better political situation in the overwhelmingly Sunni state of Syria. This, along with the rise of the Ba'th Party in Syrian politics, was another major step in diminishing Alawite insecurity.

The 1950s were a turbulent period in Syrian politics in which various communities and individuals manoeuvred to try and promote their interests. After the military coups of 1949, Sunni Arabs tried to re-establish a role in the army as it became clear that the military was the only reliable path to political power. The Sunni Arabs' lack of 'asabiyya, however, limited their ability to present a united front. Successive internecine purges of senior

Sunni officers depleted their presence in the top ranks, and members of the minorities began to filter into the middle ranks of the army. By 1963 the Alawites constituted 65 per cent of non-commissioned officers and an even larger proportion of the common soldiers.[171] This was as far as non-Sunni individuals could ascend under the prevailing social norms. In the late 1950s some of these lower-ranking minority officers began questioning the Syrian political status quo and began cooperating together behind the scenes.

The establishment of the United Arab Republic (UAR) in 1958 joined Syria to Egypt as one state. For the Ba'thists it was the first step in the consummation of their official ideology for a pan-Arab nation. For Alawites who had joined the cadres of the Ba'th Party it meant the realisation of the 'downside' of Ba'th policy to their interests. They were now part of a much larger polity with a huge Sunni majority. In Syria they were an 11 per cent minority. In the UAR they were all of a sudden a tiny minority amid a 'sea' of Sunni Muslims.[172] Moreover, Egyptian officials, in a re-enactment of the 1830s, began interfering with Alawite autonomy in their mountain territory and the neighbouring Ghab.[173] In addition, the establishment of the UAR led to the dissolution of the Ba'th Party, which removed the main vehicle of Alawite political aspirations.[174] In short, the Alawites were happy to go along with the theories behind Ba'thism, but it was not in their interests to see them fully implemented. Although the Alawites technically belonged to the UAR majority as Arabs, the spectre of their long history of oppression by the Sunnis prevented them from developing any real enthusiasm for actual pan-Arabism.[175] For them Syria was a quite big enough political arena for them to negotiate their interests.

During the UAR period many Syrian military personnel were stationed in Egypt. A group of these officers, all of whom were initially from Syrian minorities, began meeting in 1959 to discuss Syrian politics, the merits of the UAR, and possible courses of action. This group came to be known as the Military Committee and would play a major role in the events of the following years. The majority of the group was Alawite, including the most influential members Salah Jadid, Hafiz al-Asad and Muhammad Umran, while the other two original members were Ismailis.[176] Some authors have tried to prove that the Military Committee was the beginning of a deliberate plot by Alawites to capture power in Syria.[177] Others have suggested that the *raison d'être* of the Military Committee members was simple revanchism on the part of the sectarian minorities.[178] I have previously suggested that its aims were based more on the personal ambition of its members;[179] however, the truth is likely somewhere in-between.

Ideological and class interests rather than the sectarian ambitions of the Military Committee were illustrated in the expansion of the Military Committee to include six Sunnis from poor rural backgrounds.[180] In the political environment of the late 1950s, personal ambition was often limited by social background. Real political power was still the domain of the urban aristocratic families.[181] For the Military Committee members, an upheaval of the political hierarchy would remove impediments to their political ambitions.[182] So the objectives of the Military Committee could also be viewed as seeking a broad-based social revolution in Syria.[183] Alawites, especially, were frustrated at their lack of progress in the first two decades of Syrian independence. The 1960 census listed the Alawite population as 495,000, or 10.6 per cent of the total population, compared with 11.2 per cent in 1947.[184] The Alawite population was declining in proportion to other Syrian communities, which indicates a higher mortality rate from a lower standard of living.[185] Hence the independent period and Syrian nationalist policies had, so far, not provided much benefit to the Alawites.

On 28 September 1961 the UAR fell apart after a military coup by Syrian officers in Damascus. This was a blow to pan-Arab ideology and ruined the political careers of several influential figures. Akram Hawrani's influence among the peasant class, for example, was such by this time that he could have risen to political leadership himself, had he not associated too closely with the officers who orchestrated the secession from the UAR.[186] In addition, Michel Aflaq and Salah al-Din al-Bitar suffered from the ideological fallout from the failure of the UAR.[187] The Military Committee managed to avoid any association with the perpetrators of this 'reactionary' separatist coup, which, moreover, precipitated another purge of Sunni officers.[188] The way was now clear for the members of the Military Committee to assume a dominant role in Syrian politics by manoeuvring themselves into influential positions in both the military and the Ba'th Party.

The Ba'thist coup on 8 March 1963 realised the social revolution that promised to improve the situation of the Alawites and socially disadvantaged sectors of Syrian society. The urban Sunni aristocrats were jettisoned from positions of power, and the peasant classes, including the Alawites, became politically enfranchised. At first the civilian ideologues of the Ba'th, Michel Aflaq, Salah al-din al-Bitar and a Sunni officer, Amin al-Hafiz, remained as the face of the Ba'thist revolution, but the Alawite officers, Salah Jadid and Hafiz al-Asad, increasingly pulled the levers of power[189] through their influence among Alawites in key military units.[190] Both of these leaders had the potential to establish their dominance over the Alawite community.

The Ba'th Party's policies of land redistribution and the transformation of the Syrian society and economy along socialist lines 'presented a range of reasonable ambitions and general slogans', which appealed to the poor and oppressed sectors of society.[191] However, the redistribution of land was not entirely based on socio-economic principles, but rather was used as a way to entrench loyalty to the party. Hence land was often distributed to those who showed the greatest loyalty to the Ba'th. This allowed some of the former landowning elite to maintain their wealth by declaring their allegiance to the regime. This would be the case particularly after the rise of the more pragmatic Hafiz al-Asad in 1970. A new system of patronage emerged which centred on the Ba'th Party hierarchy. In the process of land redistribution many poor rural Alawites were taken away from their small farming operations to be employed in the army and security apparatus, in particular those units that were key to regime security. Hence, many ordinary Alawites went from 'serving the notables and the feudal lords to serving the new Ba'thist men' who became the new 'lords' of Syria and controlled the population on the basis of 'bestowal according to loyalty'. One former notable from Jableh was reported to have sarcastically proclaimed, 'Had we known that the Ba'th would make us gain that much property and wealth, we would have joined in …'[192]

During this period what ordinary Alawites desired was equal integration as citizens of the Syrian state. Yet common goals and social status increasingly caused Alawites to work together as a sect. In this vein, Hanna Batatu observed the close cooperation of rural groups and religious minorities in the 1960s:

In Syria … disadvantaged or previously disadvantaged rural … people—representing a level in social evolution different than that of relatively long established urban groups—tend in their political actions to adhere to or cooperate more markedly with kinsmen or members of their own clan or people from their own sect, or region, this is not so much a manifestation of narrow cliquishness, although their behaviour bears this aspect, as it is they are really acting in a natural manner, merely obeying, so to say, the logic of their fundamental structural situation.[193]

According to Batatu's explanation, the Alawites were not actively seeking sectarian domination, but rather engaged in greater levels of cooperation due to their common rural, minority background.[194] This tendency could be based on the different characteristics of rural village life. Perhaps it was the unfamiliarity of the cities and their lack of awareness of other groups due to their previous isolation.[195] Or maybe it was the insecurity of being from a religious minority that caused Alawites to cooperate together. In any case, from a political standpoint, the end result was the same: common association by members of a particular community. Opposing groups viewed this as deliberate and concerted action and therefore responded in kind.

This process of mutual distrust descending into sectarianism is illustrated by Nikolaos van Dam's analysis of Ba'th Party documents on the party's crisis in 1966, which detailed some conversations among Sunnis from Hama:

An evening gathering was held at the house of Captain 'Abd al-Jawad. There was varied conversation, which included the following: 'The wife of Lieutenant Ghassan Hamawi spoke about the bloc formation of the 'Alawis. She told what she knew of 'Alawi women forming blocs in the House for female teachers during their studies … Either 'Abd al-Jawad or Ghassan Hamawi said that the 'Alawis were trying to dominate the Army and that this made it necessary to form an opposing bloc.'[196]

Captain 'Abd al-Jawad: I told him [Sergeant Muhammad Hassun] to pay attention to the meetings of 'Alawis and started a conversation with him on the subject of 'Alawi bloc formation. I did the same with Lieutenant Ghassan Hamawi and others and he told me, 'I have started to appoint security men on the basis of their being Sunnis …'[197]

These two extracts reveal paranoia with regard to the Alawites' activities, and not just in the military sphere, as indicated by the comment about the female Alawite trainee teachers. It is quite possible that Alawite students congregated together for innocent reasons like those suggested by Batatu above. As it was, tales such as these seemed to validate fears of an Alawite takeover, mainly through the army, which was of course where many Alawites were employed. The inverse of Sunni suspicion was that Alawites felt more alienated and therefore relied on one another to an even greater extent. Even if sectarianism had little to do with Alawite participation in the political convulsions of the 1960s, it was understandable that Sunnis suspected otherwise and accused the Ba'th regime of sectarianism. As van Dam has shown, this only served to strengthen Alawite mutual reliance and their leaders' grip on the centres of power.[198]

Batatu's observation about the relative cohesion of rural and urban groups provides a new perspective of Ibn Khaldun's hypothesis that only rural tribes possess the necessary 'asabiyya to form a state or dynasty. The process described here bears some important differences from Ibn Khaldun's original formulation of the 'asabiyya concept. The Alawite political rise was not an overt and deliberate mobilisation of a group's capability to capture a state but was a chain of events which, while seemingly accidental, were possibly unavoidable due to the structural features of the state and the historic relations of the communities contained within it—in particular, mutual suspicion and insecurity. Taking into account Batatu's explanation of how rural minorities mutually support one another and van Dam's illustration of how suspected sectarianism leads to actual sectarianism, a picture begins to emerge of the process of coalescing Alawite sectarian 'asabiyya.

Alawites Ascendant

In 1966 civilian control of the Ba'th was dispensed with as a result of another coup. Amin al-Hafiz was deposed and Salah al-Din al-Bitar and Michel Aflaq fled the country.[199] The Alawite officers, Salah Jadid and Hafiz al-Asad, stood at the summit of Syrian politics, their influence assured by loyalist Alawites in the ranks of strategically vital military units.[200] Salah Jadid initially took the lead role while the more cautious Hafiz al-Asad remained active in military and security affairs.[201] Salah Jadid never assumed direct leadership of the state, however; instead he pulled the levers of power from behind the scenes while a Sunni doctor named

Nureddin al-Atassi was made president and official head of state. While the Alawite background of Salah Jadid and Hafiz al-Asad should not be over-stated, as their rise was part of a general upgrade of rural communities in Syria, their elevation in Syria proved that Alawites could ascend the heights of politics and society. But whether Alawites could openly assume the highest offices in Syrian politics remained in question. Moreover, the sect remained highly sensitive with regard to revealing any details about their religion and continued to apply taqqiya. According to one story, a non-Alawite colleague suggested to Salah Jadid that the sect should publish its secret books in order to defuse sectarian insecurities based on misinforma-tion and hearsay. In a reflection of Suleiman al-Adhani's 'crime' of exposing Alawite beliefs in the 1860s, Jadid responded that the 'shaykhs would crush us!'[202]

Salah Jadid (1926–93) was from a high-ranking Haddadin family from the mountain village of Duwayr Ba'abda, around 20 kilometres south of Asad's home town, Qardaha.[203] According to Patrick Seale, he was 'clever, high minded and pronounced in his left wing views'.[204] His political prefer-ences had at first been towards the SSNP, but after he received assistance in his military career from Akram Hawrani, he switched to the Ba'th Party.[205] As an Alawite leader Jadid was more qualified than Asad, his family held a far higher status[206] and the larger Haddadin confederation was traditionally more influential than the Kalbiyya.[207] Moreover, he made powerful external allies, something that no previous Alawite leader had managed.

The Soviet Union and East Germany were encouraged by the socialist bent of the new Syrian leadership and eagerly assumed the supporting role the United States had declined in 1946. They began financing major infra-structure, such as the Euphrates Dam, and continued to supply arms for the Syrian military.[208] Most importantly, the support of a superpower would stabilise the Syrian political system and consolidate the position of whoever claimed power after two decades of struggle.

The emergence of Alawite individuals into senior roles came as a surprise to observers of Syrian politics.[209] The key players in this ascent had kept a low profile right up until the moment when conditions were right to emerge from behind the scenes. Salah Jadid preferred to keep a low profile as he set about implementing his radical socialist reforms and foreign policy measures between 1966 and 1970.[210] While these policies alienated large sectors of the Syrian population, notably the Sunni urban bourgeoisie, they had real and tangible benefits for the Alawites who occupied the poorest and most disadvantaged sectors of society. Jadid's policies, however, threatened to undermine Alawite gains in the long term, as they provoked strong reactions from Syria's neighbours along with large sections of Syria's population.[211] In 1968 Hafiz al-Asad broke ranks with Jadid. Asad, pragmatically recognising the danger posed by Jadid's policies, moved to secure the loyalties of the important military units. By February 1969 Asad had succeeded in this task and was in a position to move against his rival for leadership of Alawite 'asabiyya.[212]

In September 1970 the showdown came after Salah Jadid's failed military expedition into Jordan in support of the Palestinian Liberation Organisation, which was locked in a struggle with the Jordanian monarchy.[213] By November 1970 Hafiz al-Asad had assumed control of the levers of power in Syria and Jadid was arrested and imprisoned. Asad enjoyed the backing of the key units in Syria's military, which by then had Alawites loyal to him in most of the key positions. Asad also consolidated his dominant position in the Ba'th Party by purging Alawite party members who were not loyal to him.[214] Incredibly, at the beginning of the 1970s, 900 years after the last Alawites had fled to the coastal mountains ahead of the Seljuk Turks, and only fifty years after they began returning to the Syrian interior in the 1920s, an Alawite was on the verge of openly assuming the leadership of the new Syrian state. But latent insecurity, chauvinism and mutual suspicion threatened a slide back towards sectarianism, even as most parties strove to establish secular systems of government.

In independent Syria, the strong sectarian 'asabiyya of the Alawites set against the weak 'asabiyya of the Sunni Arabs was significant. However, Arab (and Syrian) nationalism presented the sect with an opportunity to integrate into Syrian society in the first decades of independence. Alawite integration was buttressed by the emergence of class solidarity with poor rural Sunnis with a common interest in overturning the power structure of the urban aristocracy. For Syrians from the lower classes, from all sects, it appeared that Syria had achieved a genuine social and political revolution, which consigned primordial identities and fear to history.

3

APOGEE AND DECLINE

The rise to power of an Alawite in Syria would mark a highpoint in the sect's road towards integration as equal citizens of a diverse state. By 1973 cracks would begin to appear in the Syrian nation-building project, which the regime would attempt to remedy with the full force of the state. Fearful of surrendering their unprecedented gains, much of the Alawite sect supported the regime's resort to brutal repression of any opposition. Forcefully grasping for equality and acceptance in Syrian society against perceptions of rejection by the Sunni majority would, however, only accelerate a decline back toward social dislocation, fear and conflict. Alawite fear would, nonetheless, prove a valuable asset to the regime of Hafiz al-Asad in consolidating his hold over the institutions of the Syrian state.

Ibn Khaldun tells us that when a group has a strong leader and a high level of 'asabiyya relative to other groups, the political conditions exist for a dynasty or state to arise out of that group. Once formed, however, the 'asabiyya that brought a dynasty to power begins to erode gradually through such factors as urbanisation, luxury, decadence and corruption, resulting in the eventual emergence of a vigorous new dynasty with superior 'asabiyya to displace the senile dynasty. Hence if luxury and decadence were largely absent, urbanisation was only partial, the most blatant corruption was hidden and sectarian rather than just tribal 'asabiyya was present, would a dynasty be able to uphold the level of 'asabiyya critical to its long-term survival?

In terms of the historic development of Alawite sectarian 'asabiyya and the subsequent capture of power by Hafiz al-Asad, it seems that Ibn Khaldun does provide a cogent explanation for Alawite political history, but did Alawite 'asabiyya actually then begin to decline towards an inevitable demise of Asad rule? What factors could allow for the preservation of high levels of Alawite 'asabiyya? The small size of the Alawite community relative to the Sunni Arab majority, combined with the demographic diversity of the Syrian lands, posed challenges for the consolidation of Hafiz al-Asad's rule. He would require the broad support of the previously divided Alawite community; a necessity that Asad seemed to understand. Ultimately, insecurity remained a primary factor in the maintenance of Alawite 'asabiyya even though they supposedly became the 'dominant minority' in Syria.[1]

The thirty-year period following Hafiz al-Asad's ascension to power was an unprecedented time in Alawite history in which they were effectively 'catapulted' from obscurity into the middle of Syrian and Middle Eastern politics.[2] Ironically, the Alawite community became increasingly obscured from view over the course of Hafiz al-Asad's rule. This can partly be put down to the regime's policies, which actively discouraged sectarian discourse,[3] but also to the fact that Hafiz al-Asad himself became the focus of international scrutiny as far as Syria was concerned. The Alawite community was, however, the critical axis upon which swung the fortunes of the Asad dynasty and ultimately the Syrian state.

The stability experienced by Syria after the consolidation of Asad rule has been attributed by Syria scholar Raymond Hinnebusch to social, political and economic processes that broadened the regime's power base beyond the Alawite community.[4] This appraisal is accurate to the extent that Hafiz al-Asad successfully incorporated non-Alawite elements into his power structure, such as rural Sunnis, other religious minorities[5] and segments of the Sunni merchant class (in Damascus especially).[6] It cannot be ignored, however, that the Alawite community remained the 'keystone' of this power structure.[7]

According to Ibn Khaldun:

A ruler can achieve power only with the help of his own people. They are his group and his helpers in his enterprise. He uses them to fight against those who revolt against his dynasty. It is they with whom he fills the administrative offices, who, he appoints as wazirs and tax collectors. They help him to achieve superiority ...[8]

Hafiz al-Asad mobilised Alawites along these lines and used them to staff important posts in the government and security forces. Ultimately, it was the Alawites that allowed Hafiz al-Asad to achieve 'superiority'. If Alawite support fell away from the Asad regime, it would certainly not have survived the period of active opposition between 1976 and 1982. Moreover, the stability of Syria beyond 1982 was largely a result of the brutal example that was made of regime opponents using Alawite troops, and the omnipresent surveillance of the population by Alawites in the intelligence agencies (Mukhabarat). Yet despite the fact that Alawites underpinned the stability of the Asad regime, this still did not make it an Alawite regime.

Although Salah Jadid and Hafiz al-Asad had wielded political power from behind the scenes in the late 1960s, and both pursued political goals far beyond limited sectarian interests, the Syrian Ba'thist regime steadily came to be viewed in some quarters as an 'Alawite regime'. The official inauguration of Hafiz al-Asad as president only escalated suspicions that an Alawite cabal had usurped power. Three key factors contributed to a belief that the Asad regime was biased towards Alawites: the drafting of a new Syrian constitution in 1973, which neglected to specify that the president must be a Muslim; the placement of Alawites into important roles in the military and government; and nepotism towards relatives, such as Hafiz al-Asad's brother Rifa'at, whose open excesses produced widespread antipathy towards the regime. Conversely, from Alawite perspectives, the Sunni reaction to the new constitution and sectarian violence between 1976 and 1982 fed feelings of insecurity about continued religious chauvinism by Sunni Muslims.

In reality, it was not an Alawite regime with sectarian goals. The Asad regime needed the Alawites as its only reliable support, and Alawites felt they required Asad regime survival to avoid a return to their inferior social status, or worse, a violent Sunni backlash. As will be explained, the sect became deadlocked in a 'Faustian' relationship with the Asad regime at Hama in February 1982. Consequently, Alawite aspirations for full and sustainable emancipation in Syrian society were left unfulfilled.

In theory Asad rule represented the long-term opportunity to direct the core identity of Syria towards Syrianism, Arabism or a more inclusive broad-based Islam, all of which could assist Alawite political status,[9] yet Alawite sectarian minority status was solidified during this period. This is shown by their continued apprehension about the majority Sunni Arabs, and consequent reluctance to move out of alignment with the Asad regime, which only strengthened the Asad dynasty's hold on power. Did having members of their community in power impact favourably or negatively on Alawite political standing and security? As already shown in the previous chapter, when Alawites overstepped the bounds of Sunni Muslim toleration the repercussions were often severe for the group in general. In the context of Alawite history, the period from 1970 to 2000 went far beyond anything that had occurred previously in terms of Alawites going out on a political limb.

Early Asad Rule

At the beginning of the 1970s the Alawite situation was seemingly better than any previous period in the sect's history, including the Hamdanid period. Secular and socialist policies, first adopted by the Ba'th regime during the 1960s, were socio-economically advantageous for Alawites. Alawite security was buttressed by their predominance in the armed forces and having one of their 'own' in the presidential palace in Damascus. Syria had the Soviet Union as a superpower sponsor to buttress regime stability. Even the Sunni urban bourgeoisie were positive about the stabilisation of the political situation and welcomed Hafiz al-Asad's relaxation of Salah Jadid's radical economic reforms.[10] In this political atmosphere Alawites could understandably have felt some optimism about their future.

The Syrian Alawite population in 1970 was approximately 690,000,[11] 11 per cent of the Syrian population of 6,305,000, an increase from 10.6 per cent in 1960.[12] This represented a positive shift in Alawite demography, reversing their declining proportion in the first decades of Syrian independence. This could have been due to improved living conditions for rural populations under Ba'thist rule. Another factor was the large-scale emigration of mainly Sunni, urban professionals and businessmen from the late

1950s due to political turbulence and socialist reforms.[13] In 1970 the Alawites remained mostly rural and a majority in the Latakia and Tartous coastal districts,[14] but Alawite migration to the cities increased during the period of Asad rule.[15] The demography of Latakia, especially, changed dramatically in the 1970s, as Alawites moved into the town seeking better opportunities. The Latakia Sunnis, formerly the majority, became a minority with the Christians.

The flow of Alawites to Damascus continued as well. The Sunnis (and Christians), long established in Damascus, however, maintained their pre-eminent position in the souq (marketplace). Hafiz al-Asad staffed a majority of the government and security departments, important to regime maintenance, with more 'reliable' Alawites.[16] For Alawites, the best opportunity for stable income was the army, the Mukhabarat and the large bureaucracy. Hence there was a sectarian basis to the division of labour, with the Sunnis in the traditional private economic sector and Alawites occupying much of the public sector. While it seemed that the Alawites were finally becoming emancipated in the Syrian state, in reality it was a contrived situation.

The historic alienation of the Alawites from the majority of Syrian society continued. Now, rather than being viewed as despised, heretical and rustic mountain men, the Alawites were the threatening soldiers, or Mukhabarat, on the street corners and the 'faceless' bureaucrats in government departments. Moreover, the autochthonous Damascenes, Aleppans or Latakians for that matter, did not want these 'inferior' Alawites (or the other rural minorities) in their proud 'Islamic' cities.[17] Even so, the continuation of sectarianism in Syrian politics into the 1970s was not desired by any of the communities. This was, after all, the basis of the broad attraction of the Ba'th Party and secularism in general.

If Alawite goals had originally been based on achieving social and political emancipation in the Syrian state, did the leading Alawite individual share this aspiration, and was it his goal to help his co-sectarians achieve it? How should Hafiz al-Asad be defined? According to Henry Kissinger, Hafiz al-Asad was an extremely shrewd and pragmatic purveyor of political strategy.[18] It can be concluded, however, that he was not so pragmatic that he was devoid of idealism. Both Asad and Salah Jadid shared similar ideals of secular socio-economic political reform that would benefit disadvantaged groups like the Alawites.[19] Although Asad's more pragmatic approach saw him emerge as the victor in the contest with Jadid, this does not mean that he abandoned his ideals. Instead, he pursued a different path to their attainment.

Middle East scholar Daniel Pipes posed the question of whether Alawites like Hafiz al-Asad were primarily motivated by ideology, ambition or sectarianism; however, this assumes that these factors are separable.[20] A better perspective is to see these factors as intertwined. Abd al-Halim Khaddam, a Sunni from Banyas and a friend and colleague of Asad in the Ba'th cadres from Latakia since 1946, provided a personal perspective of the different elements of Hafiz al-Asad's personality:

Hafiz al-Asad was … like a structure, he had different sides. One of his sides was the pragmatic side, if you look at it that way, you can say he was pragmatic. From another side you can see that he was an idealist. One side you can say that his personality—you can see that he was a very decent person. But from his other side, the fourth side of the structure he was very … in the way he let his family control the power … he started corruption … for his family. It … opposes his idealistic side, and his pragmatic side. So he had all these sides to him. He was able of course to talk about people and the welfare of people and his beliefs—how he's going to help people. At the same time he was [allowing] his inner circle to become more powerful, run the country through corruption and through military control. And [on] one side he was very nationalistic, he didn't really care that he was from a minority group, he thought that everyone was equal. But again there was something about him that always—on the other side—supported his minority.[21]

According to Khaddam, Hafiz al-Asad had conflicting pragmatic, idealist, corrupt and sectarian sides to his personality. This description supports the idea that Hafiz al-Asad's intentions and goals cannot be explained by any one factor. Asad had a genuine secular ideology, which he attempted to apply to Syrian politics through a pragmatic approach, yet it cannot be ignored that he supported his minority in a way that can only be described as a type of sectarianism. While his secular ideology opposed sectarian particularism, it was only by mobilising the sectarian 'asabiyya of his community, or as Ibn Khaldun wrote 'with the help of his own people …' that he could gain a stable political platform in the turbulent arena of Syrian politics.[22]

Abd al-Halim Khaddam raises another crucial point about the corrupt role of Hafiz al-Asad's family. Khaddam had reason to be disappointed at Hafiz al-Asad granting political power to his family members; as vice-president and the most experienced and capable politician below Asad, he may have expected to be a candidate for the presidency.[23] As it happened, members of Hafiz al-Asad's family increasingly played crucial roles in the regime, especially during and after the difficult years from 1976 to 1982.[24] This was especially so of Asad's brother Rifa'at, who was 'let off the leash' in order to save the regime at its most perilous moment in February 1982.[25] The excesses of Hafiz al-Asad's family members would have implications for the wider Alawite community as they became associated with general perceptions about the nature of the Syrian regime.

A quite different perspective of Hafiz al-Asad comes from the Alawite shaykh, Naṣīr Eskiocak:

I remember before Hafiz al-Asad, in Syria, every six months there was a military coup.[26] They [Syrians] used to harm themselves, they used to fight, and they used to jail each other. When Hafiz al-Asad took the power Syria was held stable by him for thirty years. He was taking care of Syria and its rights. On one hand he ruled in a very dictatorial way but fair; he had dictatorial power, but fair and with justice. ... Hafiz al-Asad ... didn't use tyranny, he used equality and rights and the Syrian people were so satisfied with him that they replaced him with his son Bashar al-Asad. [He was] a conciliatory ruler who helped conciliate ... with righteousness and equality.[27]

The key element to take from this definition of Hafiz al-Asad is the emphasis on equality, justice and conciliation. This view may seem incompatible with commonly held estimations of Asad's iron-fisted and repressive rule; however, from Alawite perspectives, after hundreds of years of political inequality and sectarian discrimination by Sunni Muslim overlords, Hafiz al-Asad's rule may have seemed like the epitome of egalitarianism—a situation which Alawites would fight to defend.

In the early stages of Hafiz al-Asad's rule it appeared that Syrians, in general, accepted the fact of his presidency. This was, perhaps, seen by Alawites as an indication of a burgeoning Syrian nationalism, which transcended sectarianism. Asad's initial popularity seemed a far cry from previous examples of Alawite rule over populations including Sunni Muslims; Ismail Khayr Bey, for instance, was never accepted by Sunni Arabs,

Mahmud Pasha was quickly assassinated and the representative council of the Alawite State was hampered by Sunni opposition. Hafiz al-Asad, however, aided his cause by investing considerable resources to winning over the religious establishment, particularly in Damascus, with donations and generous endowments.[28] But mostly, after two decades of extreme political volatility, the Syrians desired stability, something that Hafiz al-Asad appeared capable of delivering.

In 1973 the publication of the first permanent Syrian constitution since 1961 provided a 'litmus test' of Alawite status in the new era.[29] Prior to Asad's ascension to the presidency it was taken for granted in most quarters that the president, even if only in a puppet role, should be Sunni Muslim.[30] Asad's assumption of the powers of the presidency on 12 March 1971 contravened this general rule. Moreover, the initial version of the new constitution published in January 1973 neglected to stipulate that the president need be Muslim at all.[31] It is difficult to believe that this was an oversight by Asad, who sought to demote the role of religion in a new secular Syria. For Alawites, not to mention Christians and other minorities, majority acceptance of the new constitution would show that religious obstacles to their full political emancipation were a thing of the past and that secularism had taken root in Syria. The mass protests that ensued across the country proved this was not the case.[32]

Demonstrations occurred in Aleppo, Homs and Hama, and in Damascus religious leaders circulated a demand that Islam be declared the religion of the state. In Hama, government troops and demonstrators clashed, resulting in sixty killed or wounded.[33] These events proved that religion remained of extreme importance in Ba'thist Syria and, moreover, it became quite clear that many Sunnis remained acutely aware of Asad's problematic religious credentials. Hafiz al-Asad quickly backtracked and included in an amendment to the original draft that 'the religion of the President of the Republic has to be Islam'.[34] This was a turning point for Alawites. While undercurrents of sectarianism began emerging in the 1960s, the general trajectory had appeared to be towards their eventual equal integration in Syria. The Sunni rejection of the new constitution, mandating a secular state without religious discrimination, was perceived as a profound rejection by the Alawites, which rekindled their insecurity.

The protests firmed Alawite dependence on Hafiz al-Asad, who verbally retaliated on behalf of the minorities: 'true Islam should not be narrow-mindedness and awful extremism, as Islam is a religion of love, progress, social justice and equality'.[35] This language touched on the very core of Alawite concerns about their place in Syria. This was evident in the views of the Alawite Shaykh Nasīr Eskiocak, who described Asad as 'a conciliatory ruler who helped conciliate ... with righteousness and equality'.[36]

Questions about whether Alawites were Muslim or not became of extreme importance, not only for the legitimacy of Asad's presidency but also for the security of the Alawites. Hafiz al-Asad's close ally, Abd al-Halim Khaddam, suggested that '[In] the Syrian constitution, the president has to be Muslim, not Sunni Muslim or Alawi Muslim.'[37] He implies, therefore, that there is no question over the Muslim credentials of Alawites. Unfortunately for the Alawites and the popular legitimacy of Asad's regime, many Syrians did not share Khaddam's outlook in the early 1970s. Further proof of the Islamic basis of the Alawite religion was required. Here the Alawites received assistance from influential orthodox Shi'ites.

Ayatollah Hasan Mahdi al-Shirazi (d.1980) was a prominent Iraqi Shi'a cleric who was expelled from Iraq in 1969/70.[38] After resettling in Beirut, he spent considerable time in the Alawite regions of Syria and Lebanon and developed close relations with Hafiz al-Asad. In December 1972, al-Shirazi issued a fatwa that stated: 'I found them [the Alawites]—as I expected—to be Shi'a of *ahl al Bayt* [the house of the Prophet] who are loyal and totally committed to the truth.'[39] This statement seems to conflict with contrary evidence that al-Shirazi spent considerable time and effort trying to convert Alawites to Shi'ism.[40] It is possible that al-Shirazi's fatwa had more to do with a mutually beneficial political alliance with Hafiz al-Asad, involving much-needed Islamic buttressing for the new president, in return for Syrian protection to the exiled cleric.[41] As it was, al-Shirazi was assassinated in Beirut in 1980, most likely by Iraqi Ba'th agents.[42]

Despite the endorsements of the mufti of Jerusalem, Amin al-Husayni, and Ayatollah al-Shirazi regarding the Islamic character of the Alawites, some Syrian Sunnis remained sceptical. The Muslim Brotherhood opposition worked hard to promote this scepticism in the early 1970s. After the constitution-related riots, however, Alawites received support from another

Shi'ite imam, Musa al-Sadr, who declared the Alawites' doctrinal unity with the Twelver Shi'a,[43] and in July 1973 stated: 'Today those Muslims called Alawis are the brothers of the Shi'a ... we will not allow anyone to condemn this generous creed.'[44]

The return of Shi'a support to the Alawites in the 1970s came after a long pause. This was partially due to the political marginality of the Shi'a themselves. Up until the 1970s Shi'ites carried little political weight in the Arab world. The closest Shi'a community of any size resided in Lebanon. In the period between their persecution by the Mamluks around 1305/7, and their political awakening in the 1970s,[45] the Lebanese Shi'a faced socio-economic and political disabilities similar to those of the Alawites.[46] By the 1970s, the consociational communal political structure of Lebanon meant that the Shi'ite population had begun to assume political relevance.[47] Musa al-Sadr played a key role in the mobilisation of the Lebanese Shi'ites, who would come to be important and reliable allies for the Asad regime and the Alawites.

Besides his religious defence of the Alawites, Musa al-Sadr provided vital early political support to Hafiz al-Asad's regime, otherwise isolated in the Arab world.[48] Al-Sadr never failed to support the positions of the Asad regime between 1972 and 1978—for example, he was the most enthusiastic advocate of the controversial 'Damascus Agreement' of 1976 on Lebanon.[49] In addition, al-Sadr supported the Asad regime in its confrontation with the Lebanese Druze politician Kamal Jumblatt, issues concerning the Palestinians and, most importantly, its physical intervention in Lebanon with 12,000 troops in June 1976.[50] Imam Musa al-Sadr 'disappeared' on a trip to Libya in August 1978. It is assumed he was assassinated the same day he was due to meet with Colonel Qaddafi.[51]

As Hafiz al-Asad was not a particularly religious individual,[52] it could be said that the promotion of an orthodox Shi'a religious identity for Alawites was really part of his pragmatic attempts to consolidate his own legitimacy. Many Alawites were initially not very enthusiastic about losing their separate identity and resented being lumped together with the Shi'a. This was particularly so among Lebanese Alawites, but also for some Syrian Alawite shaykhs.[53] In Lebanon, opposition to the submergence of Alawite identity led to the formation of the Alawite Youth Movement (AYM), led by Ali Eid (b.1940).[54]

According to his former teacher at the American University of Beirut, Elie Salem, 'Ali Eid was an excellent student as well as an affable and thoughtful individual, certainly not a radical.[55] He represented the new generation of educated Alawites who sought greater emancipation and open Alawite representation in Lebanese politics. In 1975, with the outbreak of the Lebanese civil war, and the entry of Syrian forces, the AYM would become the Arab Democratic Party (ADP). The armed branch of the party was called Al-Fursan al-Hammur al-Arabi (The Arab Red Knights), and was closely allied with Hafiz al-Asad's younger brother, Rifa'at.[56]

In 1973 a group of Alawite religious leaders in Syria issued a formal declaration that denied Alawite religious heterodoxy and proclaimed that the Alawites 'followed the majority of Shi'a and whatever else was attributed to them consisted of lies fabricated by their enemies and the enemies of Islam'.[57] If the reaction of some Alawites to Mamluk attempts in the early fourteenth century to channel them into religious orthodoxy is recalled, it is interesting that Alawites acquiesced so easily to having their particular creed publicly extinguished. In contrast to their inherent hostility for Sunni orthodoxy, however, Alawites have often aligned themselves with the Shi'a tradition, as is evident from their early history. Alawite sectarian apprehension, triggered by the strong reaction of Sunnis to the new Syrian constitution, possibly led to a general application of taqiyya, which precluded the open discussion of Alawite particularism. In any case, from this time, open Alawite opposition to 'merging' their identity with the Twelver Shi'a disappears.[58]

Between 1970 and 1972, Hafiz al-Asad consolidated his predominant position among the Alawite community and disposed of Alawite Ba'thists who did not align themselves with him.[59] Thereafter, a process is evident of Alawites falling into line behind the policies of the Asad regime and its political allies such as Musa al-Sadr. In short, there was a developing tendency for Alawites to let Hafiz al-Asad speak and act on their behalf, in effect placing the security of the community in his hands.

An early example of this occurred when the Syrian military intervened in Lebanon in April 1976.[60] Explanations for Syria's entry into the Lebanese arena include suggestions that Hafiz al-Asad 'considered it to be in the interest of his minority Alawite regime'.[61] Bearing in mind the sectarian tensions simmering in Syria following their supposed 'hijacking' of power, Alawites must have viewed sectarian violence in Lebanon with some trepidation.

The sectarian animosities apparent in the Lebanese conflict no doubt sparked fears among Alawites of a 'contagion' effect in Syria.[62] It may, therefore, have been the intention of the Asad regime to intervene in Lebanon in order to contain the situation and prevent an overflow into Syria. Other possible factors in Hafiz al-Asad's decision to intervene in Lebanon were the political threats posed by Lebanon, both as a refuge for political dissidents and as a model for multi-confessional democracy. With its pluralist political structure, Lebanon had long provided space for political activism by exiles and dissidents from Syria's political struggles.[63] The turmoil in Lebanon provided an opportunity for Asad to silence criticism of his regime; for example, Khalil Brayez a former Syrian army captain and critic of Hafiz al-Asad since the 1967 war, was kidnapped in Lebanon and taken back to Syria.[64] The Asad regime also disliked the thought of the Palestinians achieving political autonomy, and dreaded the prospect of the Lebanese Christians embracing Israeli protection. Overall, Hafiz al-Asad needed to control Lebanon in order to buttress his rule in Syria.

The outcome for the Alawites from the Syrian alignment with Lebanese Maronite Christians against Sunni Muslim Palestinians[65] was to help push subterranean tensions to the surface in Syria.[66] It seemed to prove for some Syrian Sunnis that the Asad regime was indeed antithetical to Muslim causes, and verified for many the suspect religious loyalties of Alawites in general.[67]

Another aspect to the sectarian conflict in Lebanon, with its pluralist democratic system, was to provide the Syrian regime with a good argument about the benefits of strong authoritarian rule. Hannah Batatu suggested that Lebanese politician Kamal Jumblatt sought the 'democratic emancipation of an entire [Lebanese] people', including his own Druze community, which 'gave the Asad regime the shivers'.[68] Sectarian strife in Lebanon had the effect of keeping Alawite insecurity on edge, preventing any slippage of 'asabiyya. Ironically, what Syrian Alawites originally wanted was something similar to a functioning Lebanese political system, where they could preserve their separate identity but still be equal citizens, which would lead to a diminution of Alawite sectarian 'asabiyya for Asad rule.

In terms of pure strategic calculations, the most obvious threat to the Syrian regime was Israel. If the Israelis took advantage of a weak Lebanon they could outflank the Golan Heights via the Beka'a Valley, which would see them in close proximity to Damascus, the industrial centres of Homs and Hama[69] and in striking distance of the Alawite heartland to the north. Overall, the nature of the Lebanese political scene with its vulnerability to external manipulation meant that if Syria did not assert its interests there, another power would.

A side effect of Syrian intervention in Lebanon, in support of right-wing Christians, was a temporary warming of US and French relations with the Ba'th regime. It was perhaps illustrative that Hafiz al-Asad went to Paris in 1976, his first visit to a Western country, while he postponed trips to Eastern Europe.[70] By the mid-1970s, Hafiz al-Asad was perceived internationally as a positive force for stability and progress in the Middle East region.[71] However, similarly to previous eras, real political opposition to the Alawites came not from major powers but from the local Sunni Arab population.

The Muslim Brotherhood Rebellion

The first six years of Hafiz al-Asad's rule saw initial Alawite hopes for genuine social and political integration in Syria gradually eroded by their continued social alienation, the constitution riots and the sectarian violence in Lebanon. The events to follow would, however, act to further galvanise the Alawites' dependence on the Asad regime.

The Syrian Muslim Brotherhood, part of the wider Sunni Islamist organisation that had originated in Egypt in 1928,[72] launched its 'all-out struggle' against the Asad regime in February 1976.[73] The direct cause of their rising against the regime was a brutal crackdown on dissent in the city of Hama by elite forces under the command of Rifa'at al-Asad in February 1976.[74] Yet the deeper causes of violent opposition to the Asad regime had been building for some time. Discontent was fuelled by the secular constitution, economic dissatisfaction among Sunni merchants, Syrian regime involvement in Lebanon and general resentment about Alawites 'usurping' a dominant role in Syria. The Muslim Brotherhood sympathiser, Dr Umar

Abdallah, revealed the sentiment behind the insurgency in his 1983 'partisan account', *The Islamic Struggle in Syria*:[75]

it has always been the consensus of the Muslim *'ulama*, both Sunni and Shi'i that the Nusairis are *kuffar* (disbelievers, rejecters of faith) ... Furthermore nine or ten percent of the population cannot be allowed to dominate the majority because that is against the logic of things, and we are quite sure that the wise men of the sect agree with us that neither we nor they are obliged to support the empire of Hafiz and Rifa'at Asad. In our case, the sectarian war was not waged by the majority trying to protect itself against the minority. It is definitely the minority that forgot itself ...[76]

This extract shows five key elements in the mentality of the insurgents. First, the Muslim credentials of the Alawites remained in question; it seems that the fatwas of al-Husayni (1936), al-Shirazi (1972) and al-Sadr (1973) were disregarded. Secondly, the Alawite sect was firmly associated with the Asad regime by the Muslim Brothers, which is indicated by the comment that 9 or 10 per cent of the population should not dominate the majority. Third, that the Asads were viewed as an 'empire' suggests that in Muslim Brotherhood eyes the regime had no legitimacy. Fourthly, the description of a 'sectarian war' reveals a mindset held by the Muslim Brothers, according to which it was a war between Sunnis and Alawites. Finally, and importantly, the comment that the 'minority forgot itself' recalls a chauvinistic attitude towards the Alawites who had stepped outside the bounds of Sunni toleration. Although Abdallah appeals to Alawites that they are 'not obliged to support' the Asads, this type of discourse would only strengthen Alawite support for the regime. To be labelled 'minority heretics' who had 'forgotten themselves' would do little to reassure ordinary Alawites that a post-Asad Syria could be favourable to their interests.

In the heart of the Alawite territory, support for the regime was as strong as ever at the end of 1976. In Hafiz al-Asad's home town, Qardaha, 20 kilometres south-east of Latakia, the local population proudly watched 'Uncle Hafiz' on television, being hailed in military processions: 'With our souls and with our blood we will sacrifice ourselves for you!'[77] Meanwhile, around the country political tensions were escalating. In Damascus, government buildings were heavily guarded and there were public hangings of 'terrorists'. In Aleppo there were bombings and civil disturbances.[78]

By 1977 the Muslim Brothers were waging an assassination campaign against high-ranking Alawites close to the regime. Victims included military personnel, such as Brigadier Hamid Razzouk and Colonel Ali Haidar. The murder of Dr Mohammad al-Fadel, the dissident president of Damascus University, initially attributed to the Muslim Brotherhood, has since been a source of debate, with some claiming it was in fact the regime who assassinated him.[79] Although the common feature was that victims were Alawites, government sources were careful not to emphasise this aspect and blamed the murders on the rival Iraqi Ba'thist regime.[80] Although Saddam Hussein would not have been displeased to see his Syrian Ba'thist rivals suffering such blows, there is little evidence to suggest he was directly responsible for the attacks. The Asad regime's reason for blaming Iraq was to avoid a portrayal of the conflict in sectarian terms, which would act against the secular pillars of the regime's legitimacy.[81] In addition, Hafiz al-Asad made special efforts to attend prayers at the Sunni Umayyad Mosque every Friday to prove his religious credentials.[82] It is important to note that the attacks were not entirely restricted to Alawites, but also Sunnis who worked closely with the regime. For instance, Asad's Sunni foreign minister, Abd al-Halim Khaddam, was wounded in an assassination attempt in early 1977.[83]

While the Muslim brothers were engaged in arbitrary acts of assassination in the hope of highlighting the Alawite political role(s), the Syrian regime was suspected of waging its own campaign of political assassinations, but for the opposite reason: to conceal the Alawite political role. On 16 March 1977, Lebanese Druze politician Kamal Jumblat was assassinated near his home village of Mukhtarah.[84] Jumblat had become an obstacle to Hafiz al-Asad's objectives in Lebanon by defying Syria's role in the Lebanese theatre.[85] It was, however, Jumblat's comments about the Alawite character of the Syrian regime that may have cost him his life. Karim Bakradouni, a member of the Lebanese Phalanges Party in the 1970s, suggests that:

when Kamal Jumblat began broaching that prohibited equation i.e. the talk about the Alawi-Sunni conflict or about a[n] Alawi-Maronite alliance; he was making what I consider a big mistake.[86]

Kamal Jumblat's son Walid, who took over the leadership of the Lebanese Druze, also believed that his father got into an 'inappropriate conversation, so to speak, against the Alawi confession in itself'.[87] It seems that the topic of Alawite political roles was highly sensitive and the Asad regime felt compelled to take any measure to stamp out the discourse altogether. The preparedness of the Asad regime to assassinate major political figures who threatened its core interests surfaced with the murder of Jumblat. According to Bassam Abu Sherif of the Palestinian Liberation Organisation (PLO), Jumblat 'was a great man, a giant, and he was killed because he was a great man and a giant'.[88] The PLO leader, Yasir Arafat, said at the time 'an era of assassinations has begun'.[89]

In Syria, despite regime efforts to defuse the domestic tensions and to eliminate accusations of an Alawite political cabal, the danger for the regime and ordinary Alawites continued to escalate. A major catalyst for escalation of the conflict occurred on 16 June 1979 when a large group of mostly Alawite cadets were massacred at the Aleppo artillery academy.[90] The massacre was intended to provoke a brutal response from the regime, which in turn would lead to a widening of the uprising among Sunni Muslims. The massacre, orchestrated by a Sunni Ba'thist officer, was a worrying sign of increasing sectarian division and hatred within two of the regime's key pillars, the army and the Ba'th Party.[91] Two months later a prominent Alawite neurosurgeon was executed outside his clinic,[92] and in late September two high-ranking Alawite officers, Colonel Mohammad Jamil Naddah, and Lieutenant Colonel Ibrahim Alia, were gunned down.[93] While most of the Sunni community did not approve of the Muslim Brothers' tactics, many could, however, empathise with the insurgents' motivation, as they felt increasingly excluded from economic and political power.[94]

With emotions rising on all sides, Hafiz al-Asad needed to perform a delicate balancing act to maintain the essential support of the Alawites without alienating the moderate Sunni majority. Crystallisation along sectarian lines (as was occurring in Lebanon) would entail a very perilous situation for Alawites. The pressure bearing on the regime produced cracks in Asad's cross-sectarian coalition. One of the rural Sunnis near the top of the security apparatus, Major General Naji Jamil, a longtime friend of Hafiz al-Asad, was 'retired' in March 1978 after 'expressing disrespect for Asad' and his policies. He was replaced by an Alawite officer, General Muhammad al-Khuli.[95] Yet Hafiz al-Asad maintained a Ba'thist and nationalist discourse while accusing the insurgents of being extremists and agents of foreign enemy interests. For example, Information Minister Ahmad Iskander announced 'We have evidence that the extremist gangs behind the current killings are connected with the Camp David camp.'[96] In other words, the regime claimed that the United States was behind the Syrian unrest with the aim of 'punishing' the regime for its opposition to the peace accord between Egypt and Israel.[97]

With the escalation of the assassination campaign to two or three murders a week by October 1979,[98] there was a genuine risk of Alawite retaliation. This would make it impossible for Hafiz al-Asad to present the situation in non-sectarian terms. In late August/early September, Alawites rioted and fought Sunni Muslims in Latakia after Youssef Sarem, an Alawite religious leader, was assassinated.[99] Although there is conflicting evidence about casualties from the rioting, it seems that the violence was at a relatively low-level.[100] However, 1,000 paratroopers under the command of Rifa'at al-Asad were quickly deployed to the city to suppress the Alawite rioters and five people were reported killed.[101] The nature and rapidity of Asad's response speaks volumes about the danger that he perceived of escalation in sectarian violence between Sunnis and Alawites. Reports that Tartous 90 kilometres to the south of Latakia, was closed to civilian traffic, indicate that sectarian tensions had already begun to spread.[102] It seemed as if the objectives of the Muslim Brotherhood in highlighting sectarian divisions were beginning to achieve results. In Damascus, Alawites clung together for security, with some military personnel even sending their families home to the Latakia region following death threats.[103]

Signs of discord among Alawites and against the Asad regime began to emerge. Alawite security bosses began demanding a stronger response to the Brotherhood attacks, while on the other hand Alawite liberals, concerned about long-term consequences for the sect, began questioning whether the president should 'include more Sunnis in his regime' to appease the Sunni majority.[104] An Alawite poet, Mamdūh 'Udwān (d.2004), decried the 'sectarian face' of the regime at a meeting of the Union of Writers and Journalists on 9 October 1979 and remarked, 'why does the regime lie? Lies stem from fear and the regime that lies fears the people, fears that the people will see it as it really is.'[105] In addition, there were some rumblings among Alawites that those with tribal connections to Hafiz al-Asad were disproportionately favoured.[106] Asad's choices lay between conciliatory approaches towards moderate Sunnis while trying to marginalise the Muslim Brothers as minority extremists, or he could ramp up security measures to stamp out criticism of the regime altogether. Initially it seemed as if Asad leaned toward the former approach.[107]

In contrast to the Ottomans in the 1850s, it seemed the Muslim Brotherhood was unable to splinter Alawite solidarity and actually achieved the reverse effect. The Syrian military, with its preponderance of Alawites, showed 'no signs of disaffection' and the Alawite community rallied around the president.[108] Political conditions had altered dramatically since the time of Ismail Khayr Bey. First, the Sunnis were no longer represented by a powerful and coherent political structure; in fact, it was the reverse and the Alawites stood on the side of the hegemonic political formation. Secondly, the Alawites were no longer restricted to their compartmentalised mountain region and had developed a much broader identity based on their common experience relative to the Syrian majority. Although Ismail Khayr Bey undoubtedly had leadership abilities, he was no comparison to the well-educated and politically astute Hafiz al-Asad in 1979. The most crucial element, however, was the extent to which the Alawites had gone out on to a political limb. The stakes of a political reversal were far too high for the Alawite tribes to risk any serious internal fragmentation of their community. Hafiz al-Asad had ruled over Syria for a decade, more than twice as long as Ismail Khayr Bey's brief governance in the Jabal al-Sahiliyah. It did seem, however, that history may have been about to catch up to the Alawites.

By 1980 full-scale sectarian civil war between Sunnis and Alawites seemed imminent in Syria.[109] Three factors contributed to an increase in tensions. First, socialist policies and high inflation (30 per cent) fuelled resentment among the merchant class, leading to strikes and demonstrations.[110] One Aleppo merchant voiced his frustration with government policy: 'We do not like socialism and we do not like the Russians ... you cannot work and make money under socialism.'[111] Secondly, the Islamic revolution in Iran also lent impetus to opposition to the Syrian regime;

even among secular Syrians. This was ironic considering the relationship that would develop between the Islamic Republic of Iran and the Asad regime. A report from Aleppo dated 31 March 1980 revealed growing anti-regime sentiments; a civil servant stated: 'There's no Shah or Khomeini here, but otherwise it's like Iran—a ruling clan with its secret police, excessive military spending, illicit wealth and thousands of political prisoners.'[112] An engineer said that 'like Iran, the people are against corruption and immorality and are with the Muslim Brothers, we're Muslims … but we don't want an Islamic republic'.[113] Comments like these highlight how the Muslim Brotherhood was winning the contest for the moral high ground in their struggle with the Asad regime.

The final factor was resentment about perceptions of corruption by the regime, in particular the president's brother Rifa'at al-Asad, which also began to undermine the credibility of Hafiz al-Asad in early 1980. Critics asked how an 'honourable man could allow corruption to spread into his own family?'[114] These sources of resentment against the regime began to find overall expression in anti-Alawite sentiment. A professional man, who requested anonymity, voiced the connection between the Alawites and the mushrooming discontent among Syrians. He said that the main problem in Syria was the domination of power by Alawites through their hold on key positions in the armed forces and the civilian and military intelligence; he suggested that most students allowed to go abroad are Alawites who return to take key jobs. 'We're a secular family but we're with the Muslim Brothers—like 90 per cent of this city [Aleppo].'[115]

The Asad regime, alarmed by the surge of sympathy for the Muslim Brotherhood among moderate Sunnis, decided on a direct course of action. On 6 and 7 April 1980, the Third Army and Special Forces units commanded by Rifa'at al-Asad entered Aleppo and Hama in force. For around two weeks both cities were swept for weapons and Muslim Brotherhood members and sympathisers.[116] The crackdown was severe with around 6,000 people arrested and thirty executed.[117] The Mukhabarat played a major, often ruthless role, in repressing the growing dissent. For instance, men were often apprehended for simply having a beard.[118] Harsh examples were made of others, such as two doctors from Hama who were taken from their homes and summarily shot and then mutilated.[119] The predominance of Alawites in both the military and intelligence units involved in the crackdowns served to increase sectarian tensions.

For Alawites, who had sought integration in Syria through secularism and a social revolution, growing negative perceptions of the Asad regime portended the failure of those aspirations. For instance, the Syrian Communist Party strongly criticised the regime in 1980, 'When the French ruled this country they failed to divide it like this regime … this regime rests on two bases: sectarianism and despotism …'[120] Nonetheless, escalating insecurity among Alawites further embedded their reliance on Hafiz al-Asad's regime.

The regime narrowly avoided catastrophe on 27 (or 26)[121] June 1980, when the Muslim Brotherhood came close to assassinating Hafiz al-Asad in a grenade attack. He was apparently saved by a bodyguard who fell on the device.[122] There is little information on the identity of the bodyguard, but assuming he was an Alawite, possibly from Asad's clan, as was the norm,[123] it shows the depth of devotion that was held for Asad.[124] According to Syria scholar and diplomat Nikolaos van Dam, the assassination attempt on Hafiz al-Asad created a 'wave of fury' in the Alawite community. Rifa'at al-Asad ordered eighty men of his defence companies to fly by helicopter to the prison at Palmyra where they massacred between 550[125] and 1,181[126] Muslim Brotherhood prisoners in their cells. The sheer savagery of this event hardly bears comprehension and gives some indication of the level of animosity that was possible between Alawites and the Muslim Brotherhood.

Hafiz al-Asad still worked to defuse tensions both with displays of force and by seeking to appease opposition leaders with promises of government reform.[127] He also continued to pursue a policy of undermining the Muslim Brothers by shifting blame for the unrest to external factors. In a speech on 8 March, Asad said he had been a devout Muslim all his life, and sarcastically derided the Muslim Brothers: 'but they do not want to accept my Islam … maybe I need a certificate of good conduct from their masters in Washington. To do that I need to go to Jerusalem to submit to the Israelis as Sadat has done.'[128] It could be read that Asad was referring to 'my' Islam as Alawite Islam, which would be a rare acknowledgement of his Alawite origins. However, he was also using a clever strategy that has become a hallmark of the Asad regime, discrediting opponents by linking them with unpopular events involving the United States and the Israelis, in this case Egyptian President Anwar Sadat's peace deal with the Israelis.

The regime also looked to its rural support base in its struggle with the urban Muslim Brothers. On 10 March 1980, Asad announced to the General Federation of Syrian Peasants plans to put half a million peasants under arms, stating: 'The peasants will exercise the role of liquidating gangs of reaction, killers and saboteurs.'[129] The 'peasants' in this case would include Alawites but also rural Sunnis who had benefited from Ba'thist policies. Asad sought to mobilise support along class lines, circumventing sectarian stress fractures that could isolate the Alawites. The regime instead sought to isolate the Muslim Brotherhood. On 7 July 1980, shortly after the failed assassination of Asad, the Syrian Peoples Council passed legislation that made membership of the Muslim Brotherhood a capital offence. The bill included an amnesty of one month for Syrian-based members, and two months for those based outside Syria, in the hope that many would abandon the Muslim Brothers' cause.[130] This new tougher policy was quickly enacted, with two Brotherhood commanders killed by 17 August.[131]

Although the situation seemed dire for the Asad regime as it faced relentless and widening opposition, if the Alawites remained unified behind the regime the chances of it being toppled were small. Opposition figures like the exiled co-founder of the Ba'th Party, Salah al-Din al-Bitar, recognised this fact when he professed that the two bases of the Asad regime were 'dictatorship and confessionalism'.[132] Al-Bitar hence tried to promote a differentiation between the Alawites and the Asad regime:

It is necessary to distinguish between the regime and the great body of Alawi who had no role in establishing it and are part of the silent majority of the people who resist its crimes, at least with their hearts.[133]

By drawing a distinction between the Alawite community and the Asad regime, al-Bitar tried to alleviate Alawite insecurity. This would weaken Hafiz al-Asad's grip on power. Hence al-Bitar flagged himself as a threat to Hafiz al-Asad's rule, and, like Kamal Jumblatt, he was assassinated a few weeks afterwards on 21 July 1980 in Paris.[134]

Meanwhile, the regime continued to grasp at any opportunity to improve its legitimacy and popularity. In September 1980, Asad quickly agreed to a political merger with Libya as a way of proving his pan-Arabist credentials.[135] The merger was only ever symbolic and was never consummated in any serious way. In October 1980 the Asad regime took steps to move closer to the Soviet Union[136] and requested a renewal of arms supplies, which the Soviets had been reluctant to deliver in recent years.[137] The official pretext for the arms requirement was the 'struggle with Israelis', but it was likely the regime's domestic problems that necessitated a military upgrade.

In late October 1980 the regime announced victory in its struggle with the Brotherhood. 'The Muslim Brothers are either behind bars or in their graves', stated Information Minister Ahmed Iskander, 'the rest are insignificant and are being hunted down.'[138] However, further security forces' crackdowns on Brotherhood cells only served to highlight how widespread the insurgency had become, especially in Aleppo and Hama, but also in Damascus. For example, seven Muslim brothers were killed and large quantities of arms and explosives were uncovered in the al-Qadam neighbourhood of Damascus on 29 December 1980. And there were reports of a mass execution in Aleppo's central square of 200 dissidents in late December.[139] Given their earlier claims that the Brotherhood was finished, the regime renewed claims of Israeli and American interference in Syrian affairs.[140]

By early 1981 it appeared that the regime was finally regaining control of the situation. There was a reduction in the levels of violence in 1981 and the information minister renewed the claim to victory: 'The Muslim Brotherhood is smashed inside Syria. Those who have been active inside Syria are running away ... the larger part of the opposition has gathered in West Germany and Britain.'[141] Yet a huge bombing in Damascus in late November 1981, which levelled four apartment buildings and killed up to 200 people, proved that the Muslim Brothers remained on the offensive.[142]

The Hama Tragedy

In early 1982 the struggle reached a critical turning point when the regime finally crushed the Muslim Brotherhood revolt with extreme force at the conservative Sunni city of Hama.[143] The Hama tragedy is significant for its repercussions on Alawite integration. The military operation against Hama destroyed the Muslim Brotherhood as a force in Syria; but it also spelt the demise of Alawite hopes for genuine emancipation in Syrian society and marked the ascendency of insecurity as the dominant feature of Syrian politics.

In January 1982 the Mukhabarat discovered a coup plot among some junior air force officers.[144] Information gained in interrogation of the conspirators led to an operation against a Muslim Brotherhood hideout in Hama on the night of 2 February 1982. A unit of around 300 soldiers from the predominantly Alawite 21st Mechanised Infantry Brigade, 3rd division,[145] and possibly some Alawite Mukhabarat agents were ambushed in a back alley and wiped out.[146] The unit apparently discovered a large arms cache prepared for a major offensive against the regime.[147] The Brotherhood was forced to launch its offensive prematurely with a call to rebellion broadcast from the city minarets.[148] By the following day much of Hama was liberated from government control with Ba'th officials either captured or executed. There is evidence to suggest that simultaneous rebellions were planned for Latakia, Tartous and Aleppo,[149] which, if successful, would have encircled the Jabal al-Sahiliyah. This perhaps demonstrates careful planning by the insurgents with the intention of decapitating the regime from its Alawite power base. Nothing came of these other planned rebellions,[150] although the Syrian army did shell neighbourhoods in Tripoli in Lebanon, after Syrian troops came under attack.[151]

The revolt forced Asad's hand also. Any chance to follow the conciliatory path, advocated by Alawite liberals, was lost. The uprising seemed to signify intractable antipathy against the perceived Alawite nature of the regime, despite the efforts of Hafiz al-Asad to suppress that discourse. It was now an existential matter for the regime. A Western diplomat in Syria at the time commented, 'It's far too early for a death watch on this government, but a year or two down the road could be a different story.'[152] For many Alawites, the final defeat of opposition to the Asad regime at Hama, and elsewhere, seemed a necessary act if their social and political elevation was not to be brutally reversed. Alawite insecurity was no doubt increased by the support of the Sunni regimes in Jordan and Iraq for the Muslim Brotherhood uprising.[153]

According to Shaykh Nasīr Eskiocak, the decision to annihilate the Muslim Brotherhood once and for all came from Rifa'at al-Asad, who told his brother: 'I have always been under your orders, but now I don't want to obey you any more, you always ask me to be patient but now I am going to hit them.' The shaykh recounted how the Muslim Brothers lived underground, so when Rifa'at al-Asad 'hit them … all the city was demolished'. Shaykh Eskiocak defended the actions of the regime in February 1982: 'why was there a problem in Hama? It was the Muslim Brothers who hit the officer cadets who were graduating from the military school, Alawite and Sunni, yes they shot them, Hafiz al-Asad couldn't stand this anymore and [allowed his brother to] hit Hama.'[154]

These types of justifications for the military operation in Hama explain why the Alawite-dominated army and security forces remained loyal throughout. A repeat of the Iranian situation three years previously, where government soldiers refused to fire on anti-government demonstrators, would have been fatal for the Asad regime. There were early unproven reports of defections among the government troops.[155] Other reports claimed that some soldiers refused to carry out orders to fire on civilians.[156] In general, however, the army's loyalty remained intact.[157]

According to contemporary sources, the regime deployed up to 12,000 troops,[158] including the 21st Mechanised Brigade of the 3rd Armoured Division and the 47th Independent Armoured Brigade, and importantly, the elite Defence Companies commanded by Rifa'at al-Asad, who oversaw the operation.[159] Although all the units were commanded by loyal Alawites, contrary to popular belief the force was not entirely Alawite. A sizeable contingent of Kurds participated as well; hence graffiti in the wake of the Hama operation included Kurds as targets for 'direct vengeance'.[160] By using Kurdish troops, Hafiz al-Asad managed to spread the 'blame' somewhat and avoided the fighting being reduced entirely to a Sunni–Alawite confrontation.[161]

Nonetheless, the battle was waged with all the brutality of two communities with a long history of social and religious hatred. The Islamist insurgents fought to re-establish the 'natural' political order in Syria against the 'heretical' Alawite usurpers. Alawites fought for the survival of the Asad regime that they believed was their best hope for security and equality in

Figure 3: Remains of the Old City in Hama, 2009

Syrian society.[162] Regime units unleashed a massive bombardment upon the city via artillery and aircraft during three weeks of fighting. Around 20,000 lives were lost as a result, not to mention the almost complete annihilation of large sections of Hama.[163]

One small, bullet-ridden section of the old city remains intact as an explicit reminder to the residents of Hama of the consequences of confronting the Asad regime. These ruins also stood as a symbol of the 'Faustian Bargain' that Alawites entered into with the Asad regime during those few violent weeks in February 1982. The bargain comprised Alawite security through continued Asad rule, but the cost was direct association with the massacre, which would hang over the sect for the following decades.

Important to the final outcome of the rebellion was the failure of the revolt to spread beyond Hama. This was no doubt the regime's greatest fear, and the insurgents' greatest hope. The regime frantically tried to conceal the scale and nature of the fighting. Accusations of American and Israeli plots escalated to a higher level than at any point previously.[164] The city was sealed off completely and reports coming from Hama were denied as outright lies.[165] Foreign Minister Abd al-Halim Khaddam tried to downplay events when he stated that there had been no incidents in the country, only a 'security search for arms dumps'.[166] The state newspaper, *Syria Times*, claimed that the people of Aleppo 'denounced the crimes committed by the Muslim Brother gangs in Hama, through which, they added another black page to their record of conspiracy against national unity and the achievements of Syria's masses'.[167] As it happened, the rest of the country, apart from some minor strikes in Aleppo, remained silent as events unfolded in Hama.

The events of February 1982 left a legacy of deep emotional scarring of the residents of Hama. This most likely explains the 'sullen uncommunicative' demeanour of the populace, observed by De Atkine in 1996,[168] and, in stark contrast to the rest of Syria, this remained clearly evident in 2009. This is likely due to what the regime did to them, but also possibly stems from the feeling that, in a cruel betrayal, their Sunni Muslim compatriots tacitly endorsed what occurred by not coming to their aid. For survivors of the Hama catastrophe, resentment against the Asad dynasty and the Alawite community would not fade with time. In 2011, for example, a mother recounted the killing of her sixteen-year-old son in 1982: 'I started screaming and the Alawite officer who grabbed me said, "your son is a criminal, he killed himself." I can never forget his face ever, ever, ever.' Another survivor's comments demonstrate the association of the entire Alawite community with the Hama massacre: 'Hama was a conservative city and its people were stubborn [and] defied submission, but the Alawites taught the rest of the country a lesson with Hama. It was a crime to be a Hamawi.'[169]

The Hama revolt was a critical moment in Alawite history. Alawite involvement in putting down the Hama rebellion proved their commitment to the Asad regime. An interesting counterfactual would be if Alawite officers and troops had mutinied and chosen not to cooperate in the 'destruction' of Hama. This may have prevented the direct association of the Alawite community with this black mark on Syrian history, and improved the prospects for genuine sectarian conciliation.

Ultimately, the efforts of the Muslim Brotherhood and its supporters to destabilise the Asad regime and bring about its downfall backfired. The end result was the destruction of all active opposition in Syria and the strengthening of Alawite–Asad 'asabiyya. For Alawites, this was not a victory, however. Attempts to integrate with Syrian society and shift Alawite political identity toward the majority as Arabs and Muslims foundered at Hama. The Alawites were now forced into a position whereby their improved status in Syria could only be maintained through coercion. In cooperation with the Asad regime, the population now had to be closely monitored and repressed where necessary in order to prevent a potentially ferocious backlash. Although members of the Alawite community dominated the state, in the minds of many Syrians, Alawites still remained a sectarian minority who 'forgot themselves'. In this negative political context, liberal Alawite voices became virtually non-existent. One exception was the Alawite Communist Party member and writer, Louay Hussein, who was imprisoned without trial for seven years in 1984, then subjected to travel bans and Mukhabarat harassment.[170]

The repressive political system in Syria, which permeated every aspect of society, largely extended from Alawite insecurity about the potential for the Sunni majority to take revenge for the Hama massacre. From the moment the dust settled after the last artillery shell on Hama in February 1982 until March 2011, Syria was in political lockdown.

The Spoils of Power

Until March 1982 the Asad regime's long-term survival was not a foregone conclusion. Having survived the difficulties of the first dozen years, especially the Muslim Brotherhood assault, the regime's hold on power was secured thanks to the broad support of Alawites and the decisive defeat of all opposition. What socio-economic benefits accrued to Alawites from this support? Would the spoils of power be distributed equally, and what would be the effect on Alawite 'asabiyya?

Despite publically disowning them,[171] Hafiz al-Asad was deeply conscious of his Alawite origins and recognised the critical importance of unequivocal Alawite support. An anonymous Syrian related how during the rule of Hafiz al-Asad there was a perception that 'an Alawite from the Latakia region could murder someone and get away with it', so protected was this group.[172] Asad's maintenance of strong links with his group of origin corresponds with Ibn Khaldun's theory that a dynasty remains close to its group in its 'first stage'.[173] A good illustration of this occurred in mid-1976 when Asad stood for four hours in the 'dusty main street' of his home town of Qardaha talking to the villagers about their concerns.[174]

Initially at least, Hafiz al-Asad did cater to Alawite socio-economic development very well. Recalling the historic socio-economic circumstances of Alawites, the material gains for the broader Alawite community in the first decades of Asad rule were substantial. Socio-economic and infrastructural developments improved the quality of life for the rural Alawite population. By 1992 the Euphrates Dam enabled electricity supply to 95 per cent of Syrian villages nationwide. Although most of Syria, including the Alawite region, was linked to the grid, consistent provision of electricity proved problematic. Daily power outages of four to six hours have been a feature of Syrian life since 1985. This was caused largely by a combination of drought, rising demand and Turkey's increasing usage of upstream Euphrates waters. Electricity shortages have been a major obstacle to Syria's overall economic development inhibiting domestic commerce and foreign investors. Yet, considering that prior to 1970 most Alawite villages had no electricity at all and 'fell asleep and awoke with the sun', the period of Asad rule brought a major advance for Alawites.[175] Also, because Alawite commercial activity in their home villages remained mainly low-tech agriculture, orchards and tobacco growing, there was a low dependence on electricity. Thus, while the unreliable electricity infrastructure was possibly a major source of dissatisfaction for urban dwellers, it was quite likely perceived in Alawite villages as a significant improvement. In another national improvement, including the Alawite region, piped drinking water was available to 54 per cent of the rural population by 1980, a 'luxury' that was almost non-existent in the Alawite region thirty years previously.[176]

Perhaps the most radical development by the 1980s was the construction of roads connecting up to 500 villages in the Alawite region.[177] This was no minor achievement considering the nature of the terrain. Although few ordinary Alawites possess motor vehicles, many mini-buses traverse the roads linking the Alawite region, providing transport to residents at extremely low cost. The impact was significant, effectively ending the historic discontinuity among the various parts, and tribes, of the Jabal al-Sahiliyah. A useful comparison can be made to the policy of Maronite Lebanese President Fuad Shihab in the 1950s. Shihab promoted the construction of new roads connecting the Maronite mountain districts as a way of enhancing Christian cohesion. For Shihab, the objective was a contingency plan in the event of the failure of the multi-confessional political project in Lebanon.[178] For Asad, increased connectivity among Alawites could only strengthen his power base, but it was also part of the overall Ba'thist ideology of improving the lot of the peasant classes.

Increased Alawite access to education was another product of Hafiz al-Asad's period of rule. According to Batatu, the number of rural primary schools in Syria more than doubled from 3,000 in 1963 to 6,302 in 1980, and rural primary school graduations increased from 3.7 per cent in 1963 to 27.9 per cent by 1991.[179] These figures suggest that Hafiz al-Asad's regime was a far greater catalyst for the educational improvements for Alawites than either Article 8 of the French Mandate or the American missionaries.

An important means of Alawite advancement under Hafiz al-Asad's rule was the establishment of informal patronage networks.[180] In the 1970s Alawite barons linked to the regime and often involved in the lucrative smuggling trade distributed proceeds to members of their tribes lacking direct access to financial resources.[181] These patronage networks bound Alawites to their particular benefactor and the regime. Ghazi Kana'an from the Kalbiyya tribe, for example, operated like a 'feudal lord' in his home village of B'hamra and its surrounds distributing favours in return for loyalty. Kana'an personally provided for the construction of a library and a community centre for the area.[182] These were some of the first infrastructural developments in villages like B'hamra since the American missionaries built schools in the 1850s and 1860s.

Although general improvements in Alawite living conditions should not be understated, improvement in living standards for the wider Alawite community was far from equal. Variation in prosperity and development occurred between the tribal groupings of the Alawite region. The development of Hafiz al-Asad's hometown of Qardaha, in particular, warrants special attention in comparison to other Alawite towns and villages.

Qardaha lies in the foothills of the Jabal al-Sahiliyah, approximately 20 kilometres south-east of Latakia. In 1986, ten years after Hafiz al-Asad stood in the 'dusty main street' of his rundown hometown, a *New York Times* correspondent visited Qardaha and observed a new four-lane highway leading into the town and 'the flush of construction and prosperity'.[183] The Asad 'palace' was located in the town behind high yellow walls guarded by elite troops.

The construction of an international airport less than 10 kilometres from Qardaha is another point of interest. Having an air terminal, no doubt, provides a useful service to the Asad elite for shuttling between Damascus and Qardaha but perhaps also a vital escape route out of the country for regime personnel, should a dangerous security situation arise. Along with a major port at Latakia, the Alawite region was developing a reasonable level of infrastructure that could support an independent state if necessary. Whether this was a primary objective of Hafiz al-Asad is debatable, but surely it was given some thought as a worst-case scenario. The development of port facilities at Jounieh in Lebanon is comparable as an example of the Maronites seeking an independent outlet for external relations without necessarily planning for actual secession.[184]

Perhaps the most telling insight about Qardaha in 1986 was the *New York Times* correspondent's observation about the contrast between 'bent over toothless old men, with worn, shabby peasant clothes', and the healthy well-heeled young men in uniform. To him, this was a palpable indication of the speed of the Alawite political transformation, or as a Western diplomat put it at the time: 'from underclass to ruling class in a single generation'.[185] To extrapolate Qardaha's prosperity to the whole Alawite sect, as suggested here, is a mistake. Wealth was certainly not distributed evenly and there remains a clear separation between those Alawites close to the regime, and those not.

In many Alawite villages people still evince the physical signs of poverty and hardship supposedly left behind over two decades before. In one Alawite village I visited, well removed according to geography and kinship from Asad's Kalbiyya tribe, living conditions are very basic. Electricity is available but not every house is connected, water for many houses is still taken from a well and the main mode of transport is donkeys, mules and minibuses arriving from Latakia.[186] Yet the inhabitants of this village too played their part in the maintenance of the Asad regime. An elderly woman, who would fit the above stereotype of hardship, proudly recounted how her deceased husband was in the army for many years under Hafiz al-Asad. And men, who worked in both Latakia and in the village, reverently took turns practising the elaborate signature of *al-ra'is* (the president Bashar al-Asad). All the while, ironically, the most frequent topic of conversation was money and the lack of it.

Latakia—An Alawite City

The demographic transformation of Latakia in the middle decades of the twentieth century tells an important story about the impact of the Asad regime. A comparison of the provincial cities of Latakia and Hama from the Mandate period up to the 1990s demonstrates how increased Alawite urban migration corresponds to the period of Asad rule (see Table 5).[187] During the Mandate period Latakia was half the size of Hama, and very much a

Table 5. Comparative Populations of Latakia and Hama 1932–94 (in thousands)

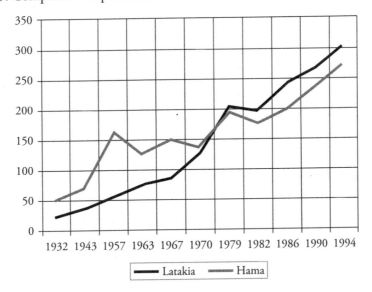

Data Source: Winckler (1999), p. 72.

backwater of Syria with a population of only 24,000 in 1932. Conversely, Hama was easily the fourth largest Syrian city at 50,000 and a thriving commercial centre dominated by wealthy Sunni landowning families.

At the same stage the majority of Latakia was also still Sunni Muslim;[188] this would change over the following decades as Alawites left the mountain in search of opportunity. In the early years of Syrian independence, rural migrants headed east towards the larger cities like Hama and Homs. Thus, the population of Hama surged between 1943 and 1957, more than tripling in size to 161,000.[189] Latakia's population in the same period maintained only a steady increase due mainly to natural increase and some minor immigration. Although during the French Mandate, Alawites technically had their own autonomous state with Latakia as its capital, this had not precipitated significant Alawite migration to this city.

The mid-1960s were a turning point in the demographic trajectory of Latakia. The 1966 coup greatly increased the influence of Alawites such as Salah Jadid and Hafiz al-Asad in the Ba'th Party. Subsequently, the influence and prevalence of Alawites in the Ba'th ranks contributed to an inflow of Alawites into Latakia. The rate of immigration into Latakia accelerated again after the ascension to power of Hafiz al-Asad in 1970, to the point that by 1979 Latakia had surpassed Hama in population. From that point on, Latakia assumed the mantle of Syria's fourth city with a probable Alawite majority. The subsequent population explosion could not have been achieved even with a high rate of natural increase among Latakia's 1932 population of 24,000[190] (which would already have included reasonable minorities of Christians and Alawites). The major factor in Latakia's growth to 204,000 by 1979[191] must therefore have been in-migration. There is no evidence of great numbers of Sunnis or other communities migrating to Latakia, thus it is logical to assume that Alawites were, through in-migration from the Jabal al-Sahiliyah, the major community of Latakia by 1979.

The brief decrease in population of both Latakia and Hama between 1979 and 1982 coincides with the period of most heightened tension in Syria's internal struggles. In Latakia the decrease was only 7,000 and was possibly due to Alawites returning to the safety of their villages. The sudden decrease in Hama's population from 198,000 in 1979 to 177,000 in

Figure 4: Central Latakia City (facing north)

1982[192] could be explained by the Hama rebellion and (chillingly) corroborates estimates of around 20,000 fatalities.[193]

There are some significant political implications of Latakia's transformation from a moderate-sized town with a Sunni majority to a large metropolitan city with an Alawite majority. For the first time in Alawite history, in a major change from their scattered distribution, the community had its own metropolitan core, a hub providing the Alawite community with a centre of social and political gravity. Another important aspect is the fact that Latakia belongs to no particular tribe; therefore, it acts as a 'mixing pot' for formerly disparate Alawite tribes, improving community cohesion.

Latakia has a very different atmosphere from other Syrian cities, with the possible exception of Tartous (which has large Alawite and Christian populations). This was especially evident during field research conducted during the month of Ramadan in 2009.[194] There are noticeably fewer symbols commonly associated with an 'Islamic city', women do not generally wear headscarves, cafes remain well attended in daylight hours through Ramadan and shops in Sharia Amerikia (American Street) unashamedly mimic Western styles and tastes.

The original Sunni Muslim population (predominant since the Crusader departure in the thirteenth century) are conspicuous by their different dress and concentration in the central old quarter of the city. Excluding the Israeli cities, Latakia is quite possibly unique in the Middle East, as a major city without a majority orthodox Muslim population (Sunni and/or Shi'a), a situation unknown since the devastation of Asia Minor's Christian communities in the fourteenth century.[195] The only possible exceptions are Muscat in Oman and the much smaller cities of Tartous, 90 kilometres to the south of Latakia; Suwayda in south-west Syria, which is mostly inhabited by Druze; the Christian city of Zahle in Lebanon; and the city of Suwaydiyya near Antakya in Turkey.[196]

The other major urbanisations of Alawites involved Damascus and Homs. The more religiously conservative cities of Aleppo and Hama were not as conducive to Alawite settlement, although some Alawite communities built up on their outskirts.[197] Damascus was the centre of bureaucratic and military administration, which employed many Alawites; hence newly arrived rural Alawites comprised a significant presence in Damascus by the early 1970s. In September 1980 the regime revealed plans for the residential development of parts of Jabal Qassioun in the north-west of Damascus.[198] Of course no information related to these plans suggested that the new residential zone would be reserved for Alawites. It is clear, however, that the area now colloquially known as Ash al Warwar (literally 'Bee Eaters Nest,' a type of Syrian bird) is populated principally by Alawites, a great many of whom are retired military personnel.[199] The residents of the Ash al Warwar seem to enjoy immunity from government building regulations and interference,[200] an indication of the special relationship between the Asad regime and its key support base. The location of this Alawite settlement is significant for two reasons: it is a very steep incline that, in the event of a civil upheaval, would enjoy strategic advantages against attacks, and being to the north-west it also allows a clear line of retreat towards the Alawite region, or if necessary, into Lebanon. Overall therefore, it was a tentative shift into Damascus by Alawites who, never comfortable in the 'Islamic cities' of the interior, were mindful to keep exit strategies.

There is a very important caveat to this process of Alawite urbanisation. Despite Alawites assuming primacy in Latakia, strong links were maintained to home villages and tribal areas. The proximity of the Jabal al-Sahiliyah, and access to frequent and cheap transport, means that it is possible for Alawites to live in their home village and work in Latakia. Many families maintain dwellings in both their villages and the city. Thus the majority of Alawites preserve a strongly rural lifestyle and outlook. Their attachment to the natural environment, cultivated throughout centuries of isolation, was obvious during visits to the Jabal al-Sahiliyah. Alawite companions were noticeably more relaxed and comfortable in their villages than the city.

So how did the social change experienced by Alawites affect their relations with the Asad regime? A major component of Ibn Khaldun's theory for the decline of 'asabiyya was that as a group becomes urbanised it is 'corrupted' by luxuries and wealth and solidarity diminishes;[201] thus 'their group feeling and courage decrease in the next generations'.[202] In the case of the tribal/clan 'asabiyya of the inner circle of the regime this was possibly true and will be discussed further below. Yet in the case of the broader Alawite group this was certainly not the case. First, for most Alawites there was only a partial urbanisation, which in itself showed the continued insecurity of the group. But, moreover, it meant that the group retained its rural outlook and characteristics. So a decline in 'asabiyya due to urbanisation was not at all a certainty for most Alawites. During field work in 2009 a comment by an Alawite acquaintance, who lives and works between a poor part of Latakia and his home village in the Jabal al-Sahiliyah, summed up the lack of 'luxury' when he despondently related, 'ana fuqeer leyun' (I'm poor Leon). Yet this same individual was staunchly supportive of the Asad regime.

In the 1980s, the socio-economic improvements noted above, Ba'thist land reform and government subsidies meant that, while still rural, Alawites were relatively better off. There is, therefore, no reason to suspect, according to a Khaldunian assessment, that the level of 'asabiyya among the wider Alawite group was in serious danger of decline in the first decades of Asad rule. Overall their lives were much improved, without coming anywhere near decadent luxury. Nonetheless, the roots of Syria's socio-economic crisis of the early twenty-first century can be traced to the first period of Asad rule.

Syria's population grew at an unprecedented rate, even by Middle Eastern standards, from the 1970s onwards. Between 1970 and 1990, Syria's population doubled from 6.4 million to 12.8 million.[203] At first Hafiz al-Asad was not overly perturbed by this population explosion and saw it as quantitatively strengthening the country against the Israeli enemy as part of his pursuit of 'strategic parity'.[204] In addition, the proceeds of the 'oil boom' of the 1970s helped to ameliorate the negative effects of population growth.[205] However, by the end of the 1980s, with the Syrian economy and infrastructure in a poor state, the greatly expanded population began to pose a serious dilemma for the regime. Nonetheless, Hafiz al-Asad failed to implement anti-natalist policies to try and lower the rampant population growth. In a comprehensive study of Middle East demography, Onn Winckler could not 'find any expression of Hafiz al-Asad … or any other senior official publicly advocating a family planning program'.[206] Such a policy could have been seen as un-Islamic, which could have sparked a renewed wave of religious antipathy for the Alawite nature of the regime. Instead, Asad adopted an indirect approach by setting up voluntary clinics but kept a safe distance from any potentially unpopular policy to do with family planning.[207] The lack of definitive action to combat rapid population growth has led to severe socio-economic and environmental challenges, which rank among the most serious facing Syria in the twenty-first century.

In education and religion the regime promoted a syllabus based on Ba'thist Syrian and Arab nationalism and a homogenised version of Islam. Monique Cardinal notes how Syrian classrooms during the 1990s did not even discuss the two main Sunni and Shi'a Islamic branches, let alone the Alawites and other unorthodox sects.[208] This refusal to allow discussion of Syria's diverse religious make-up was intended to create a new generation of Syrians who were non-sectarian in their social and political ideas. The Norwegian researcher Torstein Worren has suggested, however, that this institutionalised lack of knowledge about different sects promotes distrust and suspicion of the 'other' in Syrian society. To navigate this social undercurrent of distrust, Syrians developed techniques to discover people's sectarian affiliation indirectly by asking after family names and areas of origin.[209] Alawites are also recognisable by their pronunciation of the consonant ق (qaf), transliterated as a Q in English, which has become a glottal stop among most other Levantine Arabic speakers.[210]

Rather than promoting the inclusion of Alawites in Syrian society, the education policy pursued by Hafiz al-Asad actually served to maintain the alienation of Alawites. Historically the Alawites were feared and mistrusted by orthodox Sunni Muslims because of their ambiguous religious identity, and thus the prohibition on discussing the differences (and similarities) between sects in the modern period only served to perpetuate ill-informed perceptions. This sentiment was voiced in a declaration by Alawite religious leaders near the start of Asad rule in 1973:

The factor contributing most to divisions among people … is that they are wanting in knowledge of the facts about one another … no society is free of alien deviations and a concomitant susceptibility to abuse … diseased souls are still burrowing in the past and reiterating inventions by the enemies of Arabism and Islam …[211]

The policy pursued by Hafiz al-Asad of submerging Alawite identity seems to oppose this appeal by Alawite leaders for improved inter-faith dialogue. One outcome of sustained Alawite alienation and insecurity was, however, the preservation of Alawite 'asabiyya for the Asad regime.

Struggle for the Asad Dynasty

Although there is no evidence suggesting that Alawite 'asabiyya was declining by the 1980s, in 1983–4 a serious crack occurred in the 'asabiyya of the Asad clan. In November 1983 Hafiz al-Asad, who had obviously come through a very difficult period personally, became acutely ill with heart problems.[212] Asad's younger brother Rifa'at immediately took steps to make certain that political power fell to him in the event of his brother's demise. As the regime elite came to the hospital to visit the president, Rifa'at reportedly told them, 'Why don't we use our meetings here to deliberate on who will succeed [Hafiz al-Asad]? … I do not believe that you will prefer another man to me.'[213]

It is not entirely certain what Hafiz al-Asad planned for his brother in terms of the succession. According to then foreign minister and key adviser Abd al-Halim Khaddam:

when [Hafiz] first had his illness, his main concern was to have his brother be president after him. When his brother saw that Hafiz was sick he rushed to control the country before his brother died ... this was when all the problems began. They all stood—they opposed Rifa'at and they protected Hafiz.[214]

It is apparent that many Alawites viewed Rifa'at al-Asad negatively. He had, of course, been instrumental in the preservation of Asad rule by ruthlessly pursuing the Muslim Brotherhood and supervising their final defeat at Hama. To an extent, therefore, Alawites owed their position after 1982 to Rifa'at.[215] It was his ruthless tactics and open corruption, however, that now made him a liability to the continued security of the Alawite community. Rifa'at's poor public image was potentially very damaging to long-term regime maintenance. Key Alawite supporters of the regime recognised this fact and strongly opposed Rifa'at's bid for the presidency.

The intra-Alawite struggle that broke out over the following months was the first obvious sign of a serious rift in Alawite solidarity since the Asad–Jadid struggle of the late 1960s. The first indications of the struggle were the posters of Rifa'at al-Asad that appeared around Damascus in February 1984.[216] The posters were quickly pulled down or covered up with posters of Hafiz al-Asad by republican guardsmen and internal security agents.[217] By 27 February tensions had escalated to the point that a military standoff took place in Damascus between Rifa'at's Defence Companies and the units of Alawite Generals Ali Haydar, Shafiq Fayyad and Adnan Makhlouf, and shots were reported near the Presidential Palace.[218]

The struggle between Hafiz al-Asad and his brother threatened to open Syria up to external interference as Rifa'at sought external allies in his attempt to seize power. Notably, the Saudi Crown Prince Abdullah, who was an ally of Rifa'at al-Asad, visited Damascus in late February 1984.[219] Rifa'at al-Asad's association with the Saudi monarchy would likely have been viewed with concern in the Jabal al-Sahiliyah. The Wahhabi school of Islam practised by the Saudis is considered hostile by Alawites, being largely derived from the ideas of Ibn Taymiyya. Shaykh 'Ali Yeral explained Alawite concern over Wahhabi intolerance in 2011:

The Wahhabis don't like anyone, we hope from God that [their] wrong and hypocritical ideas … will change and disappear … they hate Iran, the Shi'ites, Syria, Hizballah, the Alawites, they don't like anyone.[220]

By forging an external alliance with the Saudis in his bid to succeed his brother in early 1984, Rifa'at al-Asad threatened to undermine Alawite 'asabiyya. A recovering Hafiz al-Asad moved to defuse this situation, potentially ruinous to his regime. On 11 March, Asad appointed three vice presidents, including Rifa'at, the Sunni foreign minister, Abd al-Halim Khaddam, plus another Sunni, Zuhayr Mashariqah, the undersecretary of the Ba'th Party Regional Command.[221] This was a way of appeasing his brother Rifa'at and maybe lessening the intra-Alawite appearance of the power struggle.[222] Asad also hoped to 'buy some time' to allow the situation to settle down.[223]

These efforts were in vain, however, and on 30 March 1984 the crisis came to a head. Rifa'at seemed intent on capturing power and ordered his troops to block the entrances to Damascus and move on the capital in force. Alawite commanders Shafiq Fayyad and Ali Haydar once again engaged in armed confrontations with Rifa'at's Defence Companies and bloodshed seemed inevitable.[224] President Asad determined to deal with his brother personally, and once and for all. According to Hanna Batatu, Hafiz al-Asad told his brother in no uncertain terms, 'I am all out of patience with you … If you do not abide with what I tell you and comply with my orders, I will send you to your death and will have dirges sung over you.'[225] Patrick Seale's version contends that Hafiz al-Asad, undefended, confronted his brother at Rifa'at's residence in front of their mother and challenged him to act, saying: 'Here I am. I *am* the regime.'[226] Either way, Rifa'at, who knew by this point that the Alawite powerbrokers, whom he had been trying lobby to his cause, were aligned against him, yielded to his brothers demands and stood down his Defence Companies.[227]

When further incidents of intra-Alawite violence broke out in Latakia in May 1984, Hafiz al-Asad became convinced that the only way to preserve the regime and Alawite solidarity was to exile his brother.[228] Initially all three main Alawite antagonists, Rifa'at, Ali Haydar and Shafiq Fayyad, were sent to the Soviet Union in late May.[229] This was possibly a reminder to Alawite elites that Hafiz al-Asad was firmly in control at the head of the regime and would not tolerate other centres of power regardless of their allegiance. Haydar and Fayyad were, however, allowed to return, while by September 1984 Rifa'at was permanently exiled.[230] The struggle for the dynasty was over and 'asabiyya among the Alawite elite remained intact.

Rifa'at al-Asad had commanded loyalty from his Defence Companies and the Lebanese ADP, along with political support from the Saudi monarchy and possibly even the United States. He did not, however, possess the necessary influence to steer Alawite 'asabiyya to his political advantage. In a rare reference to the role of the traditional Alawite leadership on Syrian politics, Hanna Batatu observed from rumours circulating Damascus in 1984 that '[Hafiz] al-Asad was abetted by the sages of the Alawi community who ... perceived Rifa'at as a threat to the survival of the regime as a whole.'[231] This assistance was evident in the Murshidi Alawite shaykhs' order to their followers, who made up a large proportion of Rifa'at's Defence Companies,[232] to abandon the younger Asad. At this time, the only effective means of controlling the country was command of Alawite loyalty, and it was clearly demonstrated that Hafiz al-Asad retained the confidence of the majority of the Alawite community.

Alawite loyalty to Hafiz al-Asad during the succession crisis demonstrates two key elements of the Alawite-Asad 'asabiyya by the mid-1980s. First, Alawite tribal and military leaders firmly attached the sect's interests to the survival of the Asad regime, which they felt Rifa'at endangered. Secondly, how the community apportioned its loyalty was in fact dependent on what they viewed as regime policy decisions beneficial to Alawites. It was not simply a case of unquestioningly supporting the Asad regime but rather who could best serve the interests of the community. Clearly the policy directions promoted by Rifa'at were not seen as desirable. By evaluating Rifa'at al-Asad's political outlook it may therefore be possible to comment on the general political outlook of the Alawites in the mid-1980s.

In domestic affairs Rifa'at endorsed a more capitalist economy,[233] which won him supporters among those who advocated in favour of economic liberalisation.[234] Ironically, these would include Sunni merchants, the class that gave rise to the Muslim Brothers whom Rifa'at had been instrumental in destroying. Nonetheless, it seemed most ordinary Alawites preferred the retention of the leftist social policy pursued by Hafiz al-Asad.

Rifa'at's political ideology can be seen in his founding of the al-Rabitah (the Association of Higher Education Diploma Holders). Rifa'at himself held a doctorate from Moscow University.[235] The association, however, took the form of a 'quasi-political party' which advocated an elitist approach to politics.[236] This was in complete contradiction of Ba'thist doctrine, which expounded the virtues of the peasants and the masses. Although Alawite elites enjoyed privileged educational opportunities, the majority of Alawites, who were still rural peasants, identified with the Ba'thist ideology championed by Hafiz al-Asad.

In foreign policy, Rifa'at openly advocated a shift towards the West. He made overtures to the United States and developed close links with the Saudi monarchy. Moreover, Rifa'at had 'serious reservations about the alliance with Iran'[237] and openly opposed unity talks with Iraq.[238] Once again Rifa'at's politics seemed to contradict what could be considered core Alawite interests. In religion, Shi'ite Iran was a natural ally of the Alawites, whereas Saudi Arabia represented the heart of Wahhabi–Sunni fundamentalism.[239] A move towards the United States would also imperil Soviet and Iranian support for the Asad dynasty. In addition, Iraqi unity talks bolstered the appearance of regime commitment to the ideals of Ba'thism and pan-Arabism, which remained the best available mainstay of domestic legitimacy for the Asad regime.

Rifa'at al-Asad's blunt approach to asserting Alawite particularism was also potentially dangerous as it went against the community's long history of dissimulation. His popularity among the more militant Lebanese Alawites reflects this aspect of his approach. The political situation in Lebanon was very different for Alawites, however. In Syria the Alawites were on a political limb facing a potentially hostile majority, and therefore veered towards taqiyya and a homogenous Arab identity.

Lastly, Rifa'at al-Asad, like Ismail Khayr Bey in the 1850s, took full advantage of his influential position to enrich himself and his followers. He accumulated a vast fortune by monopolising the smuggling trade and the 'military–commercial complex' established between military elites and Damascene merchants.[240] As such, he became an open symbol of the nepotism, corruption and immoral hedonism that regime critics railed against. Rifa'at could thus perhaps be categorised within Ibn Khaldun's definition of corruption caused through the luxuries bought by power. Patrick Seale describes how Rifa'at 'travelled abroad, explored foreign capitals [and] acquired a taste for Western luxuries ...'[241] Conversely, Hafiz al-Asad lived a fairly moderate lifestyle and kept himself firmly rooted in the realities of Syrian and Alawite politics.

Based on the negative response by most Alawite military and religious leaders to Rifa'at al-Asad's leadership bid in the mid-1980s, it seems Alawites inclined towards socialist economics, the Iranian and Soviet alliances, an inconspicuous Alawite identity and modesty in presenting the material trappings of power.[242] The key to maintaining Alawite 'asabiyya was therefore found in abiding by these principles—which is exactly what Hafiz al-Asad did.

The Alawite–Iranian Axis

According to Ibn Khaldun, when a 'ruler seeks the help of clients and followers' outside of his group, it can be seen as a symptom of the dynasty's decline.[243] In this sense, the Islamic Republic of Iran became the most significant external influence on the Asad dynasty. Iran came to represent a renewal of Shi'a political and religious support to the Alawites. After the 1979 Iranian revolution the Asad regime immediately reversed its previous hostile foreign policy towards Iran and sought close relations with the revolutionary Islamist regime in Tehran.[244] This seemed an unusual step for an avowedly secular Ba'thist regime engaged in a bitter struggle against Islamists at home. Also, as already discussed, many Syrian Muslims took inspiration from the Iranian people's overthrow of the 'corrupt' and 'repressive' rule of the shah.

Hafiz al-Asad quickly looked to bolster Alawite religious legitimacy through the new relations. The grand mufti of Syria, the regime-appointed Sunni Kurd Ahmed Kuftaro (d.2004), 'praised the Iranian revolution' and declared that 'there was no difference between Sunnis and Shi'ites'.[245] The policy of equating Alawism with orthodox Shi'ism, begun in the early 1970s, now paid political dividends. Iranians are predominantly Shi'a and in Alawite history Shi'a political powers had been, with the exception of the Mirdasids (1024–80), favourable to Alawite interests. Shi'ite clerics had already come to the aid of the Asad regime in the 1970s by endorsing

Alawite religious credentials, but now the Alawites had, for the first time since the Hamdanids, a major Shi'a state as a political ally.

Recalling Ottoman concerns about Alawites serving as a bridgehead for Persian designs in the Levant, it is interesting that it was through precisely this channel that the Iranians began to assert influence in the region in the early 1980s. The Asad regime became a vital conduit for the Iranians to the major Shi'a community of the Levant based in southern Lebanon. For its part, the Syrian regime gained another valuable political ally in Lebanon to add to the Shi'a 'Amal movement, launched by Musa al-Sadr, and the Alawite ADP in Tripoli. This was the Iranian-backed militant Islamist Shi'a movement Hizballah (Party of God).

Hizballah's political influence among Lebanese Shi'ites grew as a result of Israel's occupation of southern Lebanon from 1982. Their militia's active resistance against the Israeli forces provided a Khaldunian 'external threat', which occupied the minds of the country's citizen's, without Syria having to engage directly in the confrontation.[246] Hizballah therefore provided benefit to the Asad regime in maintaining its domestic situation. Moreover, the Lebanese Shi'ites provided strategic depth in the Asad–Alawite struggle against Sunni Islamists now operating out of Tripoli.

Hafiz al-Asad himself was always cautious in his dealings with Iran and Hizballah, always looking to maintain firm control over what he viewed as his Lebanese sphere of influence. Religious extremism was a threat to Alawite interests and was not tolerated from either Sunnis or Shi'ites. For example, when fighting broke out again in June 1985 between Sunni Islamists (now under the name Tawheed) and Alawites of the ADP,[247] Asad pounded Tripoli with artillery in similar fashion to Hama three years prior.[248] In 1987, Alawite colonels, Hisham al-Mouallaq, Ali Deeb and Abd al-Halim Sultan, all veterans of the 1982 Hama campaign, were dispatched with their units to curb Hizballah overzealousness. This included the summary execution of twenty-three Hizballah militiamen in Beirut.[249] This sent a strong message to Iran that Syrian supremacy in Lebanon was not to be challenged.[250]

Nonetheless, by 1988 the Syria–Iran partnership had 'evolved into a durable regional alliance'.[251] Successive international actors have misinterpreted this relationship. Outwardly it seems that 'secular Arab' Syria should be amenable to positive inducements to leave the alliance with Islamist

Persian Iran and radical Hizballah, yet successive attempts to do so have failed. The former Syrian foreign minister, Abd al-Halim Khaddam, was emphatic when he explained in 2009 that '[Bashar] is not dividing himself from Iran.'[252]

There is of course a geopolitical logic underpinning Iran–Asad relations which had nothing to do with religious affiliation. The long-standing durability of the Syria–Iran alliance is, however, understandable in the context of Alawite 'asabiyya. First, while the original secular ideals of Hafiz al-Asad were genuine, they also cloaked the religious particularism of his Alawite power base. Secondly, Alawites have only ever benefited from political relations with Shi'a powers, and indeed consider themselves closely associated to the Shi'a creed. It is understandable, therefore, that they would trust this alliance over Sunni Arab or Western states. Shaykh 'Ali Yeral illustrated this perspective of the Syrian–Iranian alliance:

[The relationship] is important in religion or in politics. This creates a common sentiment ... the Alawites and the Shi'a are one community, which unites them to the *ahl al-bayt* (family of the Prophet Muhammad). During the Iran–Iraq war, Syria was on the side of Iran. Why? Because Iran was the one that was oppressed. So Iran will be on the side of [Alawites in] Syria if there is a political, economic and religious problem.[253]

Another aspect to the Syrian–Iranian alliance came to prominence after the end of the Cold War. The demise of the Soviet Union meant that the Asad regime needed allies that would not pressure it to reform in a way that would risk weakening Alawite support. Structural economic reforms, like those pressed on Jordan by the International Monetary Fund (IMF), for example, would negatively affect those employed in the public sector, which of course meant Alawites. Iran therefore provided an ideal economic, political and religious ally in terms of maintaining Syria's domestic political equation. It is important to note, however, that Hafiz al-Asad never allowed any of his external allies, including the Soviet Union, Hizballah or Iran, to surpass his Alawite power base in terms of strategic importance in the maintenance of his rule. This was a vital element in maintaining his domestic and regional autonomy and influence.

Overall, Hafiz al-Asad was able to manipulate regional circumstances, emphasising external threats, to help uphold the 'asabiyya of Syrian

Alawites. The Israeli conflict provided the Asad regime with the quintessential Khaldunian external threat. The constant presence of a menacing threat over the horizon distracted Syrians from their country's poor economic performance and lack of freedoms. For Alawites, this served as a second layer of anxiety to add to their apprehension about Sunni Arab desires for revenge after the violence of Hama in 1982.

According to Ibn Khaldun, the cultivation of external allies outside of the ruler's group is symptomatic of a dynasty's decline.[254] However, the Iranian and Hizballah alliances amplified the strategic clout of the Asad dynasty, enabling it to manipulate regional events to its domestic advantage. Moreover, the Shi'a identity of both these regional actors was attractive to Alawites whose history and religion has significant connection with the Shi'a tradition. Hafiz al-Asad was also mindful to keep these allies at arm's length to maintain the autonomy of his regime, while keeping his primary power base in the Alawite community.

Preparing for Succession

In the 1990s a major preoccupation of Hafiz al-Asad was ensuring the continuance of the Asad family dynasty. Abd al-Halim Khaddam, who was a close observer of the lead up to the hereditary succession, related how Rifa'at al-Asad's 1984 coup attempt did not lessen Hafiz al-Asad's determination to keep Syrian political power within the Asad family:

Even though this [coup attempt] happened with his own brother he still wanted the succession to be from one of his own family members if not his brother. He concentrated on his sons. He started building the security and military forces around that idea that he wanted his son to take over. So in the 1990s he started reforming [the] security and military in order to make it easier for his son to succeed.[255]

Initially, Hafiz al-Asad's eldest son, Basil, was groomed for the job. With Basil's death in a car accident in 1994, the second son, Bashar, was taken out of his medical training as an ophthalmologist to assume the role of successor. It was questionable, however, whether the young and inexperienced Bashar had the ability to manage the political balancing act of preserving the status quo in Syria and providing for Alawite security.[256] Some doubted that the 'secondary regime strongmen'—which essentially meant top Alawite generals in the military and intelligence services—would be willing to transfer their loyalties to the unqualified and inexperienced Bashar al-Asad.[257]

The prospect of a post-Asad Syria would certainly have been contemplated by many Alawites in the latter part of the 1990s as the health of the president declined. The spectre of Sunni revenge for the Hama massacre hung over the Alawite population as they waited to see who could assume responsibility for the security of the community. After all, a successful transition of Alawite political power would be a novelty. For example, the demise of Ismail Khayr Bey ended that family's political fortunes and brought a thorough repression of the whole Alawite community, and Suleiman Murshid's son met a similar fate to his father when he attempted to resume the former's autonomist aspirations.

If there had existed a genuine and widely held belief among Alawites that Bashar could not fulfil the position established by his father, it is possible that Alawite 'asabiyya for the Asad regime would have declined. In Bashar's favour was the fact that a considerable amount of political capital had been invested in legitimising the Asad name as synonymous with Syrian and Arab national aspirations. Moreover, to transfer political power to another Alawite clan or family would have been highly inflammatory to the Sunni majority as a flagrant demonstration of Alawite dominance in Syrian politics.

Most importantly, however, was the fact that over the previous three decades Hafiz al-Asad had made certain that no alternative power bases existed among the Alawite community. One notable example was former Alawite strongman, Salah Jadid, who remained 'safely' incarcerated for twenty-three years until his death in 1993.[258] To be doubly certain, in 1998–9 Hafiz al-Asad conducted a ruthless purge of any potential rivals for power, including many of his closest friends, in order to ensure his family's retention of power through his son. In addition, several influential Sunnis were removed from their positions in the lead up to the succession. The long-time prime minister, Mahmoud al-Zouabi, ostensibly committed suicide and in 1998 the Army Chief of Staff Hikmat Shihabi fled to the United States.[259] Both had been key figures of Hafiz al-Asad's regime, but it would seem they could not be trusted to remain on the sidelines during a dynastic transfer of power. Hafiz al-Asad's diligence in eliminating potential rivals to Bashar was shown in the common refrain around Damascus after his death in June 2000, '*ma fi gheiru*' (there is no one else).[260]

Apprehension about their continued security in the event of Hafiz al-Asad's death led to renewed efforts to promote the Islamic credentials of the Alawite sect. Hence in the 1990s numerous 'scholarly' publications appeared arguing the close linkage of the Alawite religion to the Ja'afari school of Shi'a Islam.[261] It is possible that recognition of Hafiz al-Asad's deteriorating health and the failure after Hama to integrate Alawites into Syrian society through Arab nationalism and a broadened Islamic identity led to renewed Alawite efforts to prove their Shi'a Islamic credentials. This policy was made easier by the willingness of Shi'a scholars, with close links to Syria's Iranian allies, to provide documentary evidence of Alawite-Shi'a unity. The readiness of Alawites to present themselves as orthodox Shi'ites was evident in an interview with the Alawite shaykh, Muhammad Boz, in 2011. He portrayed Alawite origins in terms of the original split between the Sunni and Shi'a communities: following the burial of the Prophet Muhammad and the designation of Abu Bakr as the successor, Boz said, 'the ones who accepted the will of the Prophet were called Alawites and the ones who followed the choice of Abu Bakr became the Sunni'.[262]

By 1999 the necessary preconditions had been established for Bashar al-Asad's accession.[263] Bashar was promoted as the only viable option to protect Alawite interests. Simultaneously, the Muslim identity of the sect was buttressed in preparation for a potentially turbulent power transfer. However, the most significant legacy that would be passed on to the second generation of the Asad dynasty was an acutely dilapidated economy, which had deteriorated steadily since the mid-1990s due to low rates of economic growth, depleting oil reserves and the inefficient public sector.[264] In 1999 Hafiz al-Asad deflected the blame for the state of the economy to the long-serving prime minister, Mahmoud al-Zouabi, and his government. Ironically, in light of events in 2011, Hafiz al-Asad stated his readiness to 'step into the street to demonstrate' against the corruption and incompetence of the government, which he described as the 'worst ever witnessed by the country'.[265] This was a hallmark of Hafiz al-Asad's special talent for manipulating propaganda to buttress the stability of Asad rule against all odds.

Overall, under Hafiz al-Asad, Alawite 'asabiyya was maintained at a high-level and the regime, after some initial crises, consolidated its power. Hafiz al-Asad's careful pragmatism and shrewd manoeuvring on the regional and domestic fronts played a major part in preserving strong Alawite support for his rule. Alawite loyalty was clearly demonstrated during the struggle with the Syrian Muslim Brotherhood, culminating in the brutal destruction of resistance at Hama in 1982. The possibility of repercussions from this 'Faustian bargain' always hung over the Alawite community as the next generation of Asad rule in Syria approached.

Ibn Khaldun wrote that famine, overpopulation and pestilence occur at the end of dynasties; moreover, rulers born to power often do not possess the necessary qualities to rule.[266] At the dawn of the second generation of the Asad dynasty, economic stagnation and population growth were already threatening to bring the former two of these outcomes. The rise of Hafiz al-Asad in 1970 represented a high point of Alawite socio-political progress; however, the next three decades saw a regression into insecurity and rigid authoritarianism. Whether or not Bashar al-Asad would possess the necessary qualities to manage the political complexities of modern Syria and arrest the descent back into fear and conflict remained to be seen.

4

RAPID DESCENT

On Saturday 10 June 2000, Hafiz al-Asad died of a heart attack aged sixty-nine.[1] Abd al-Halim Khaddam, who was scheduled to have a meeting with Asad that day, was returning to Damascus. When he arrived at the president's house he found the inner core of the Syrian regime gathered there. Khaddam was informed that the president was dead and they told him 'since you were not in the house we have agreed to have Bashar as the successor'.[2] Khaddam, one of two vice-presidents and the senior politician in the country, did not agree with the dynastic succession but he could not dispute the decision; as he later reflected:

When they told me that, I couldn't really say no because, first, the president had just died, so it wasn't appropriate to actually discuss that at the time. Second, I saw that the assembly of the leaders of the party all said that they wanted Bashar to succeed, so by me saying no it would create a disturbance in the country.[3]

Despite his reservations, Abd al-Halim Khaddam, who was nominally running the country during the transition, provided the official pronouncements for the rapid promotion of Hafiz al-Asad's thirty-four-year-old son, Bashar.[4] Bashar al-Asad had no genuine background in politics or the military—being Hafiz al-Asad's eldest surviving son was his only qualification for the presidency. Bashar al-Asad's succession confirmed that Syria was now ruled by a hereditary dynasty. Following the successful upholding of Alawite 'asabiyya during the previous thirty years, the Alawite community remained the mainstay of the Asad regime.

Alawite support was, understandably, strong among those closely connected to the Asad family. A forty-four-year-old Alawite woman from Qardaha illustrated this with a comment shortly after the death of Hafiz al-Asad: 'for us the most important [thing] is that the president should come from the Asad family'.[5] The strength of feeling among Alawites further removed from the centre of power for continued Asad rule in 2000 is more difficult to establish. Yet given the widespread Alawite approval of Hafiz al-Asad's leadership, it could be assumed that Bashar al-Asad, at least, began his rule with broad Alawite support. According to Ibn Khaldun, however, the second stage of a dynasty brings an accelerated decline in 'asabiyya as the ruler separates himself from his group:

with the approach of the second stage, the ruler shows himself independent of his people, claims all the glory for himself, and pushes his people away from [his power] with the palms of his hands. As a result, his own people become in fact, his enemies.[6]

Did Alawite support for the Asad dynasty begin to decline in the first decade of Bashar al-Asad's rule? If so, what factors contributed to the lessening of Alawite support? And what factor[s] could act to prevent the sect's abandonment of the Asad dynasty? If ordinary Alawites became detached from the Asad regime this could indicate that the insecurity that underpinned their support for Hafiz al-Asad had finally begun to diminish, reopening the way again for genuine integration and security in a pluralist Syria.

A Modernising Reformer?

The transfer of power to the next generation of the Asad family was outwardly greeted with singular enthusiasm in Syria. On the streets of Damascus crowds chanted 'God, Syria and Bashar only.'[7] The excitement of many Syrians was genuine. After three decades of iron-fisted rule, the death of Hafiz al-Asad portended a welcome change from the status quo. An indication of broader Sunni feelings for continued Asad rule was pos-

between Shawkat and Shaker al-Abssi, the leader of the Fatah al-Islam fighters at Nahr al-Bared.[96] Another report suggested that Asef Shawkat personally travelled to Libya in July 2007 to ask for financial support from Colonel Qaddafi for its activities in Lebanon.[97]

Although it cannot be categorically proven that the Syrian regime was responsible for the fighting at Nahr al-Bared, the tactic of inciting instability in northern Lebanon was one that the regime had employed previously. The goal, in this latest case, could have been to demonstrate the consequences of continuing with the establishment of the Special Tribunal for Lebanon (STL). The content of a meeting between Bashar al-Asad and UN Secretary-General Ban Ki-Moon in Damascus on 24 April 2007, one month prior to the start of the fighting in Lebanon, supports this conclusion. In response to remarks by the UN secretary-general about Syria's role in Lebanon, President Asad said:

Lebanese society is very fragile and it has been at its most peaceful when Syrian forces were present in the country ... now there was great instability in the country. Moreover this instability would intensify if the Special Tribunal were established. This was particularly the case if the Tribunal were established under Chapter 7 of the [UN] Charter.[98] This could easily ignite a conflict which would result in civil war and provoke divisions between Sunni and Shi'a from the Mediterranean to the Caspian Sea.[99]

Bashar al-Asad was therefore equating continued regional stability with the stability of his regime. Asad had already convinced many Alawites of this logic, demonstrated in the comments of the Alawite shaykh 'Ali Yeral in 2011, when he also predicted a far-reaching Sunni–Shia conflict if the Asad regime was toppled.[100] Regardless of Bashar al-Asad's threat about possible repercussions for regional stability, the Special Tribunal for Lebanon was established under Chapter 7 on 30 May 2007,[101] ten days after the outbreak of fighting at Nahr al-Bared camp on the Lebanese Mediterranean coast. The fighting at Nahr al-Bared, which seemed like a realisation of Bashar al-Asad's warning to Ban Ki-Moon, lasted for three months, only ceasing after a mass assault by Lebanese troops on 2 September 2007.[102]

In March 2008 the STL was formalised, with a venue at The Hague in the Netherlands, along with the appointment of judges, a registrar and a prosecutor.[103] In April 2008, one of the STL's key witnesses, Muhammad Zuhayr as-Siddiq, disappeared from Paris, and the Beirut home of Judge Ralph Riachi, who was assigned to the Tribunal, was ransacked twice.[104] Another early informant to the UNIIIC investigation, Ziad Wasef Ramadan, was imprisoned in Syria and has not been heard from since September 2007.[105] Although it is unclear whether or not the Syrian regime was involved in all of these events, the possibility cannot be discounted.

The decision to launch a case into the Sudanese president, Omar al-Bashir, for his role in South Sudan at the International Criminal Court (ICC) in 2008, added to the Syrian president's apprehension about the STL.[106] The eventual indictment of Al-Bashir in March 2009 set a precedent that sitting presidents were, in fact, not immune from international proceedings.[107] The Syrian Foreign Ministry quickly issued a statement that revealed Bashar al-Asad's anxiety about this development:

Syria views with concern … the arrest warrant issued for Sudanese President Omar Al-Bashir, and that the decision to issue it is a grave precedent that disregards the immunity of all heads of state under the Vienna Convention … harmed Sudanese sovereignty, and constituted disgraceful interference in its internal affairs.[108]

In 2008 the vigour of the international effort to pursue justice in Lebanon slowed. In January 2008 the original UNIIIC head investigator, Detlev Mehlis, criticised the lack of progress of the investigation under Serge Brammertz.[109] And in May 2009 Judge Mehlis commented that he did 'not see any murder indictments [against the Syrian regime] in the foreseeable future'.[110] By November 2010 the Syrian regime appeared to have escaped any immediate indictments from the STL, which instead narrowed its focus to suspects from Syria's main Lebanese ally, Hizballah.[111]

New Opposition Alignments

The regime's apparent weakness after 2005 gave encouragement to the Syrian Muslim Brotherhood to renew its opposition to the Syrian regime. The day after the decision to retreat from Lebanon was announced, the Islamist organisation's leader, Dr Hassan Howeidy, made a demand from Jordan for democratic elections and a new constitution in Syria, warning, 'if the situation continues, potentially there is great interior pressure, as yet unrevealed, that will cause savage behaviour—as has happened in the past'.[112] This was an explicit warning about the possibility of renewed Sunni–Alawite violence, and likely referred to the struggles of 1976–82. Social pressures in Syria were not necessarily religion-based, however, but rather stemmed from socio-economic and political frustration among large portions of all Syria's communities. Yet in the Alawite collective memory, Howeidy's remarks may have recalled the numerous violent repressions of the past against their community by Sunni Muslims. Also, although most Alawites were excluded from any benefits or role in Syria's political system, Howeidy still placed the Alawites together as a single dominant group when he added, 'All the problems in Syria are because the power is not with parties but with the Alawites … the majority of Muslims hate following Alawite rule.'[113]

To be sure, the domestic stability of the regime still rested with Alawites in the military and security apparatus. During the rule of Hafiz al-Asad, statements from the Muslim Brotherhood singling out the Alawite community and threatening sectarian retribution had only served to rally Alawites around Asad and bolster 'asabiyya. However, considering the signs of discord among Alawite security elites in 2004–5, some Alawites began to doubt the capability of Bashar al-Asad to protect their community against such threats. In this context, the possibility of a coup by elite Alawites emerged. An anonymous Syrian political analyst referred to this possibility in late 2005: 'Either Bashar will have to make his coup, or someone will make it against him.'[114]

For many ordinary Alawites, Bashar al-Asad, who was born and raised in Damascus and had married a Sunni, seemed detached from their community.[115] Conversely, 'old guard' figures such as Ghazi Kana'an still commanded tremendous respect in the mountain villages of the Alawite region as a protector of Alawite interests. There was potential, therefore, for an Alawite maqaddam, like Kana'an, to establish a separate power base among the Alawite community. The United States was possibly led to believe by anti-Syrian Lebanese politicians that Kana'an was the only man capable of assuming control in a post-Asad Syria without a descent into sectarian strife.[116]

Another figure with no power base and pushed to the fringes of the regime but who possessed long experience in Syrian and Middle East political affairs was the vice-president, Abd al-Halim Khaddam. Following Hikmat Shihabi's departure from Syria in 1998, Kana'an and Khaddam remained two of the last key figures from the previous regime capable of challenging Bashar and forming a viable alternative.[117]

A Kana'an–Khaddam alliance could have been the Alawites best chance for retaining key community interests of physical and socio-economic security. Kana'an possessed sufficient competence and respect among Alawites to coordinate the various Mukhabarat branches and reconcile with the Sunni majority. Khaddam skilfully helped facilitate the retention of an Alawite-led regime in Syria for over three decades, all the while providing an important Sunni face to the regime. In many ways, Abd al-Halim Khaddam had long been a good servant of Alawite interests. Significantly, both Kana'an and Khaddam (along with Hikmat Shihabi) enjoyed good relations with the late Rafiq al-Hariri. Khaddam was the only member of the Syrian regime who attended the funeral of the former Lebanese prime minister in Beirut.[118]

After returning from Rafiq al-Hariri's funeral, Abd al-Halim Khaddam's position in Syria became increasingly difficult—he and his family were under constant surveillance, and he found himself ostracised. Khaddam chose the tenth Ba'th Party regional conference in June 2005 to deliver a scathing condemnation of recent regime policy; he announced his resignation and immediately left Syria for Paris.[119] Khaddam's departure from Syria seemed less a panicked flight than a calculated tactical move. Khaddam's first step was to ally with another 'old guard' figure in exile, Hikmat Shihabi, and he maintained contact with Ghazi Kana'an in Syria.[120] On the morning of 12 October 2005, Ghazi Kana'an was found dead in his office at the Ministry of the Interior. State media reported that he had committed suicide.[121] Many observers deemed it more likely that Kana'an was executed at the orders of the Syrian regime.[122] Although it is impossible to determine how Kana'an died, a major consequence of his demise was that the last prominent Alawite with the potential to challenge Bashar al-Asad had now been removed.

By the end of 2005 the Asad dynasty had avoided an internal coup but was reduced to a small and isolated clique. Bashar al-Asad was at the top but remained influenced by his brother-in-law, Asef Shawkat. Bashar's brother Maher al-Asad was very influential as the commander of the Republican Guard, the key praetorian unit since the downgrading of the Defence Companies in 1984. How much influence female members of the family had, including Bushra al-Asad (Bashar's older sister and Shawkat's wife) and Anisa Makhlouf (Bashar's mother), is difficult to determine. Bushra al-Asad is apparently a strong-willed and intelligent individual who could have been a candidate for the presidency if not for her gender.[123]

A new element in the power structure, not evident in the former stage of the Asad dynasty, was the establishment of a corporate wing to the regime. This role fell to the Makhlouf clan of Bashar's mother and was led by Rami Makhlouf.[124] Rami Makhlouf had already amassed a vast fortune in the first few years of Bashar's rule through business monopolies, such as the mobile phone networks. On the periphery of this inner clique were other Asad cousins such as the Shaleesh clan, who oversaw business interests, in conjunction with the regime, in such areas as smuggling contraband in and out of Iraq.[125]

Regime Consolidation and Isolation

Although Bashar al-Asad and his inner core had succeeded in consolidating their hold on power and seeing off potential adversaries such as Rafiq al-Hariri, Abd al-Halim Khaddam and Ghazi Kana'an, the process of achieving this consolidation had left them extremely isolated and vulnerable both internationally and domestically. On the international front, the UN investigation of the murder of Rafiq al-Hariri posed a clear danger to the regime if its top officials, or even the president himself, were found culpable. This could destroy the legitimacy of the Ba'thist regime, bring tough sanctions and possibly even a UN authorised intervention in Syria. The progress of international justice would prove a slow process, so the threat of the UN investigation was not imminent; however, in 2005/6 the threat posed by the UNIIIC appeared very real. Domestically, the demise of the influential Alawite figure, Ghazi Kana'an, meant that the regime severely tested the loyalty of a great portion of the Alawite community who already felt abandoned and betrayed by the policy directions and actions of the regime.

Abd al-Halim Khaddam pointed out that it cannot automatically be assumed that Kana'an was assassinated;[126] however, many Alawites were convinced that Bashar al-Asad had ordered him to be killed, adversely affecting their approval of the regime. At Kana'an's funeral in his home village of B'hamra, women wailed, 'Why did you kill him?'[127] A relative of Kana'an was disparaging of the idea of suicide: 'he was a man of confrontation, suicide is an escape—he wasn't a man to run away from something'.[128] Kana'an's brother Ali attacked the regime by going public with his belief that Bashar al-Asad, his brother Maher and Asef Shawkat were responsible for Rafiq al-Hariri's death. He was found dead on 9 November 2006, (once again 'officially' by suicide) on the Tartous–Latakia rail line.[129] This brutality against the Kana'ans, a fellow Kalbiyya clan from the town of B'hamra, would not be easily forgiven.[130] It was this type of crumbling Alawite 'asabiyya which posed the greatest danger to the future of the Asad regime.

Hafiz al-Asad was also suspected of ordering politically motivated murders, which were no more morally defensible than the actions of his son; yet from a purely political perspective, a distinction can be made. Hafiz al-Asad sought to suppress suggestions that sectarianism was the foundation of his regime. This was possibly a contributing motive in the, as yet unsolved, assassinations of Kamal Jumblat and Salah al-Din al-Bitar. Bashar al-Asad and his key advisors were suspected of conducting political assassinations purely from the point of view of protecting their own interests, even if at the expense of Alawites. Thus it seemed that the Asad dynasty was at odds with the Alawite majority and, true to Ibn Khaldun's words, it appeared many of Bashar al-Asad's 'own people, in fact, bec[a]me his enemies'.[131]

In this context of diverging Alawite–Asad dynasty interests, the Alawite community had a potential opportunity to exit its 'Faustian bargain' with the Asad dynasty in 2006. Abd al-Halim Khaddam, now based in Paris, understood the Syrian regime better than anyone else, having developed an intimate knowledge of its structure and mechanics over the course of his long political career. In 2005–6 he believed that the regime's Alawite power base was possibly wavering and if he could remove this 'keystone' in its power structure the dynasty might fall. This required alleviating Alawite anxiety about a sectarian backlash against their community in the absence of the Asad regime.

On 30 December 2005 Abd al-Halim Khaddam launched his counter-attack against the regime in an interview with Al-Arabiya television. He proclaimed his knowledge of the Syrian regime's responsibility for the Hariri and related assassinations, and his belief that the new ruling clique was leading Syria to ruin.[132] This testimony from a long-time regime insider like Khaddam was a heavy blow to the Syrian regime and added to its isolation and vulnerability. It was Khaddam's next move, however, that posed the biggest threat to Bashar al Asad. By joining forces with the Syrian Muslim Brotherhood, now led by Ali Bayanouni, and forming the National Salvation Front (NSF) on 16 March 2006, a novel opposition alliance was created. The partnership of Abd al-Halim Khaddam and Ali Bayanouni gave the NSF potency in two important ideologies, Ba'thism and Islamism, and therefore held potential to gain significant traction in Syria. Admittedly, Ba'thism had waned in terms of its genuine popular appeal, yet Alawites still clung to its secular and socialist principles as a means to alleviate their insecurity.

Khaddam was certain of the success of the NSF; in the press conference at the formation of the movement he said he expected an uprising in Syria 'in a few months'. 'Bashar al-Asad is making a lot of mistakes and he's digging himself into a hole.'[133] Having assisted Hafiz al-Asad in the delicate balancing act of retaining Alawite support without overly antagonising the Syrian majority, Khaddam understood the key factor to regime change was the position of Alawites. Any uprising that was uniformly opposed by Alawites in the military/security apparatus had little chance of success, a lesson harshly learnt at Hama in 1982.

Hence, in early June 2006, Abd al-Halim Khaddam made a public commitment to protect the Alawite minority from any potential backlash against their community in a post-Asad Syria.[134] Although Sunni himself, Khaddam is better defined according to his secular Ba'thist outlook. Alawites required these types of reassurances from a Sunni Muslim leader, the group from which they could expect to suffer renewed discrimination and possible retribution in a post-Asad Syria. On 17 August 2006, Syrian Muslim Brotherhood leader Ali Bayanouni delivered such a message via an Al-Jazeera television interview:

The Alawites in Syria are part of the Syrian people and comprise many national factions ... [The] present regime has tried to hide behind this community and mobilize it against Syrian society. But I believe that many Alawite elements oppose the regime, and there are Alawites who are being repressed. Therefore, I believe that all national forces and all components of the Syrian society, including the sons of the Alawite community, must participate in any future change operation in Syria.[135]

Dissection of this message reveals a significant understanding of the political situation of Alawites, which perhaps indicates the influence of Khaddam on the choice of language. Bayanouni rejected the idea of sectarian particularism, present in previous statements about the Alawites; instead he said the Alawites 'comprise many national factions'. Secondly, he makes an implicit distinction between the 'present regime' and the previous Asad regime, a possible attempt to disconnect Bashar's regime from the strong loyalty many Alawites felt for Hafiz al-Asad and his policies. Where many Alawites felt the late President Asad strongly defended Alawite interests, Bayanouni suggested that the present regime exploits the community in order to preserve itself. Finally, Bayanouni invited Alawites to join as equal partners in a civil uprising to bring 'change' for Syria.

The tone of Ali Bayanouni's message was radically different from previous Muslim Brotherhood pronouncements, which had implicitly, and explicitly, labelled Alawites as heretics and usurpers who were unified in their complicity with the Asad regime. Bayanouni made a distinction between those Alawites closely connected with the regime and the rest of the Alawite community. This resonates with the idea of a division of the Alawite 'asabiyya into two branches: those attached to the inner core whose 'asabiyya remained intact for agnatic and material reasons, and those whose 'asabiyya for the Asad dynasty was upheld only by their insecurity about a Sunni-dominated state. Considering the reduction in size of the former group, due to the directions pursued by Bashar al-Asad in his first six years of power, it can be assumed that the latter group was the larger.

Bayanouni's outreach to the Alawite majority was a similar concession to Alawite aspirations for a secure place in Syrian society as the fatwa of the grand mufti of Jerusalem, al-Husayni, in 1936.[136] At that time Alawites felt their choice was either unity with Muslim Syria or autonomy under French guardianship. The choice in 2006 was unity with the other communities in a new post-Asad Syria, or to hope for continued protection under the seemingly unstable Asad dynasty.

Several factors weighed on this opportunity for a major shift in the political direction of the Alawite sect. First, what chance did Bashar Al-Asad have of surviving the UN investigations into the Hariri murder? If the regime was in fact doomed, a better option could have been to seek the best alternative for community security in a new power reality as had occurred in 1936 when the prospect of continued French protection became unlikely.[137] However, over a period of forty years the Asad regime had worked to ensure that no alternative source of political authority existed among the Alawite community. In contrast to 1936, when influential tribal leaders and shaykhs debated and decided on courses of action, in 2006 few (if any) authoritative decision-makers existed outside of the regime structure. The final factor was: could the Sunni majority actually be trusted to uphold an 'amnesty', as advertised by Bayanouni and Khaddam, and not seek violent retribution against the Alawite community for the Hama massacre and subsequent political repression?

The point should be raised that ordinary Alawites, especially those living in rural areas, may not be fully aware of, or understand, the complex challenges facing their community. This, however, would be a misapprehension. As Abd al-Halim Khaddam told this writer, the average Syrian is politically aware, 'they understand what is going on'.[138] Ordinary Alawites are no exception to this—an Alawite cleaner in Latakia, for example, knew the names, backgrounds and roles of every politician in a local newspaper and recognised the late model Mercedes convertible in the business district of Latakia as belonging to the president's first cousin.[139] Although Alawites are not ignorant of political affairs and their implications, the lack of community leadership inhibits any ability to mobilise effectively and take political steps in the community's interests independently of the regime.

The most likely approach for Alawites was to withdraw into the security of their tribal and family groups and wait to see what would transpire and, if necessary, activate their traditional tactic and fall back to their mountain redoubts. An Alawite village grocer, at the height of the regime crisis in October 2005, said that in the event of conflict in the country, 'the people in Damascus will return to the village, and they'll find protection with their people ... they're going to hide behind the rocks and the stones. In the city there are no rocks and stones.'[140]

In June 2006 the UN Security Council passed Resolution 1686 which endorsed the UNIIIC report on the Hariri murder, extended the investigation's mandate and expressed determination to hold 'all those involved in this terrorist attack accountable'.[141] One month later, on 12 July, the Syrian regime's remaining Lebanese strategic ally, Hizballah, entered into a conflict with Israel in southern Lebanon.[142] This conflict, in which Hizballah kept the Israeli Defence Forces heavily engaged for thirty-four days, provided a major boost to the Asad dynasty in several ways.[143] It was a timely reminder for Syrians of the ongoing threat posed by Israel and provided a rallying effect, comparable to the boosting effect for Hafiz al-Asad from the relative Syrian success in the 1973 October war.

Bashar al-Asad sought to maximise the propaganda benefit of the 2006 war by strongly declaring his backing for the 'courageous resistance'. The Hizballah fighters were well provisioned and supported via Syria (and Iran),[144] a point that Asad used to strike a blow at his enemies in the Arab world, especially the Saudi monarchy, going as far as calling them 'half men' for their lack of support for Hizballah.[145] In view of the beneficial effects of the 2006 Lebanon War for the Syrian regime, it is possible that Bashar al-Asad's regime, with the consent of the Iranian regime, prompted Hizballah to provoke the hostilities with Israel. Speaking in 2009, Abd al-Halim Khaddam was certain of this interpretation: Bashar 'has been using Hizballah in Lebanon to somehow remove the danger of the Tribunal [the investigation into the Hariri murder]'.[146] From 2006 onwards the resistance ideology took on greater significance for Bashar al-Asad in buttressing his rule. He actively promoted himself in Syria alongside resistance figures such as the secretary general of Hizballah, Hasan Nasrallah, and the president of Iran, Mahmoud Ahmadinejad.

This was a significant deviation from the propaganda strategy of Hafiz al-Asad, who never included others in his personality cult apart from members of his family and occasional Islamic symbols.[147] This change in policy also represented a shift in the balance of power in the Syria–Iran–Hizballah alliance in favour of Iran and Hizballah. Where Hafiz al-Asad relied only on Alawite support to give domestic stability to his regime, which allowed

Figure 5: Damascus poster showing leaders of the resistance

him to follow a more independent foreign policy, Bashar, from the mid-2000s began to rely more heavily on his external allies. This development corresponds with Ibn Khaldun's theory that a declining dynasty moves away from his own group of origin and instead 'seeks the help of clients and followers ... and cares only for [its] new [allies]'.[148]

By the end of 2006, several months after Abd al-Halim's prediction for a Syrian uprising, no such event had materialised; many Syrians, fearful of political instability and international sanctions, patriotically rallied around the regime.[149] There was little evidence of Alawites joining opposition movements, or of any disloyalty among the military and security services. The effect of the 2006 Lebanon War no doubt played a part in this. But wiping away centuries of mistrust and hostility between Alawites and Sunnis was not going to happen overnight. Moreover, the fear of retaliation for Hama still lingered among Alawites, despite the efforts of opposition leaders like Khaddam and Bayanouni to dispel this. Syria would not emerge from international isolation for another two years, but in the first real test of Alawite loyalty the resilience of sectarian 'asabiyya was clearly evident.

Overall, the period between 2003 and 2007 was a difficult time for the Asad regime and the Alawite community. Bashar al-Asad's inexperience was starkly demonstrated by his tendency for reckless behaviour. Regardless of whether this was due to his own hubris or as a result of an impressionable character and faulty advice from those surrounding him, he brought the Syrian regime perilously close to crisis. He critically upset the careful and firmly controlled equilibrium, established by his father, between Alawite interests and appeasement of the Sunni majority. True to Khaldunian predictions, Bashar had jeopardised many of the fundamental elements of Alawite support for his rule by 2007. When the opportunity arose, however, Alawites did not abandon the Asad dynasty. Why was this? The short answer is fear. Sectarian insecurity, a key factor that Ibn Khaldun failed to recognise in his theory for the decline of a group's 'asabiyya, was the critical ingredient that maintained the rule of the Asad regime. For Alawites, the survival of the regime meant some level of protection against Sunni revanchism, despite the paradoxical fact that the regime was directly and indirectly promoting an upsurge of Islamist sentiment. Overall, the sect's insecurity meant that Alawite 'asabiyya remained intact.

Alawite Socio-Economic Conditions under Bashar al-Asad

Throughout their history it has been an unfortunate reality that the Alawite community has only made a lasting imprint on the historical record during times of difficulty or conflict. For centuries since their reduction to the Jabal al-Sahiliyah, the construction of an academic perspective on Alawite socio-economic circumstances has been limited to piecing together glimpses from, often calamitous, moments for the group, including: the Jablah revolt and Mamluk repression; the short career of Ismail Khayr Bey and Ottoman repression in the nineteenth century; the unionist/separatist dilemma of 1936; the violent sectarian conflict of 1976–82; the Asad dynasty crisis of 2005–7; and now the Syrian uprising of 2011–14.

Outside these events, the Alawites become very hazy to scholars. From 2007 to 2011, with the start of regime reconsolidation, this pattern resumed and Alawites once again receded from view. As a result of this sporadic record of the Alawite community, there is a temptation to view the group as heterodox religious extremists, violent insurgents (Jablah revolt), disordered and savage tribesmen (Ismail Khayr) or shadowy and ruthless security operatives ('sectarian Stasi'). Yet the reality of this community is less dramatic than these depictions.

This section attempts to portray the everyday characteristics and dilemmas of this community in the twenty-first century. In drawing out the ordinary aspects of the Alawite community, the tragic consequences of sectarian insecurity are poignantly highlighted. Overall, the political system, which stems from Alawite–Asad 'asabiyya, limits the potential of all Syrian people including the great majority of Alawites.

One major trend stands out when assessing general Alawite socio-economic circumstances under Bashar al-Asad. There is a widening income gap between Alawites who are well connected to the regime, and those who are not. As discussed previously, there has been a disparity in this regard since the beginning of Asad rule, but the extent of this gap became extremely pronounced after 2000.[150] Moreover, the size of the privileged Alawite elite shrank as Bashar al-Asad withdrew into greater reliance on his trusted inner core of family and close friends. According to opposition sources, in 2007 the combined wealth of the regime inner circle, including the wider Makhlouf, Shaleesh and Asad families, was approximately 40 billion US dollars.[151] In the same year the total projected revenue of Syrian fiscal operations[152] was 442.5 billion Syrian pounds (SP) (approximately 8 billion US dollars) while government debt stood at 725.7 billion Syrian pounds (13 billion US).[153] The 'corporatisation of corruption' among the dynasty's inner core, which Abd al-Halim described, reached into the very heart of the Syrian economy. In 2004 and 2006, the Commercial Bank of Syria (CBS), for example, which controls nearly 90 per cent of all deposits and controls most of Syria's foreign currency reserves, was listed internationally as a 'financial institution of primary money laundering concern'.[154]

In 2009 Abd al-Halim Khaddam estimated that the majority of wealth in Syria was under the control of around 500 people.[155] This is probably an exaggeration; however, in a country of over 23 million, even if the actual figure was double or triple Khaddam's estimation, it still represents an enormous concentration of wealth in a few extended families. In considering only the Syrian Alawite population of around 3 million, it shows that the distribution of wealth is very unequal within that community. Official figures are not available for income distribution in Syria; therefore, evaluation of this aspect is only possible through primary and secondary qualitative observations. In 2009 and 2011 the great majority of Syrians, including Alawites, suffered very difficult economic circumstances. This stands in contrast to occasional signs of extreme wealth in the form of mansions and luxury vehicles.

The relative socio-economic security the rural Alawite majority had enjoyed under Hafiz al-Asad waned as Bashar al-Asad shifted the focus of development towards the cities. For example, the new regime's liberalising economic reforms led to the reduction or cancellation of agricultural and

Figure 6: The Asad Residence near Qardaha

fuel subsidies. In 2008 the price of diesel jumped from 7.3 SP to 25 SP per litre,[156] and agricultural subsidies were cancelled in favour of arbitrary 'cash transfers'.[157]

Compared to the rapid improvements for rural Alawites under Hafiz al-Asad, the extension of essential services like running water and electricity slowed. According to World Bank data, from 2000 to 2005 access to improved water sources in rural areas in Syria increased by only 3 per cent.[158] In 2009, in the Murshidi village of Kdeen, many houses still did not have electricity connected and water was stored inside houses in large drums. In the village of Jobat Berghal, near the summit of the Jabal al-Sahiliyah, the school, sports club and community centre built in the 1970s and 1980s stood in disrepair or had been closed by 2005, and villagers still waited for the provision of running water.[159] For many Alawites it seemed the regime had abandoned them; for instance, a retired government employee from the village of Qarir complained: 'It's like people don't even know we live in the country … every person sitting in the chair of power cares about money, not about the people.'[160]

There are indications of the changing nature of the Alawite–Asad relationship even in the Asad hometown, Qardaha. In 1986 there was a general flush of prosperity in Qardaha with abundant construction and development projects underway. In 2009 and again in 2011, the town had not seemingly advanced considerably in recent times and appeared somewhat rundown. There was no evidence of disproportionate wealth among most residents of the town; in fact, the taxi driver who drove this author in 2009 was himself a local resident and a distant relative of the Asad family. In 1986, the Asad residence was located within Qardaha, while in 2009 the palatial Asad residence stood some distance away atop a hill north of the town.

Qardaha is a rarity among Alawite towns in possessing a mosque, a sure sign of its purely symbolic political function. It is ironic that the Latakia region's best supplied and cheapest liquor stores are located nearby.[161]

It is possible to see the changing nature of the Alawite–Asad dynasty relationship from a comparison between Qardaha in 1986 and 2009. First, it seems symbolic of how the Asad dynasty distanced itself from ordinary Alawites, even those from the Kalbiyya tribe, that the Asad 'palace' was relocated away from the town. Also, the way that development of Qardaha township seemingly ground to a halt indicates that the material benefits of power have further reduced to only the Asad family and its clique. The building of an elaborate mosque in Qardaha is more representative of the political priorities of the regime than providing infrastructure for the Alawite community. The Asad regime's tightening alliance with the Iranian regime and Hizballah, no doubt, makes it politically expedient to provide suitable religious facilities for their frequent visits.

In Damascus, Alawite-populated satellite suburbs like Ash al Warwar appear largely undeveloped and the residents display similar, if not worse, signs of poverty as those living in the mountain villages of the Latakia region. Meanwhile, the regime elite live in luxury, with more lavish lifestyles than at any other stage in the Asad dynasty. Despite this widening socio-economic gap between the Alawite community in general, and the

Figure 7: Mosque in Qardaha

Asad dynasty, many Sunni Damascenes generalise about Alawite dominance over their city.

A study on contemporary Damascene social identity by Christa Salamandra illustrates the extent to which Sunnis resent what they see as the degradation of Damascus's cultural and economic heritage by the 'invading' Alawites.[162] A young Sunni translator from Damascus demonstrated this:

I've noticed over the past five years that I have become proud of being Damascene. I see this also with my father, who was one of the founders of the Ba'th Party. The Ba'thists used to think Syrians were all simply Syrian. Now many of them regret this. Now they feel that they are distinct from all the villagers, especially the 'Alawis. They think the 'Alawis may have the money, they may have the power, but we have the tradition.[163]

The feeling that Alawites have all the money and the power is no doubt fuelled by the extravagant wealth and lifestyles of conspicuous Alawites close to the Asad dynasty like Rami Makhlouf. This echoes the resentment that Syrians felt about the extravagant wealth of Rifa'at al-Asad in the 1970s and 1980s. In that case, however, Hafiz al-Asad boosted his own popularity and the stability of the Asad dynasty by being seen to crack down on the corruption of his brother, culminating in his exile.

Despite the false presumption by some Sunnis that Alawites in general are politically and financially dominant, their perceived inferiority in Syrian society is shown by the comment above, whereby they are still referred to as 'villagers' lacking in 'tradition'. This mentality recalls historic perceptions of the Alawites and indicates that the sect had not made much progress in elevating their status in Syrian society during Asad rule. An anonymous Alawite writer from Latakia summed up the modern situation of Alawites:

They say that this regime is 'Alawi, but I don't think so. Or you can say that there is a coalition of 'Alawis who are benefitting, but not the rest ... If you ask a Damascene, he will answer in a way that reflects his prejudices. He will say that they [the Alawites] have come and dominated everything, stolen everything and so on. But those who came in from other areas live in the suburbs, in illegal sub-standard housing, while those in the centre are [Sunni] Damascene and Christian.[164]

When asked in 2005 if the Asad dynasty benefited the Alawite community disproportionately, a retired government employee from Jobat Berghal, near the summit of the Jabal al-Sahiliyah, responded angrily, 'The opposite! The opposite! We're all Alawites here and when you come here, you can't find anything.'[165] In this rare outburst the middle-aged man bemoaned the corruption in the country that protects the privileged few, while he still hand-pumps water into his home. He made a clear distinction between the first stage of the dynasty and the current ruler, 'President Hafiz al-Asad said it was the right of any citizen to raise his voice if he sees injustice … now they say it's not your right to talk.'[166] These remarks from an Alawite source give an indication of declining 'asabiyya at the community grass roots.

The outbreak of severe drought in Syria in 2006–9 had a major impact on Alawite socio-economic conditions.[167] In the Jabal al-Sahiliyah, Alawites

Figure 8: Parched terraced fields in the Northern Jabal al-Sahiliyah in 2009

struggled to maintain their limited incomes from small agriculture and tobacco growing as water shortages impacted terraced fields and orchards.

Despite facing severe socio-economic challenges, the 'asabiyya of ordinary Alawites was under strain but intact. In general, Alawites remained mostly positive in their assessment of Bashar al-Asad despite their economic predicaments. In 2009 a twenty-four-year-old Alawite acquaintance pleaded with this author to buy him some shoes as his were worn through. Yet when I showed him a souvenir cap that I had bought from Qala'at al-Hosn (Krac de Chevalier), with the words 'I love Bashar' emblazoned on it, he told me that the president was *'qua'is'* (excellent) and asked if he could have the cap. Conversely, a Sunni taxi driver from Homs, who was much better off than my Alawite acquaintance, angrily tried to throw the cap out the window when I showed it to him a day earlier. Why was my Alawite friend so admiring of Bashar al-Asad who lived in luxury, while he could not afford to buy shoes? According to Ibn Khaldun, group 'asabiyya declines as 'profits are distributed amongst … the privileged few'.[168] Despite growing discontent among Alawites in general, their support for the Asad dynasty did not appear to be declining to any serious extent. Their latent insecurity seemed to cause Alawites to overlook inequality within Syria and their own community. To further understand this phenomenon it is helpful to examine the situation of an Alawite population outside Syria.

The 'Precarious' Security of the Lebanese Alawites

In Tripoli in northern Lebanon there is a small Alawite population of around 100,000–120,000.[169] Like their Syrian counterparts, Lebanese Alawites originally resided on the rural margins. After 1976 they began moving into Tripoli from the Akkar region north of Tripoli, protected by the presence of their co-sectarians in the Syrian army stationed in Lebanon.[170] Jabal Mohsen, where around half of Lebanese Alawites live, ranks among the poorer areas of Lebanon. Despite the small size and poverty of the Lebanese branch of the Alawite community it plays an important part in Syrian political equations. To Syrian Alawites the situation of their Lebanese co-sectarians seemed to illustrate the precarious situation of

Alawites not under the direct protection of the Asad dynasty. This perception stems from the frequent Sunni–Alawite violence that occurs in Tripoli.

After Sunni–Alawite hostilities in Syria were terminated at Hama in 1982, many of the Muslim Brothers and their supporters fled across the border and found refuge among Tripoli's Sunni community and in Palestinian (PLO) bases.[171] Here they confronted the Alawite, Arab Democratic Party (ADP),[172] led by Ali Eid. Clashes in Tripoli commenced in June 1983 after attacks on Lebanese Alawites and Syrian soldiers led to strong Alawite reprisals against Sunnis.[173] Thereafter, intractable sectarian hostility emerged between the suburbs of Jabal Mohsen and the neighbouring Sunni suburb of Bab al-Tebbaneh. Intermittent outbreaks of Sunni–Alawite violence have been a feature of life in Tripoli for nearly three decades.

An episode of intensive Alawite–Sunni conflict in Tripoli occurred between 21 June and 8 September 2008.[174] In an attempt to stem the fighting and draw Lebanese Alawites away from their reliance on the Asad regime, the leader of the Lebanese Sunni community, Sa'ad al-Hariri,[175] tried to alleviate Alawite insecurity: 'We are both Lebanese and we will not let anyone tamper with us.'[176] Nonetheless, the ingrained insecurity of Tripoli's Alawites was revealed in the words of ADP leader Rifa'at Eid: 'we are a minority; we need weapons before we need food'.[177]

By exploiting the insecurity of Tripoli Alawites, the Asad regime created a useful instrument to manipulate its Lebanese political interests. A good example of this occurred in August 1983 when the United States was applying pressure on Damascus to remove its troops from Lebanon. Syrian troops stationed in Tripoli 'abruptly withdrew to the city's outskirts', upon which a devastating bombing of a Sunni mosque occurred and intensive Sunni–Alawite fighting broke out.[178] The intended message was possibly that Syrian forces were essential to Lebanese stability. A parallel can be drawn with the fighting in 2008, when Bashar al-Asad also sought to prove Syria was instrumental in Lebanese stability. It could be argued that the Asad regime's interests were served by the promotion of violence in Tripoli—it consolidated Alawite 'asabiyya by promoting sectarian insecurity, but it also provided them with an argument that Lebanese stability could only be achieved through Syrian intervention.

166

There are, however, genuine security concerns for Tripoli Alawites from an upsurge in fundamentalist ideology among Sunnis.[179] A lack of job opportunities for Tripoli's youth provides fertile ground for recruitment by Salafist clerics. The Tripoli journalist, Fakher al-Ayoubi, commented in 2008, 'A lot of young people are joining the Salafists since May, some of them don't even know how to pray, but they like the idea of fighting the Alawites.'[180]

On 8 September 2008 the respective leaders of the Alawite and Sunni communities in Tripoli signed an accord ending the fighting.[181] This agreement was achieved against the backdrop of Syrian troop deployments around the northern Syria–Lebanon border, and even included reports of incursions by Syrian Special Forces into Lebanon.[182] Thus, despite claims by Rifa'at Eid that the Syrian regime was not involved in the Tripoli conflict,[183] the favourable terms of the Tripoli Accord for Alawites, combined with the heavy presence of Syrian troops near Tripoli, indicated strong Syrian support to the Tripoli Alawites.[184]

In terms of Alawite–Asad 'asabiyya it seems that the Alawites of Lebanon look to the Syrian regime to provide for their security. It could be read that Rifa'at Eid was referring to the Syrian regime when he stated, 'only the capable state that has a strong army and active institutions can protect the Alawites and minorities'.[185] This was despite the 2005 Lebanese 'Cedar Revolution' that appeared to transcend sectarian divisions in a way that could prove beneficial to long-term Alawite political interests. Ultimately, however, the lack of institutional stability in Lebanon, and the perceived threat of Sunni hostility, causes Lebanese Alawites to gravitate towards their co-sectarians in Syria. Overall, Sunni–Alawite conflict in Lebanon serves as a reminder of the potential for a renewal of a similar conflict in Syria and helps keep Syrian Alawites firmly behind the 'bulwark' of the Asad regime.[186]

The tiny Alawite village of Ghajar in the Israeli-occupied Golan Heights provides an interesting contrast to the Lebanese Alawites' reliance on the Asad dynasty. According to local residents, the village of Ghajar, with a population in 2010 of approximately 2,200, was established during the Ottoman conquest of the Levant in 1516.[187] This Alawite village was separated from Syria by the Israeli occupation of the Golan Heights in 1967. Because this community was beyond the reach of Damascus at the outset of Hafiz al-Asad's rule, it is an interesting case of Alawites outside the Alawite–Asad 'asabiyya who pursue their interests independently. The Ghajar Alawites willingly accepted Israeli citizenship in 1981 and, according to some sources, even requested Israeli annexation of their village.[188] Conversely, most of the Golan Druze community refused to accept Israeli citizenship.[189] Many of the Ghajar residents commute from the village for employment in the industrial zones of northern Israel, in the orchards of the Golan, or in hospitality in Haifa, Tel Aviv or Jerusalem.[190]

In 2009 moves to incorporate Ghajar village into Lebanon provoked a strong reaction from the village leaders who lobbied the Israeli government to reconsider.[191] The Ghajar Alawites appeared apprehensive about the Islamist Hizballah forces that control southern Lebanon. The Ghajar Alawites, for the time being, prefer the security and opportunities afforded by Israeli citizenship. Their official argument for wanting to remain in the Israeli-controlled Golan is that they hope to be returned to Syria along with the rest of the Golan. This type of pragmatic manoeuvring between competing forces seeking the best outcome for Alawite security is reminiscent of pre-Asad Alawite approaches. In Syria, however, the bulk of the Alawite community, increasingly neglected by the new generation of the Asad dynasty and suffering the negative effects of drought, were limited in their room for pragmatic manoeuvre. Their fates were seemingly tied to the Asad dynasty. In the period from 2007 to 2010 Syria approached a dramatic turning point.

5

REVOLUTION

As the first decade of the twenty-first century drew to a close, the Syrian regime outwardly appeared to consolidate and rise triumphantly over its external and internal challenges. In parallel, beneath the surface of Syrian society, signs emerged of an impending revolution. For Alawites, the political upheaval that eventually erupted in March 2011 would present both potential for conflict with a resurgent Sunni Muslim majority, but also historic opportunities for the sect's long-term security and integration in a new political system based on a pluralist, civil-democratic state. Fear and insecurity would be the key determinants of which path the sect and the country would take.

The first seven years of Bashar al-Asad's presidency had brought increasing discontentment among Alawites about the performance of the regime. Most Alawites gained little material benefit from the new generation of Asad rule. The regime favoured external allies over Alawites and incurred the wrath of the international community, and there had also been a potentially dangerous resurgence of Islamic fundamentalism in the country. Despite this downward pressure on Alawite 'asabiyya, sectarian insecurity prevented any serious decline of Alawite support for Bashar Al-Asad.

Ibn Khaldun suggested that rulers born to power and privilege often lack the necessary qualities to rule effectively.[1] Major elements to consider in this regard are Bashar al-Asad's disconnection from the socio-economic challenges facing ordinary Syrians, overconfidence in his popularity, his capacity to maintain regime unity and his preoccupation with external threats. Abd al-Halim Khaddam commented in 2009: 'The real threat to Bashar al-Asad is Bashar al-Asad himself. The way he is. That's the threat that every dictator at the end comes to—that threat of himself.'[2] All the while, socio-economic and political pressures were reaching a critical level in Syria.

Diplomacy and Rehabilitation

In early 2007 the Syrian regime's position at the international level remained precarious. The United States, European governments and the UN continued to apply economic, political and legal pressure on the Syrian regime for its suspected destabilising roles in Lebanon and Iraq, and the STL had been formally established at The Hague. Bashar al-Asad was almost entirely isolated among Arab states, with Hizballah his only major Arab ally. In addition, in September 2007, the regime suffered a humiliating blow when the Israeli air force easily breached Syrian defences to destroy a suspected nuclear facility in north-east Syria.

In order to confront these challenges, Bashar al-Asad worked closely with his Iranian allies. Shortly after the UN decision to establish the STL, the Iranian foreign minister, Manouchehr Mottaki, arrived in Damascus on 1 June 2007 to discuss options. High on the list of priorities was the situation in Lebanon where the two sides agreed to 'cooperate on achieving unity and stability'.[3] In the months following this meeting, the Lebanese political system was effectively paralysed. Lebanese presidential elections slated for September 2007 were postponed due to ongoing political assassinations and a boycott by pro-Syrian Lebanese MPs.[4] The elections were postponed a staggering twenty times before an agreement was finally signed at Doha on 21 May 2008.[5] The Doha Accord gave major concessions to Syria's Lebanese political allies, including the right to veto government decisions.[6] Thus, the Syrian and Iranian regimes, less than a year after their crisis meeting on 1 June 2007, re-established a strong political footing in Lebanon.

The other main avenue open to the Syrian regime to alleviate external threats was regional and Western diplomacy. Despite the consolidation of

Iranian–Syrian ties in 2007, Syria gave signals that it was open to a strategic realignment away from Iran in return for concessions from Western and Arab powers. While the US and French administrations remained unconvinced of Syrian intentions,[7] the prospect of a Syrian strategic realignment appealed to Israeli decision-makers who were feeling vulnerable after their unconvincing performance in the 2006 Lebanon War.[8] For Syria, a renewed peace process with Israel could provide an opening to split the international consensus about holding the regime accountable for the political assassinations in Lebanon. Owing to US reluctance to be drawn into the process, Syria and Israel instead began negotiating via indirect talks with Turkish mediation in June 2007.[9]

The election of a new president in France in May 2007 presented another opportunity, under the aegis of its Iranian allies, for the Syrian regime to reconsolidate.[10] According to the *Al-Hayat* newspaper, shortly after his inauguration President Sarkozy received a letter from Tehran offering France the opportunity to regain some of its lost influence in the Levant by playing an important role in regional peace initiatives.[11] Tehran perhaps recognised the ambition of the new right-wing French president and the persistent desire of France for a role in the Eastern Mediterranean, and saw an opportunity to further break up the international coalition against their Syrian allies.

It was not France, however, that first broke the Western diplomatic embargo on Syria. In early June 2007, the Italian foreign minister, Massimo D'Alema, travelled to Damascus to discuss events in Lebanon and the prospect of an international tribunal to try suspects indicted by the UNIIIC.[12] Even though the talks reportedly did not proceed well and broke down over Italian demands for Syria to stop interfering in Lebanon,[13] the main outcome was to give an invaluable boost to the Asad regime from the re-opening of diplomatic dialogue.

In early July 2007 there were indications of a change in approach by the French government from its previous hard-line stance against Syria.[14] By the end of July France had sent an envoy to both Damascus and Tehran carrying a message: 'Such visits will not take place in the future unless France sees tangible changes in Syria's behaviour in Lebanon and the region.'[15] Yet the diplomatic procession continued, with Spanish envoys arriving in Damascus in August 2007.[16] In this fashion, Bashar al-Asad gradually emerged from his isolation of 2005–6. Asad's need for international rehabilitation coincided with a period when southern European states were heavily engaged in diplomatic competition for prestige and influence in the Mediterranean basin.[17] The players in this intra-European political competition appeared to pay little attention to the possible impact of their actions on diluting the STL and they also harmed wider efforts to confront impunity for acts of political violence in the Levant.

Following these successes on the diplomatic front, the Asad regime suffered another setback. On 6 September 2007, eight unopposed Israeli aircraft bombed a military installation in north-east Syria, which the Israelis believed to contain a nuclear facility.[18] This graphically demonstrated regime weakness in the face of Israeli aggression. Bashar al-Asad's domestic legitimacy was strongly hinged upon 'steadfast resistance' against the Israeli enemy; hence opposition figures used the opportunity to accuse the regime of weakness in all areas except 'oppressing the Syrian people'.[19]

The Israeli aggression came as a shock to the Asad regime because the Israeli prime minister, Ehud Olmert, had seemingly been responding positively to Syrian overtures for peace talks through Turkish channels.[20] Within days of the attack the regime mobilised part of its large army reserve in preparation to defend against further Israeli incursions.[21] In reality, Syria was poorly equipped to repel conventional Israeli attacks.

The neglect of Syria's armed forces was a source of Alawite dissatisfaction with Bashar al-Asad's rule. Although Hafiz al-Asad had all but bankrupted the Syrian economy in an effort to modernise the Syrian military in the 1980s,[22] for Alawites this was recognition of their valuable role as the protectors of their community and Syria. By prioritising external allies such as Hizballah over its own community, Bashar al-Asad risked alienating senior Alawites in the security forces. In general, Alawite confidence in Bashar al-Asad to protect their interests was sorely tested by the Asad regime's weakness in the face of Israeli aggression.

In this light, reports from late October 2007 that Alawites demonstrated in Latakia against Bashar al-Asad's performance seem credible. According to the report, some protesters even waved placards of Rifa'at al-Asad.[23] For some Alawites, Rifa'at was perhaps recalled as a stronger protector of their interests than Bashar al-Asad. He had, after all, defeated the challenge of the Muslim Brothers. In 1979, when Latakia Alawites had previously expressed frustration at the Asad regime's performance, it was Rifa'at al-Asad who was sent to repress Alawite dissent. In 2007 Asef Shawkat was charged with cracking down on the protesters, many of whom were arrested.[24]

Against these new internal and external challenges, the regime maintained its strategy of diplomacy and a few months later activated its two key diplomatic assets: its roles in the Arab–Israeli peace process and Lebanese domestic politics. Indirect Syrian–Israeli peace negotiations were officially announced under Turkish mediation on 21 May 2008.[25] On the same day, the Doha Accords, mentioned earlier, were signed under Syrian auspices. This agreement finally unlocked Lebanon's political paralysis and left Hizballah greatly enhanced in Lebanese politics.[26]

At the international level these moves by Damascus proved a diplomatic master stroke; they had an immediate effect on liberal politicians in the United States, who viewed them as proof of the Syrian regime's good intentions.[27] This was very encouraging for Damascus, considering the forthcoming elections in the United States and the likelihood of a Democrat victory. The presidential candidate Barack Obama suddenly became a popular figure in Damascus.[28]

Another positive development at the international level for the Asad regime was Bashar al-Asad's invitation to the Mediterranean Union summit, hosted by the French President Nicolas Sarkozy, in Paris on 13 July 2008.[29] This was the Syrian president's first visit to a Western country since the assassination of Rafiq al-Hariri in 2005. Bashar al-Asad was invited by Sarkozy to stay on in Paris as a special guest at the Bastille Day celebrations on 14 July.[30] This event was identified by many observers as a major symbol of Bashar al-Asad's international rehabilitation and the end of Syria's isolation.[31] These 'victories' at the international level were significant in terms of the recovery of the Asad regime from crisis, yet they also served to gloss over growing domestic challenges.

A Confident Bashar al-Asad

Ibn Khaldun suggested that 'the second stage is one in which the ruler … is concerned with gaining adherents and acquiring clients and followers in great numbers'.[32] In other words, rulers who have inherited power may seek the adoration of the masses and be prone to delusions of grandeur. As Bashar al-Asad confronted the numerous challenges facing his rule, his self-belief steadily increased. This confidence, however, evolved into a dangerous disconnection from ordinary Syrians, including Alawites, and a lack of awareness of the social and political pressures building in Syrian society in the latter part of the decade. The major factors in Bashar al-Asad's developing hubris would be his stance on the 2009 Gaza War and his apparent victories against his various internal and external opponents.

On 27 May 2007, Bashar al-Asad was returned as president in a referendum with 97.29 per cent of the vote. Like previous referendums, the president was the only candidate.[33] David Lesch, a Middle East scholar who gained personal access to Bashar al-Asad, suggested that Bashar's self-belief began to increase after the 2007 presidential referendum. Lesch observed in Bashar al-Asad, 'a cathartic expression of gratification that the people really liked him'.[34] The 'resounding endorsement' of the referendum and the easing international pressure in the first half of 2007 gave Bashar al-Asad the confidence to begin harshly cracking down on internal dissent.

After the demise of Saddam Hussein's regime in 2003, a feeling had endured among Syrian political dissidents that the regime could be challenged. According to the Syrian human rights lawyer Anwar al-Bouni, this was only because of 'the fright [the US invasion of Iraq] gave our rulers'.[35] By June 2007, however, ten reform activists—including Michel Kilo, Kamal Labwani, Mahmoud Issa, Suleiman Shummar, Khalil Hussain, the Muslim Brotherhood member Abd al-Jabar Allawi, Ahmed Sheikho, Faisal Ballani, the Kurdish activist Ziad Ismail and Anwar al-Bouni himself— were imprisoned on political charges.[36]

In 2008 Bashar al-Asad also cracked down on challenges to his power from within his own regime. Power struggles over regime policy, personal interests and the distribution of wealth among the elite[37] amounted to 'a quiet civil war' within the upper echelons of the Syrian regime.[38] The infighting coincided with the murder of the top Hizballah operative, Imad Mughniyeh, in Damascus on 12 February 2008 by a car bomb.[39] Tensions ran high between Asef Shawkat and the president's brother, Maher Al-Asad, head of the Republican Guard, and senior security personnel were reorganised with loyal Alawites replacing non-Alawites in many sensitive urban areas.[40] Asef Shawkat was subsequently demoted from his prominent role in military intelligence.[41]

Other extraordinary events included the assassination of Alawite Brigadier General Muhammad Suleiman, Bashar al-Asad's top security aide responsible for special nuclear projects on 1 August 2008.[42] In September 2008, Hisham al-Labadani, the top aide to Damascus-based Palestinian Hamas leader, Khaled Meshal, was reportedly hauled from a car in Homs and executed.[43] Two weeks later, on 27 September 2008, a car bomb exploded in Damascus near the Palestinian branch of Military Intelligence in the Sayeda Zeinab neighbourhood. The bombing involved 200 kilogrammes of explosives and killed seventeen people, including a high-ranking officer, Brigadier General Abd al-Karim 'Abas, and his son.[44] Significantly, the head of the Palestine branch of Military Intelligence, Suleiman Dayoub, was a close ally of Asef Shawkat.[45] Thereafter, the internal disturbances dissipated and Bashar al-Asad consolidated his control of the regime.

As with the 2004 Kurdish riots, Bashar al-Asad used the 27 September explosion—the first such event in Damascus in twenty-seven years—to emphasise the need to avoid any political upheaval in Syria. Asad placed the blame on his March 14 enemies in Lebanon for orchestrating the attack via the Sunni extremist group, Fatah al-Islam.[46] This increased the Syrian regime's justification for intervening in Lebanon's internal affairs to protect Syria's domestic security.[47] Also, by blaming the attack on Muslim extremists emanating from northern Lebanon, another timely reminder was delivered to Alawites about the ever present threat of 'Islamist terrorists' to their security.[48] This of course helped to consolidate Alawite sectarian 'asabiyya.

After a parting shot by George W. Bush when US Special Forces raided Syrian territory in October 2008,[49] the US threat dissipated with the election of Barack Obama, who subsequently launched a policy of re-engagement with Syria. The threat from the STL, while still present, receded. Moreover, Syrian interests in Lebanon were being re-established, albeit in a diminished capacity in contrast to Hizballah and Iran's expanded influence in Lebanese affairs, and Bashar al-Asad consolidated control of his regime.

During these diversions the promise of modernising reform, which Bashar al-Asad had brought to the presidency, seemed a distant memory and was almost completely replaced by the rhetoric of 'resistance'. Bashar al-Asad appeared to believe that steadfast resistance against Israel and the West would be enough to sustain his popularity among the Syrian population. In March 2009, for example, the Syrian culture minister, Dr Riyad al-Agha, told the UAE newspaper *Al-Ittihad*, 'I believe that resistance is [the only] practical option, despite its heavy toll; indeed, resistance demands from a people, that choose it, numerous losses and sacrifices.'[50]

Hafiz al-Asad also utilised the resistance discourse to buttress his rule; however, he had also been careful to maintain a balance between the discourses of resistance and reform, the provision of the basic needs of Syrian citizens and the support of his Alawite community. Hafiz al-Asad crafted his regional strategy with a view to sustaining the Ba'th regime, which included consideration of Alawite concerns. For example, Hafiz never allowed any serious increase in religious fanaticism, even from his allies, Hizballah. Conversely, Bashar al-Asad operated in the regional arena with the prime objectives of escaping from the threat of the STL and boosting his personal popularity, often through religious rhetoric about 'resistance' to Israel and the West.

Bashar al-Asad's ambition to increase his popularity in the Arab–Muslim world beyond his Alawite community was demonstrated in his stances on the Gaza War, which began in December 2008.[51] Speaking at the Doha Summit on 16 January 2009, Bashar vented:

We will take care to remind our children of the Gaza slaughter. We will save the pictures of the children of Gaza with their wounds and blood, and we will teach our children that the strong believer is better than the weak.[52]

This type of religious rhetoric ran counter to Alawite preferences for secular political approaches. Strong religious feelings among the Sunni Muslim majority had always been dangerous for Alawites. However, Bashar al-Asad's personal profile was elevated enormously in the Muslim world and he became almost a cult figure of the 'resistance' in large sections of the Arab 'street'. A pop song was even written about him named 'Bashar the Lion',[53] and the Ibn Khaldun Center for Development Studies in Cairo awarded him the title of 'the most popular leader' in the Middle East.[54] This newfound popularity came at the expense of Western-aligned Egypt,

Jordan and Saudi Arabia, whose muted responses to the Gaza War placed severe strains on these governments as their populations demanded stronger responses.[55]

Bashar al-Asad also used the Gaza War as an excuse to suspend the Turkish-sponsored Syrian–Israeli indirect peace talks.[56] The Asad regime arguably only ever engaged in these talks as a means to escape from international isolation by improving its standing with Western countries. The peace talks were clearly disingenuous as Bashar al-Asad's strong alliance with Iran and Hizballah precluded any chance he would unilaterally come to terms with the Israelis.[57] The Gaza War consequently provided Bashar al-Asad with a convenient opportunity to exit the peace talks without losing face with the Turkish government, France, Britain or the incoming US administration, all of whom had recently offered Syria concessions based on its (potential) 'constructive' regional role.[58]

The Syrian president's other victory stemming from the Gaza War was a temporary truce with the Syrian Muslim Brotherhood. Bashar al-Asad strongly supported the Palestinian Islamists, even while it remained a capital offence to be a member of the Muslim Brotherhood in Syria. An Egyptian official raised this irony when he said, 'The difference between Hamas and Hama is just one letter.'[59] Nonetheless, Bashar al-Asad's newfound popularity from his support of Hamas in the Gaza Strip made it difficult for the Syrian Muslim Brotherhood (now based in London) to continue active opposition against the regime, and in January 2009 they called for a truce with the Syrian authorities.[60]

The Syrian Muslim Brotherhood's temporary normalisation of ties with the regime had another important implication. It led to the termination of their alliance with Abd al-Halim Khaddam and the demise of the NSF.[61] The end of effective opposition, the easing of international pressure and his newfound popularity in the Muslim world gave the Syrian president cause to feel confident about his prospects.[62] However, Bashar al-Asad's miscalculation of Syrian domestic circumstances and his overconfidence in his popularity among the Syrian people spelled danger for the regime and the situation of Syria's Alawites.

Rising Internal Challenges

Ibn Khaldun's theories about the rise and decline of dynasties included a great deal of consideration for economic and environmental factors and the resulting social and political implications. Concerning the end of dynasties he wrote:

In the later years of dynasties famines and pestilences become numerous ... as people refrain from cultivating the soil ... [due to] attacks on property and tax revenue ... [and] trouble occurs as a result of unrest of the subjects and the great number encouraged by the senility of the dynasty to rebel.[63]

Like Ibn Khadun's theoretical dynasty, environmental and socio-economic problems posed serious challenges to Syrian stability in the late 2000s. The income gap increased visibly and economic hardship became pronounced through population growth and inflation.[64] In addition, Ibn Khaldun's 'attacks on property and tax revenue' were perhaps reflected in the 'predatory self-enrichment' of regime figures like Rami Makhlouf.[65] If the Syrian economy continued to deteriorate, the potential for domestic upheaval or rebellion would threaten the position of the regime. Moreover, tough economic times could pose a threat to Alawites from rising religious conservatism among the Sunni majority. The 'Little Ice Age' and related socio-economic decline of the thirteenth century had, for example, helped shape the fundamentalism of people like Ibn Taymiyya.[66] Thus, Bashar al-Asad's handling of the challenging economic times ahead carried direct implications for Alawite security.

In September 2009, five months after the collapse of the NSF coalition, Abd al-Halim Khaddam expressed to this writer grave concerns about rising pressures in Syria:

Thirty per cent of the workforce in Syria is currently unemployed and the inflation has gone way out of control. The rising prices of the basic goods people need have gone to nearly five times since 2000. All the corruption that you can see happening in Syria means that the government cannot control what's happening in Syria, it has gone out of control. There was a middle class in Syria that was actually involved in every aspect of political, economic and social life. This class, this middle class is completely vanished. There are only two classes of people now. There is the bottom one, which is the majority of the people, they are very poor. On the other hand, you see the other class that consists of maybe 500 people, which are in control of all the wealth, all the businesses, everything.[67]

Khaddam's evaluation of the Syrian economy and wealth distribution painted a picture of a country on the edge of upheaval and revolution. This was possibly wishful thinking on the part of an ardent regime opponent. However, as the events of 2011 showed, his appraisal of the potential impacts of rising socio-economic pressures was relatively accurate.

Bashar al-Asad's management of the Syrian economy was made more difficult by the numerous challenges the country faced in the latter half of the decade. These included dwindling oil reserves, US economic sanctions, the global credit crisis in 2008 and the severe drought in 2007–10.[68] Yet from 2007 onwards the Asad dynasty also struggled to address rising pressures within Syrian society. These pressures can be grouped into four categories: economic, political, environmental and religious.

Economic pressures

At the end of the decade Syria's population growth remained high at 2.5 per cent; around 4.6 million Syrians were aged between fifteen and twenty-four, requiring 400,000 new jobs each year. In 2009 inflation had peaked at 17 per cent.[69] Since the beginning of Asad rule in 1971, Syria's modest oil reserves had been a vital safety net propping up the Syrian economy and financing the regime's operations, including its large security apparatus.[70] Thus declining proceeds from oil became a serious problem, especially after Syria lost most of its economic interests in Lebanon in 2005.[71] Oil production lowered from 548,000 barrels per day in 2000 to 380,000 in 2009, and was set to decline further in the absence of new oil deposits.[72] The Asad regime's main compensating strategy was to promote itself as a regional transit hub for oil and gas.[73] An example was the proposed reopening of an oil line from Kirkuk, in Iraq, to Banyas on the Syrian coast.[74] However, political imperatives conflicted with this potentially lucrative economic opportunity.

Despite promises by the Syrian prime minister, Mohammad Naji al-'Otri, that Syria would stop the flow of Sunni fighters into Iraq, the Asad regime soon reopened its border for al-Qaeda and other fighters.[75] The deal was scrapped shortly thereafter by the Iraqis.[76] The Asad regime was possibly worried about Iraq stabilising into a US-backed, democratic multi-sectarian state.[77] This would also set a dangerous precedent for its Alawite support base that Asad rule was not essential to their long-term security. In addition, constrained Islamist fighters could turn their sights back on to the 'Alawite regime' in Syria. The implications of placing its political security ahead of Syria's economic prosperity proved hazardous by adding to rising social pressures inside Syria. One more economic setback attached to the Syrian regime's Iraq policy was the renewal of sanctions against Syria by US President Barack Obama on 8 May 2009.[78]

Another lost economic opportunity was the re-opening of discussions in 2009 between the European Union (EU) and Syria for an economic association agreement, shelved since the Hariri murder in 2005. Despite signs that Bashar al-Asad was not reform-minded, or inclined towards the West, the EU offered to complete the agreement with Syria. This agreement could have opened lucrative trade and investment opportunities for the struggling Syrian economy.[79] Yet, as with the Iraqi deal, Bashar al-Asad chose political priorities over economic opportunities and the agreement was left unsigned by the Syrian government. Provisions calling for improvements in human rights, appended to the document by the Dutch government, were partly the cause for the Syrian regime's reluctance to commit itself to the agreement.[80] But other considerations such as loyalty to Iran and newly established good relations with Turkey convinced Bashar al-Asad that he did not need the EU association agreement.

The international financial crisis that began in 2008 also had a detrimental effect on the Syrian economy. Although the primitive state of the Syrian financial sector sheltered the country from the worst effects of the recession, there was an indirect effect as an estimated 50,000 Syrians, who had been working abroad in the Gulf States, were laid off and returned home.[81] This had two negative consequences: the loss of remittance income, and upward pressure on Syria's unemployment figures, which already officially stood at 12 per cent in 2008,[82] but more realistically stood at around 20–25 per cent.[83]

Despite a healthy overall growth rate of 5 per cent, the partially liberalised economy distributed benefits very unevenly. According to international measures, by 2007 a third of the population lived in poverty on less than $50 US per month, while 12.3 per cent of Syrians lived in extreme poverty with a maximum monthly income of $32 US.[84] The Syrian regime tried to speed up liberalising economic reforms to combat the recession. These measures proved inadequate, however, and in many instances only served to increase economic problems. One prime example was the establishment of the Damascus Securities Exchange (DSE) on 10 March 2009, initially listing six companies.[85] The regime tried to entice Syrians to invest in the DSE and put their money into banks. The governor of the Central Bank of Syria (CBS), Adib Mayaleh, said 'We want to encourage the Syrian public to subscribe to these public offerings and change the mentality of keeping cash under the mattress.'[86] Yet in the absence of transparent financial institutions, Syrians were reluctant to trust the government with their money.[87] Overall, the partial liberalisation of the Syrian economy appeared only to increase the earning potential of those close to the regime, such as Rami Makhlouf.[88]

Growing disaffection and anger with the regime's economic performance emerged among the Ba'th Party's traditional support base, the rural peasantry, workers and the bureaucracy, among whom ordinary Alawites were heavily represented. The Syrian General Federation of Trade Unions published a statement in 2009 saying: 'Where are the results of economic reform? … The rich have become richer and the poor poorer … low-income earners who make up 80 per cent of the Syrian population are looking for additional work to support themselves.'[89]

Another income source the Asad dynasty favoured was tourism.[90] This sector did indeed hold considerable promise for Syria. In 2008–9 tourism contributed US 3.9 billion dollars to Syria's economy,[91] and according to the Syrian Ministry of Tourism, accounted for 11 per cent of GDP by 2009, with an average of 5.4 million visitors per year (mostly Arabs from the Gulf States).[92] In addition, a cooperation deal with Turkey held promise for Syria's tourist trade,[93] and more European visitors began to venture to Syria in 2009.[94] By 2009 16 per cent of Syria's labour force was engaged in some way with the tourism sector.[95] Many of the country's main tourist sites are located in the Alawite coastal region. Similarly to the 1920s, there was good potential for Alawites to profit from their natural environment through international tourism. Over-reliance on tourism would prove hazardous, however, as it is an industry heavily dependent on a stable and secure domestic situation, and the country was unable to preserve this level of stability.

One outlet for economically challenged Syrians was Lebanon's labour market. In 2009 an estimated 300,000 Syrians worked in Lebanon, mainly in construction. However, the pay and work conditions of these workers were very poor and they often suffered discrimination and abuse.[96] A poignant moment for this researcher came when speaking to a Syrian shoepolisher hunched in an ostentatious Beirut waterfront street. When asked why he came to Lebanon, he said he had eight children and there was no work in Syria. Yet despite his obvious destitution, when asked his opinion of the Syrian president he said, with a worried expression, 'qua'is' (excellent). This response may have come from genuine admiration, but it seemed to come from an ingrained fear of criticising Syria's leadership, which was apparent even outside Syria.

Political Pressures

Harsh political repression was a fact of life in Syria since the internal troubles of the 1970s and early 1980s. However, there had existed an unspoken 'social contract' guaranteeing economic security through subsidies, government jobs and free education and healthcare in return for forgoing political freedoms. Under Bashar al-Asad, this social contract was compromised. More people began seriously questioning their lack of political freedoms. In late August 2007, large posters of the US-based Reform Party leader, Farid Ghadry, appeared in Damascus, Aleppo and Idlib.[97] According to Reform Party sources, the posters had been put up by a group of young Syrians.[98] Bashar al-Asad reacted by taking the measure, often considered illegal under international law, of revoking Ghadry's Syrian citizenship.[99] Farid Ghadry had already raised the ire of the Syrian regime by addressing the Israeli Knesset and raising possibilities for resolving the Syrian–Israeli conflict,[100] a key platform of the Asad regime's legitimacy. The appearance of the posters demonstrated that Ghadry enjoyed some support in Syria, which no doubt infuriated and concerned Asad.

REVOLUTION

The Syrian president's response to the problem of political dissent remained repression. Dutch diplomats, involved in the EU association agreement, had questioned the ongoing human rights record of Syria, which had not improved by the end of Bashar al-Asad's first decade in power.[101] Syria's prisons remained full of political prisoners, who even when released complained of being subjected to intimidation and discrimination.[102] Conditions inside Syria's prisons were harsh with torture a common event. Two riots were put down with lethal force at Sednaya Prison, north of Damascus, in July[103] and December 2008.[104] Dozens of bodies from the riots were reportedly secretly buried at night to keep the massacres from public exposure.[105] Moreover, human rights activists were arrested in greater numbers, and the State Security Court remained accused of arbitrary rulings.[106] In the absence of economic security, continued repression by the Syrian state only pushed people towards exasperation, despair and resentment against the regime. In short, there was a growing deficit of basic dignity afforded to the Syrian population.

Environmental Pressures

Perhaps the most critical challenge to state stability was caused by the drought that gripped the country from the summer of 2006.[107] The drought lasted for four summers, peaking in 2007–8; it sent 2–3 million people into extreme poverty and decimated Syria's agricultural sector, which accounted for 23 per cent of Syria's GDP.[108] Previously a net exporter, Syria became a net importer of wheat and corn, with the regime having to import a record 1.8 million tonnes of corn in 2009.[109] The drought also exacerbated Syria's chronic electricity production problems with a 1000 megawatt deficit in 2009 that resulted in daily (twice daily in some areas) outages across the country.[110] A Syrian official in charge of development and investment stated that the drought could pose a bigger problem for Syria than the global financial crisis: 'it adds to the misery of less income and less spending, and this affects economic growth'.[111] While the official was using the term 'misery' to describe the macroeconomic implications for Syria's economy, it was also an appropriate term for the physical misery that was being experienced by ordinary (particularly rural) Syrians.

Ordinary Alawites in north-west Syria were equally susceptible to the problems caused by economic stagnation and drought. Tobacco crops in the Latakia region were adversely affected and many Alawites illegally began cutting down oak trees to make charcoal to sell for use in *nargile* pipes popular in cafes around the country. This practice threatened to cause extensive deforestation of the Jabal al-Sahiliyah.[112] Despite having experienced poverty throughout their occupation of the Jabal al-Sahiliyah, the Alawites had always managed to preserve its forests. The Alawites attached great spiritual value to the natural features of their mountain, so to be forced to degrade that environment indicated the severity of their socio-economic hardship. During visits to Alawite villages in 2009 and 2011, conversations invariably revolved around dire financial circumstances, lack of work opportunities and the detrimental effects of the drought on crops.

Rural Syrians from all communities faced severe struggles to sustain their livelihoods. The drought forced tens of thousands of rural Syrians into the cities, and 160 villages in northern Syria were completely abandoned.[113] One student from the Hasakeh region in north-east Syria explained how virtually his entire village left to look for work in Damascus.[114] Another badly affected region was southern Syria around Dera'a and Suwayda.[115] The regime failed to address the suffering of rural Syrians or recognise the potential for civil unrest from growing socio-economic pressures. In one incident, a government decision to tighten building regulations resulted in the demolition of temporary housing near Damascus, which led to a clash with the authorities that killed four rural migrants.[116]

Rising Religious Pressures

When asked whether he thought increasing corruption, inequality and rising poverty could translate into renewed sectarian tensions in Syria, Abd al-Halim Khaddam's initial reaction rose from his strong Ba'thist instinct to downplay sectarianism: 'In Syria there are both Christian and Muslims. They are very religious but they are not radicals.' However, he conceded that he had concerns about rising resentment among the Syrian majority against a perceived sectarian bias in Syria stemming from socio-economic hardship:

The people are starting to see that, whenever an employment position comes up for anything—a normal person cannot just go and take that place, there is a somehow, a racial background to that … Now you can see that there are some racial tensions in Syria. These tensions are growing now; they can of course pose a threat on the unity of Syria … if the regime continues the way it is now, radicalism is going to grow in Syria. At some point something is going to happen, it's going to explode.[117]

Abd al-Halim Khaddam's prediction of a social explosion in Syria with possible 'racial' (sectarian) fault lines carried serious implications for the Syrian Alawites and their future security. If Khaddam was correct it would show that while the Asad dynasty had been focused on reconsolidating its position against external threats, a far greater threat was emerging within Syria itself.

To examine latent sectarian tensions in Syria it is helpful to compare the ongoing tensions in Tripoli between Alawites and Sunnis.[118] A major factor in the tensions in Tripoli has been socio-economic hardship caused by scarce work opportunities.[119] Thus it could be argued that similar socio-economic problems in Syria contributed to the emergence of sectarian tensions in Syria. During Hafiz al-Asad's rule the centralised command economy of Syria, while failing to enrich the country, provided a basic economic safety net and restrained disparities in wealth.[120] Sectarian tensions, caused by perceptions of inequality and injustice, were however, becoming clearly evident during this writer's second trip to Syria in March 2011.

On one occasion I went with two (Sunni) Syrian acquaintances from drought-stricken north-eastern Syria to the beach a few kilometres north of Latakia. Beyond a fence was a long and inviting stretch of sand. When our small group rounded the fence a man in civilian clothes and a dog quickly appeared and told us this was government property and we must leave. Directly across from where we stood, the Afamia Rotana resort, frequented by regime figures, was visible with its own private beach. As we walked back to the public enclosure, one of my Syrian friends remarked below his breath, in surprisingly good English vernacular, 'fuck the government, they take everything from us'. I was later told, without any prompting, that the man who expelled us from the beach was Alawite. The implicit association between Alawites and government control was palpable.

Returning from the beach by taxi, the driver, who was also Alawite, was drinking a can of beer and jokingly offered a sip to one of my Sunni companions who replied angrily, '*la! Ana Muslim*' (No! I'm a Muslim). The taxi driver responded that he too was Muslim (Alawite Muslim), and the conversation threatened to become heated. My other friend recognised the danger in the subject and quickly made a light-hearted quip to defuse the situation. These incidents gave a glimpse of the 'tinder box' residing beneath the surface of Syrian society with dangerous implications for Alawite security. On one hand the Alawites were directly associated with the Asad regime and its deprivation of basic liberties to most Syrians; and on the other hand they were still not considered 'proper' Muslims by much of the Sunni Muslim population of Syria.[121]

When I first arrived in Syria in August 2009 the country was still gripped by economic recession and drought. Upon leaving the airport the first question I asked the taxi driver was, 'why does everyone smoke?' He acerbically replied, 'Life is hard.' Smoking was a small comfort for Syrians in their otherwise bleak socio-economic circumstances. An indication of the disconnection of Bashar al-Asad in this regard can be seen in his decree of December 2009, which banned smoking in cafes, restaurants and public places.[122] Meanwhile, in the Jabal al-Sahiliyah, strict penalties were imposed for tree felling, and the regime expended considerable funds in registering individual oak trees. Around Slunfeh, at the peak of the Jabal al-Sahiliyah, every single tree was numbered with a steel plaque. While these measures may have seemed progressive, and in line with the policies of many Western countries, for ordinary Syrians they were further cause for rising frustration.

The lack of appreciation by the Syrian regime of the building social tensions was illustrated by Prime Minister Naji al-'Otri, who said in December 2009:

in spite of the climate changes and drought which Syria suffered during the past three years, reflecting negatively on the agricultural sector in addition to the world financial crisis and its repercussions, Syria has managed to alleviate their impact thanks to precautionary and pre-emptive measures.[123]

In reality the dire socio-economic situation of Syrians at the end of 2009 held many of the ingredients for a 'social explosion'. The fact that most ordinary Alawites shared in the economic difficulties with the rest of the country, however, actually served as a point of cross-sectarian commonality. On the other hand, the resilience of sectarian 'asabiyya could mean that if Alawites remained firmly attached to the regime, when the 'explosion' came it could lead to negative consequences for communal relations.

Overall, the cumulative social pressures from economic, political, environmental and religious factors constituted a grave risk to the stability of the Syrian state. The lack of opportunity in Syria was evident in the sheer numbers of idle men sitting around smoking, or engaged in petty hawking, shoe polishing or even begging. The everyday challenges faced by most Syrians could not be alleviated by their president's rhetoric about 'steadfast resistance' against Israel or America.

A Rising Islamic Tide?

In early 2007, an editorial in the state newspaper al-Thawra read: 'Syria has a great deal of confidence now ... The country is convinced that the major pressures that once faced us have disappeared. We want to offer security—that's what we offer. The Americans, they offer Iraq, which is chaos.'[124] The sectarian chaos in Iraq provided Alawites with a demonstration of the consequences of political upheaval. Regime rhetoric about offering security from the 'chaos' sweeping the region was a persuasive tool in the hands of the Asad regime, and assisted greatly in the maintenance of Alawite 'asabiyya.

Alongside the immediate threat of Sunni radicalism, a general rise in conservative Islamic values in Syria posed a challenge to the ongoing security of Alawites. While the regime presented itself as the Alawites' protector against these rising threats, it actually played a large part in their development. Paradoxically, therefore, the best chance for Alawite security in Syria was to abandon the Asad dynasty and finally seek genuine integration in Syrian society, as was the original intention of the Alawite political and religious leadership in 1936.

Throughout Bashar al-Asad's rule there was a general erosion of the strict secularism which was the aspect of Ba'th ideology so important to Alawite political status and security. By 2007, Syria's first Islamic banking institution received the go ahead from the government.[125] This was partly a result of Syria's new alliance structure (now without the Soviet Union), which was heavily reliant on Muslim states. Dwindling Syrian oil and gas reserves negated the ability to operate a low-level rentier economy and necessitated the need to encourage foreign investment, particularly from the Gulf region.[126] For Iran and the Gulf States, Syria is a vital cog in regional politics. Hence the Asad regime was forced to focus on the Muslim world for the bulk of its foreign investment and economic support, which meant pressure continued to be exerted on the secular nature of the Syrian state.[127]

Although Alawites preferred strict secularism, in a well-functioning regional economy, even if the predominant political-economic system was Islamic-based, Alawites could hope to enjoy reasonable security. This was the case at various times during the Ottoman period; for instance, in the seventeenth and eighteenth centuries Alawites carved out a niche in the tobacco industry and were relatively well tolerated by the Ottoman authorities. It was only during more turbulent times, such as the Mamluks' strategic and economic crises of the fourteenth century, that fundamentalist Islam increased and posed critical threats to Alawite security. The regional equation in 2007–8 more closely resembled the latter definition. The economic situation was bleak across most of the region, which, combined with conflicts in Iraq, Afghanistan and the ongoing Palestinian issue, had the effect of swelling the importance of religion in Middle Eastern society.

Both the Damascus Spring and the fall of the Iraqi Ba'thists had raised the expectations of many Syrians for political change, yet both had ended in disappointment. Several years on, disillusionment and frustration, exacerbated by high unemployment, high inflation and the effects of the ongoing drought, were setting in among a growing portion of Syrian society. A veteran political dissident from the Syrian Communist Party, Riad al-Turk, voiced these concerns in May 2007:

An earthquake can be avoided if Bashar chooses the path of reconciliation, democratic change and ousting of the corrupt … It could happen, but I don't expect it … Where does the ordinary citizen go? He goes towards God to save him from this misery and he is embraced by the clerics. When the citizen has no option he becomes an easy prey in the hands of the fundamentalists.[128]

In this context of rising religious sentiment, the Asad regime's double game of restricting fundamentalism in Syrian society while encouraging it elsewhere as a foreign policy tool became increasingly difficult to balance. Signs emerged that the regime was losing control of the situation. On 28 September 2007 the jihadist preacher Abu al-Qa'qa' was shot dead outside his mosque in Aleppo. Al-Qa'qa's aide claimed that 'his killers do not want Muslims to unite'.[129] This could be read as an accusation against the Syrian regime, who perhaps felt that al-Qa'qa' was becoming too influential as a Muslim leader. Another interpretation is that he had fallen out with other Muslim fundamentalists for his collusion with the 'heretical' Alawite dynasty.[130]

Both interpretations are plausible, and either could indicate negative developments for the Asad regime in its dealings with Islamist forces. If al-Qa'qa' was becoming so influential that he had to be killed, it signals that the regime was losing control. Conversely, if al-Qa'qa was killed because of his cooperation with the Asad dynasty, it shows that Bashar al-Asad could not control the Islamists within his borders who were turning their sights towards his regime. The latter interpretation could explain the effects of Syrian fighters returning from Iraq imbued with al-Qaeda ideologies for restoring Islamic rule to 'Bilad al-Sham'.[131]

Al-Qaeda and similar groups began turning their sights on the Syrian regime from late 2005, and increasingly so from 2007 after the US 'troop surge' in Iraq.[132] On 27 May 2007, a militant Islamic group named the 'Monotheism and Jihad Group' led by a man named Abu Jandal al-Dimashqi urged the assassination of Bashar al-Asad in an audiotape posted on the Internet. In addition, Abu Jandal, citing Ibn Taymiyya's fourteenth-century fatwas, advised the 'physical annihilation' of the Alawites.[133] Talk about the 'kuffar' (infidel) Shi'ites and 'Nusayris' also began emerging among radical Sunni elements in Lebanon.[134] Signs of domestic instability paralleled the increase of Islamic extremism, with a large explosion at a military installation in Aleppo on 26 July 2007, for example, killing fifteen soldiers. Official sources blamed high summer temperatures for setting off stored munitions.[135] However, other sources claimed that the blast occurred at 4.30 a.m. when temperatures were cool,[136] which raises the possibility that it was an attack by an anti-regime group. Islamic extremists, such as al-Qaeda, still only represented an extreme fringe element of the Sunni majority, who remained moderate in their religious views. Nonetheless, the re-emergence of Ibn Taymiyya's radical ideas and intolerance of Alawites was a cause of concern for the community, and reinforced their insecurity.

In late 2007, Bashar al-Asad appeared to try and change course and mitigate the effects of religious radicalism, which he had helped unleash. The regime attempted to reconsolidate Syria's standing as the 'beating heart' of Arabism by emphasising the Arabic language as the primary source of identity for Syrians.[137] Bashar al-Asad announced guidelines for protecting the purity of the Arabic language from foreign corruption.[138] This was a belated step back towards Alawite interests, which are served by retaining secular Arabist-Ba'thist ideology based on emphasising Arab identity over sectarian identity. For instance, the education system promoted under Hafiz al-Asad even tried to suppress any acknowledgment of divergence between the main branches of Islam.

Bashar al-Asad, perhaps mistakenly confident in his popularity and acceptance by the Sunni majority, allowed orthodox Sunni Islam to become the dominant religion in education and matters of state.[139] Meanwhile, the Alawites and other heterodox sects became increasingly submerged in terms of their religion and identity. Thus the Alawite elites of the Asad regime were actually cutting themselves off from their own community at the same time as exasperation and resentment against the regime was building in Syria's Sunni majority.

Integration at Last?

Much of the previous discussion has focused on the rising potential for religious conflict in Syria, but was sectarian tension still acute three decades on from the 1982 tragedy at Hama? A snapshot of Syrian society in 2010 would have shown Alawites present in all the interior cities of Syria, often in mixed neighbourhoods with high levels of interaction and social exchange; therefore social integration had been gradually developing, especially among Syria's younger generations.

For the Alawites to maximise their chances to continue this trajectory toward genuine integration in Syrian society, they would need to recognise the hazardous path Asad was leading the country down and break free of the regime when the opportunity arose. Two factors were critical to the achievement of this outcome: first, Syria's overwhelmingly youthful population was not necessarily as affected by sectarian thinking as their parents;[140] and second, the communication technology 'revolution' that has occurred in Syria connected this young generation in ways that the regime struggled to control.

Driven by a common desire for greater political freedoms and economic opportunities, non-sectarian civil society had been occurring at the grassroots level among Syria's younger generation, facilitated by new communication technologies like the Internet, satellite television and cellular phones.[141] In 1996, the Internet was unavailable to ordinary Syrians, and in 2000 less than 1 per cent was 'connected'. By 2010, however, at least 21 per cent of Syrians regularly used the Internet.[142] These communication tools provided new platforms for open discussion that circumvented government prohibitions around political and religious discourse.

The Syrian authorities revealed their concern about the threat posed by the Internet in June 2007, when seven Syrian students were sentenced to prison terms for online dialogues about political reform.[143] It is likely that two of the students were Alawite, as they were given seven-year sentences, like those imposed on Alawite dissidents Aref Dalila in 2001[144] and Louay Hussein in 1984.[145] The other five students received five-year sentences.[146] A comment to the father of one of the students by the arresting Mukhabarat officer was revealing: 'these youths are more dangerous than al-Qaeda, because they come from all sects'.[147] This showed how the security establishment considered cross-sectarian dissent, involving Alawites, as a threat to the regime. A gradual reduction of Sunni–Alawite insecurities would finally indicate the decline of Alawite sectarian 'asabiyya. These rare glimpses of Alawite dissent in the years before the uprising challenged the outward appearance that the Alawite community was relatively monolithic in its political behaviour, as well as being generally supportive of the regime. The harsher punishments meted out to Alawites for political crimes highlight how fear of state repression was a major factor in the inability of Alawites to express alternative views.

The regime directed substantial resources to monitoring online activity to confront the threat of internet activism. In September 2007, 350 Mukhabarat recruits were dispatched by Asef Shawkat to Bonn, Berlin,

London and North Korea to study advanced communications interception. It is unclear whether the German and British authorities were aware of this activity, or if private consultants were covertly enlisted; the latter seems more likely. These recruits were themselves monitored closely and restricted in their movements and ability to interact with expatriate Syrians.[148] Despite these measures, the Syrian regime would continue to struggle to control online political dialogue and dissent.

In June 2009, the Syrian minister of defence, General Hassan Turkmani, told army officer graduates, 'The communications' revolution that we witness nowadays requires us to possess qualifications and capabilities in all military performance fields to defend the homeland.'[149] He was possibly referring to popular social networking sites like Facebook, which accelerated the process of connecting Syrians from different backgrounds within Syria and exposed them to political currents across the Arab world and beyond. Recognising the potential danger of social media, the regime found a pretext to ban Facebook in September 2009. They justified the measure as a protest against Israeli users in the Golan Heights, who submitted their home address as 'Israel'.[150]

In the years immediately before the 2011 Syrian uprising, Internet cafes proliferated in every Syrian city, invariably full of young people in their twenties or early thirties. For monitoring purposes, customers at these establishments had to surrender their identity cards while using the Internet. Great care was taken by Internet users to avoid politically sensitive language that would trigger online monitoring by the Mukhabarat. Government restrictions were not particularly successful, however; many Syrians accessed banned social media sites by using 'proxy' addresses. The Internet provided an important tool for evading government restrictions on political discourse, thus, despite operating in some of the most repressive conditions in the world,[151] Syrian Internet users from all communities defied the state's attempts to suppress them and began establishing a 'cyber' civil society based around online forums and discussion groups.[152]

Another communications revolution that the Asad dynasty struggled to control was the proliferation of cellular phones, many of which are Internet-enabled and have digital cameras. According to official Syrian government figures, 38 per cent of Syrians had mobile-cellular connections by the end of 2008,[153] which grew to as much as 60 per cent by 2011.[154] It seems incredible that many Syrians, given their dire economic circumstances, could afford to buy and operate these devices, though this is partially explained by the availability of cheaper Chinese generic brands.[155]

Paradoxically, top regime figures like Rami Makhlouf profited immensely from the rapid proliferation of cellular phones among Syrians. Makhlouf monopolised the mobile telecommunications industry in Syria with his control of the company 'Syriatel'.[156] Hence it would seem that one of the main avenues of enrichment for members of the Asad dynasty also facilitated the infrastructure for the revolution that erupted against them in 2011. This provides an interesting variation of Khaldun's theory that 'commercial activity on the part of the ruler' leads to a dynasty's decline.[157]

The major threat to the Asad regime from the communications revolution was the fact that young Alawites were very much involved in it. Internet and cellular technologies are connecting young Alawites in Latakia to young Sunnis in Hama, Damascus or Aleppo. Centuries-old misconceptions and suspicions between communities were slowly being broken down.

Outwardly, Bashar al-Asad seemed set to finish the decade triumphantly having risen above all his external and internal challenges.[158] The Syrian populace, afraid to speak or act openly for fear of arbitrary imprisonment, or even torture, gave no indication that they would soon challenge the authority of the Asad dynasty. The Alawites, despite having their religion and identity submerged and being increasingly neglected by the regime elite, appeared broadly loyal to the regime, with the exception of glimpses of liberal dissent among Alawite youth and a few Alawite intellectuals.

While Alawites clung to Asad rule, under the surface rumblings of civil unrest in Syria steadily increased due to socio-economic, environmental, religious and political pressures. Developments, such as new communication technologies provided both threats and opportunities for the Alawite community. The resilience of sectarian 'asabiyya could cause Alawites to stay strongly supportive of the Asad dynasty, even as it moved towards a dangerous decline. On the other hand, Syria's increasingly youthful population, willing and increasingly capable of engaging in cross-sectarian political dialogue, provided a possible historic opportunity for Alawites to overcome sectarian insecurity and finally become sustainably integrated into Syrian society.

Shaykh Qasim al-Tabarani led the Alawites into the inhospitable Jabal al-Sahiliyah sometime after 1008 due to religious persecution and intolerance. A thousand years later, on 12 December 2009, the core members of the Asad family, Bashar, Maher and Bushra, gathered in Qardaha for the funeral of their brother, Majd.[159] A few days later, another funeral took place—that of the former president, Amin Hafiz, the last person to rule Syria since its independence who was not an Asad.[160] The dynasty established by Hafiz al-Asad had ruled Syria for forty years. Ibn Khaldun observed, quite reasonably, that 'every dynasty has an expiry date'.[161] Whether the Asad dynasty's expiration arrived sooner or later, it would no doubt come, but what fate would befall the Alawite community when that moment arrived remained in the balance.

The Syrian Uprising

By late 2010, it seemed that the Tunisian scholar Ibn Khaldun's theory for the decline of 'asabiyya in groups would, in Syria's case, fail to manifest into the rapid decline of the Asad dynasty. The resilience of Alawite sectarian insecurity appeared to ensure the continuation of Asad rule, into the foreseeable future at least. Then, on 17 December 2010, a Tunisian street vendor named Muhammad Bouazizi set himself on fire to protest the indignity, corruption and injustice in his country.[162] The incident ignited smouldering Arab discontent, and was transmitted rapidly and widely in the Arab world by modern communications technologies and social media. Starting in Tunisia, Bouazizi's act preceded a wave of Arab uprisings that, despite Bashar al-Asad's pronounced belief in his own popularity,[163] cascaded into southern Syria on 15 March 2011.

There have been many different explanations of the particular circumstances of the Syrian uprising. Was it a genuinely democratic emancipatory movement, a socio-economic reaction to neoliberal economic reforms of the previous decade[164] or a result of the severe drought in 2006–9? Some argued the case of foreign intervention and regional geopolitics,[165] while others explained the uprising in Syria in religious and sectarian terms, as a Sunni Islamic movement seeking to throw off the minority rule of the Alawites and the secular Ba'th regime.[166] The uprising most likely contained many of these elements; however, it was essentially a spontaneous social movement with no discernible leadership or specific objective other than a desire for change and a rejection of fear. Yet perhaps the best explanation of the nature of the uprising came from the protesters themselves. In the mixed Sunni, Alawite and Christian coastal city of Banyas in September 2011, a protester tried to explain events to the international community:

In these days we make demonstrations to claim our rights, our justice, and our freedom. [But] they say we are Salafi, we are Al-Qaeda, we are terrorists and we want to make an Islamic state here. I say it's a big lie … They say we want to [incite] sectarianism. No! In Banyas, in all of Syria … Christian and Muslim are brothers. In the street you can see the mosque and the church. Sunni, Alawi, Shi'a, Kurdi, Druze, we are all brothers, we are all friends, we are all neighbours … Why do they [the Syrian regime] kill us? Why [do] they kill people in Dera'a? … [Look at this] demonstration in Banyas … hundreds of people to say that they want freedom, they want their rights, they want justice in Syria. We want to make *real* Syria, *true* Syria.[167]

This common narrative of the early protests rejects sectarian, religious and conspiracy theories about the nature of the uprising in Syria. Moreover, the vision that is portrayed for a 'real', 'true' Syria, involving all the different ethnic and religious groups, reflects the political and social reality of the diverse Syrian state, and invokes a diverse civic nationalism that transcends religious and ethnic identities.[168] If this was the real nature of the political shift in Syria, it marked a historic opportunity for the Alawites to achieve genuine social integration and sustainable security in Syria based on diverse citizenship, rather than limited ethnic, religious or ideological identities.

From the very beginning of the uprising, Syrian protesters tried to reassure Alawites of their security and bring them on board with the revolution. The individual who filmed the first major anti-regime protest in Damascus declared, 'The date is March 15 … this is the first open uprising against the Syrian regime … Alawite or Sunni, all kinds of Syrians; we want to bring the regime down!'[169] Ten days later anti-regime protests broke out in the 'Alawite city' and regime stronghold of Latakia.

For Alawites, these events instantly changed the political landscape, forcing them to confront the reality of their relationship with the Asad regime. The challenge for the Syrian Alawite community was whether they could overcome their fears and abandon the Asad dynasty. In a fashion reminiscent of the pragmatic Alawite approach of 1936, rumours circulated in late June 2011 that Alawite religious leaders had already approached Sunni imams seeking guarantees of Alawite security 'in return for abandoning the Asads'.[170] And in September 2011, three prominent Alawite shaykhs, Mohib Nisafi, Yassin Hussein and Mussa Mansour, denounced the killing of civilian protesters and tried to distance the Alawite community from the regime, stating: 'We declare our innocence from these atrocities carried out by Bashar al-Assad and his aides who belong to all religious sects.'[171] In addition, long-silent Alawite liberals like Aref Dalila and Louay Hussein again emerged to try and bridge the gap between the Alawite and Sunni communities in Syria.[172]

Numerous Alawites participated in the early peaceful demonstrations in Homs' Clock Square and in protests in Damascus.[173] Organised Alawite opposition was shown by the Party of Modernity and Democracy, which represented Alawites from the Hama district at an opposition conference in Antalya, Turkey, on 1 June 2011.[174] The party claimed that the regime was manipulating Alawite insecurities, and that the sect's best prospects lay in embracing a path towards a liberated, democratic Syria.[175] In late March 2013, 150 Alawite notables held a conference in Cairo to voice opposition to the regime and show support for a pluralist state beneficial to the security of minorities. One delegate at the conference, the Alawite lawyer Issa Ibrahim, feared that if a real change to a democratic system could not be achieved, the impetus for change would transform into religious fundamentalism.[176]

For many Alawites, the decision whether to abandon the regime came down to pragmatic considerations. Through the first year and a half of the uprising, supporting Bashar al-Assad seemed a pragmatic choice. The internal and external opposition was fragmented, the international community was not intervening in the crisis and Aleppo and Damascus remained quiet. Thus it seemed the uprising would eventually be brought under control. A potential turning point for Alawites came in mid-2012 when the regime suffered severe setbacks with large scale rebel assaults on Damascus and Aleppo, and the successful assassination of four top regime figures in central

Damascus on 18 July.[177] Rare Alawite defections also began to increase in the Syrian Arab army,[178] as the regime struggled to control its borders, large parts of the countryside and the two major cities. Some Alawites began to feel that supporting the regime was a lost cause, as one Alawite explained, 'It doesn't seem to be in our interest, the regime is losing.'[179]

In general, however, the majority of the sect remained, at least tacitly, supportive of the regime throughout the crisis. There are several key factors which negatively influenced Alawite perceptions of the uprising and kept them from joining the opposition movement in significant numbers. First, collective memories of the sect's long history of subjection to Sunni Muslim domination raised concerns among Alawites about a return to second-class status. As anthropologist Christa Salamandra has pointed out, the term 'Alawi often carries connotations of both class and religious identity in Syria.[180] Alawites are therefore sensitive to references to their rural origins. Many Alawites in Latakia were reportedly outraged to hear an anti-regime protest chant, which suggested that Syrian President Bashar al-Asad should 'go back to the farm'.[181] Second, Alawites remain disproportionately employed in the public sector, including the military and security services as well as in the still extensive bureaucracy.[182] Many, therefore, remain reliant on the state for their livelihoods, which provided strong disincentives to join the opposition.

Thirdly, a general fear of sectarianism hung over the Alawite community as the uprising unfolded. This fear became self-fulfilling as the security situation deteriorated in contested parts of the country. Sectarian kidnappings and murders escalated in Homs in mid-2012, with both pro-regime and opposition sides blaming the other for attempting to incite sectarianism.[183] Many Alawites were convinced that the uprising was an attempt to create an Islamic state in Syria, and suspected the involvement of the Muslim Brotherhood in seeking retribution for the Syrian government's massacre in Hama in 1982.[184] Anti-Alawite sentiment also began to rise among Sunnis as the regime escalated its repression against the opposition.

Alawite insecurities about a social reversal, income security and sectarianism made them easy targets for political manipulation. From the very earliest days of the uprising the regime stood accused of exploiting Alawite insecurities. The veteran political dissident Aref Dalila claimed the regime played the 'sectarian card' in its response to anti-regime protests in Latakia in late March 2011.[185] There was evidence to support this view as intelligence officers actively funnelled groups of Alawite youths towards the protests in central Latakia to incite sectarian violence, while unidentified snipers fired arbitrarily into the crowd from rooftop positions.[186]

In Alawite villages on the coast, the regime actively promoted Alawite fears in the early period of the uprising. Armed intelligence agents and militia were dispatched to village junctions, ostensibly to guard against terrorists who planned to target Alawites. The state media played a key role also; in one example related by an Alawite student, Al-Duniya TV, which is funded by Rami Makhlouf, reported eyewitness accounts that Alawites were being killed in rural Idlib. In order to confirm these allegations the student telephoned an acquaintance in that region who informed him that he had not seen or heard of any such thing. Elements of the opposition also played a part in elevating Alawite insecurities. Religiously oriented satellite television stations' use of sectarian language in relation to the uprisings caused Alawites who had initially supported the uprising to start doubting whether the revolution was for all Syrians or just for Sunnis.[187]

The situation of Alawite revolutionaries became increasingly difficult. Efforts to convince their co-sectarians that the best option for the sect was to join with the uprising met with solid resistance in most cases. The fear felt by the majority of Alawites was difficult to penetrate, as it rested on three bases: historic insecurity regarding the Sunni majority, the 'evidence' that was being propagated by the regime of terrorism and extremism and increasingly sectarian discourse coming from some quarters of the opposition. Alawite revolutionaries often found themselves ostracised by their own communities and families or facing prison and torture. In parallel, opposition groups increasingly came to view Alawites as untrustworthy and potential spies.[188]

Predominantly Alawite militias known as 'Shabiha' were mobilised by the regime to confront the opposition, which added to the escalation of sectarian tensions. These groups originated from the organised criminal gangs who operated with a high-level of impunity in the 1980s in and around Latakia.[189] The Shabiha groups were used as shock troops to break up protests with lethal force, and to spread terror in an attempt to stem the tide of open dissent sweeping the country. One of the primary functions of the Shabiha was to provoke violent reactions from the protestors, who remained determinedly peaceful for several months in 2011. The spread of peaceful protests threatened to destabilise the foundations of the regime far more than armed opposition.

Atrocities perpetrated by the Shabiha against civilians, such as the bloody massacres which occurred in the village of Houla in May 2012, and in Bayda and Banyas in May 2013, indirectly implicated the wider Alawite sect in these crimes and raised the stakes of a regime collapse.[190] Between November 2012 and January 2013, the Asad regime further escalated the overtly sectarian mobilisation of Alawites by organising the various Alawite militias into loyalist armed units called the 'National Defence Forces' (NDF).[191] Mirroring Iran's support to the Shi'a militias of southern Lebanon in the 1980s, the NDF is trained and overseen by Hizballah and the Iranian Quds Force, entrenching Alawite dependence on the regime's Shi'a allies.[192]

The major turning point in transforming the peaceful demonstrations into armed resistance came in the northern Syrian town of Jisr ash-Shugour in early June 2011, when defectors from the security forces engaged in the first major battles with the regime.[193] The Syrian government's narrative of the incident was that 'terrorists attacked the police and security centers ... and used rooftops to sniper and shoot at citizens and security forces'.[194] The residents of Jisr ash Shugour, many of whom fled to Turkey, claimed they were participating in peaceful protests when fired upon by security forces. Soldiers who refused to fire on the protesters were executed by their officers.[195]

After the potential turning point in mid-2012 mentioned above, passed without any significant increase in Alawite defections, the general trajectory was towards a protracted and bloody conflict, which was officially declared a civil war (or non-international armed conflict) in June 2012.[196] The declaration of civil war lessened the chance of international intervention on humanitarian grounds, and essentially equalised the parties to the conflict as far as the international community was concerned.

It became clear that neither the United States nor NATO was going to intervene militarily. This fact was underlined when the 'red line' threshold for intervention in Syria, set by US President Barack Obama regarding the use of chemical weapons, passed without any action despite the use of chemical weapons against the Damascus suburb of Ghouta on 21 August 2013. The Syrian regime denied the attack, which killed around 1,400 people, including women and children, but rapidly agreed to dispose of its chemical weapons stockpile in a last-minute deal mediated by Russia to forestall US military strikes.[197]

The US withdrawal from its commitment to intervene in Syria was a significant moment for the Alawites due to the effect it had on the character of the opposition. The secular, Western-supported moderate opposition groups (such as the secular Free Syrian Army, FSA) lost credibility and support among the broader opposition movement. Hence, from mid-2013, Sunni Islamist groups increasingly assumed the lead role in fighting the regime. A new opposition structure was formed, the Islamic Front, combining a number of smaller opposition groups—including some formerly aligned with the FSA—into an armed force of approximately 50,000–60,000 fighters.[198] The conflict consequently took on a more explicitly sectarian nature and limited the scope for dialogue between Alawites and the opposition. Regardless of the ideology of the various opposition groups, a common demand is an insistence that Bashar al-Asad step down as president. Hence, to a significant degree, persistent Alawite 'asabiyya in support of the Asad dynasty effectively undermined their ability to adapt pragmatically to political change in Syria, like they had in the past.

Two events signalled the possible future trajectory for the Syrian Alawites in mid-2014. First, in the midst of the ongoing civil war, Bashar al-Asad won a widely criticised presidential election with 88.7 per cent of the vote in regime-held areas.[199] Many Syrians labelled them the 'blood elections' due to the brutal repression of the preceding three years. Shortly afterwards, the al-Qaeda offshoot, the Islamic State of Iraq and al-Sham (ISIS), which had been building its strength in the al-Jazira region between Syria and Iraq, captured the major city of Mosul in northern Iraq on 10 June 2014. From this territorial foothold, now including large parts of both Syria and Iraq, the group's leader, Abu Bakr al-Baghdadi, declared a new Sunni caliphate. ISIS conquests in Iraq and Syria constituted a symbolic challenge to the incumbent geopolitical structures of the entire Arab–Islamic world.

For the Alawites, the growing ideological and strategic strength of extreme Islamist forces raised the spectre of the sect's historic persecution at the hands of previous Sunni Muslim powers.[200] From Alawite perspectives, the ISIS fighters' view of their community is simple: 'Alawite equals infidel.' Moreover, similar to the Mamluk and Ottoman states, the ideology of this new wave of Islamism sees heterodox Islamic sects like the Alawites, Ismailis, Druze, Yazidis and even Twelver Shi'ites as weak points in Islamic solidarity.[201]

In 2014, fear mixed with despair settled heavily on the Alawite population in the villages of north-west Syria. Some recognise the futility of continuing to fight for the regime's survival; one sixty-year-old man complained, 'at least half of the village's youth are spread among the fighting fronts. Dozens have been killed.' Another man said, 'Asad has failed as a leader; he is sacrificing our lives to stay in power.' However, the most common view is that there is no choice but to continue to support the regime in view of the religious radicalism of much of the opposition fighters. 'If we stop fighting now this would mean certain death for all of us,' was the view of one woman.[202]

Persistent Alawite support for the Asad regime has coincided with a rise in the very thing that the sect has always feared most—fundamentalist Sunni Islamist ideology. Against this threat, Alawites can be expected to continue to cling to the regime of Bashar al-Asad. In their long struggle for integration and security in Syria, this may not prove a sustainable solution, and will only feed the cycle of hatred, war and fear. In the coming period the Alawites could well see the pragmatic benefits of abandoning the Asad dynasty and look to establish cross-sectarian alliances with moderate opposition groups. The idea of democratic pluralism articulated in the 2011 Syrian uprising may well form the only effective counter-ideology to the spread of extreme Islam.

CONCLUSION

The fear and insecurity that has shaped Alawite identity and political behaviour explains the establishment, consolidation and durability of the Asad regime. The case of the Alawites has shown that there is a need to rethink Khaldunian theory in order to consider both sectarian identity and insecurity as factors in the maintenance of group solidarity and related identity-based conflicts. The implications of a resilient sectarian 'asabiyya have great relevance to the post-2011 Syrian conflict, as well as to the increasing role of identity politics in the Middle East.

While contemporary conflicts may suggest otherwise, the case of the Alawites shows that sectarianism is not an inevitable component of Middle East politics. The Asad dynasty, while made possible by Alawites, is not an Alawite regime, but rather a 'self-reproducing and narrow elite' who have benefited from Alawite 'asabiyya that was made resilient by sectarian insecurity.[1]

As this book has shown, the cycle of fear that governs recurrent conflict can be broken, if the opportunities to do so can be recognised and acted upon. Considerable efforts were made by Alawites, Sunnis and other minorities to achieve genuine political integration in Syria as it gained its independence, and many courageous Syrians attempted to do so again in 2011. Without the influence of fear, or if there had been a greater awareness of the nature of insecurity and its vulnerability to political exploitation, the outcomes may have been different.

There were many causes of the Alawites' high levels of insecurity. The main cause was most certainly the persecution and discrimination they faced at the hands of Sunni Muslims, first in Iraq, then Syria and in their mountain refuge, the Jabal al-Sahiliyah. Another factor was the community's transition to a rural, tribal society—the direct result of their marginalisation. Isolated in their mountain refuge for centuries, the Alawites became self-reliant and 'wild'. Ibn Khaldun equated this situation to the development of high levels of 'asabiyya; however, the fractured topography of the Jabal al-Sahiliyah, inter-tribal fighting and interference by external powers prevented any substantial broad sectarian 'asabiyya from occurring for many centuries. The Alawites were ostracised from the Muslim world of which they were originally a part, gradually developing their own strong identity that would later become politically relevant when they made efforts to re-enter mainstream Muslim society.

As the Ottoman Empire declined and modern Syria emerged, Alawite 'asabiyya played an important role in the development of the state. Political flux provided favourable conditions for Alawite individuals to establish their superiority and mobilise Alawite 'asabiyya. As Ottoman authority in the Levant began to wane in the 1850s, the Alawite strongman Ismail Khayr Bey achieved political significance, however, his career was curtailed when central authority resumed as a result of wider strategic and geopolitical factors. In contrast, Hafiz al-Asad's rise came within a quite different geopolitical context. Within the truncated Syrian sovereign state, the Alawites' political significance was amplified. Alawite significance was made even more salient when viewed in the context of their high 'asabiyya; thus, when Hafiz al-Asad consolidated his superiority among the Alawites, he was able to dominate the Syrian state.

Once again, it must be emphasised that sectarianism was not the initial impulse of those groups and individuals who were trying to build a diverse independent state; however, a type of ethno-religious security dilemma occurred between communities as they struggled to come to terms with a fluid political arena and their centuries-old sectarian insecurities. The Alawites had more cause for insecurity than most, having been at the receiving end of discrimination for much of their history, which explains why they clung to the Asad regime and its upholding of Ba'thist secular ideology. Hafiz al-Asad remained firmly rooted in his Alawite community, and his careful pragmatism buttressed his stature with many Alawites. He provided at least some benefit to the wider Alawite community, and pre-sided over a relatively inclusive patronage system. The Muslim Brotherhood revolt, from 1976 to 1982, and the massacre at Hama, changed the situation. Thereafter, sectarian insecurity became a primary factor in Syrian politics, and brutal, Alawite-enforced, repression descended on Syria.

While many Alawites expected a dynastic succession to continue the socio-economic security they had experienced under Hafiz al-Asad, downward pressure soon came to bear on Alawite 'asabiyya. This occurred as a result of Bashar al-Asad's poor understanding of Alawite interests and the importance of preserving their support. The economic policies he implemented were unpopular among ordinary Alawites, especially as wide disparities in wealth developed between individuals close to the regime and the bulk of the Alawite community. Basic infrastructural and socio-economic advances for Alawites, achieved under Hafiz al-Asad, stalled or even regressed under Bashar. Moreover, the 'corporatisation of corruption' and neglect of rural Syria became a major element in the rising resentment against the regime, which led to the events of 2011.

In terms of statecraft, Bashar al-Asad lacked the careful pragmatism of his father. This was most evident in foreign policy, where, following some serious miscalculations based on poor judgement and the influence of close advisors, Bashar brought almost the entire international community down upon the regime. As the regime came under pressure, Bashar al-Asad allowed his external allies, Iran and Hizballah, to become increasingly dominant in their relations with Syria.

Many factors with the potential to cause a rapid decline in Alawite 'asabiyya were present in the first decade of Bashar al-Asad's rule; however, the effect of sectarian insecurity prevented any real reduction in Alawite support to the regime. This was partly due to the perpetuation of Alawite sectarian paranoia, which was only reinforced by the sectarian chaos in Iraq, Lebanon and during the Syrian uprising.

Regardless of the outcome of the Syrian revolution, there will be a new political reality in Syria sooner or later. It is quite possible that in a fluid political environment, a 'security dilemma' between communities will set off another Khaldunian cycle. It could well be that the group with the highest level of 'asabiyya, sectarian or otherwise, could give rise to another authoritarian dynasty. This is the dilemma facing all transforming states. It is likely we could see the emergence of a tribal 'asabiyya in Libya, a Shi'a, Kurdish or Sunni 'asabiyya in Iraq or a tribal-sectarian 'asabiyya in Yemen.

So what are the possible answers to the problems of social integration in the Middle East? Arendt Lijphart says that 'consociationalism is ... the only realistic possibility [for] ethnically and religiously divided societies'.[2] In reply, Donald Horowitz has argued that 'there is a circularity of cause and effect in consociational theory, and its application to the more severely divided societies of Asia and Africa remains problematic'.[3] In other words, organising politics along ethno-religious lines can only lead to the reification of distinct identities and eventually back to conflict. The Lebanese state is the archetypal case showing the dangers inherent in a power-sharing system based on institutionalised sectarianism. While its citizens have in general enjoyed greater liberty than in most Middle Eastern states, competition and insecurity between politically mobilised communities has caused catastrophic violence and frequent paralysis in the functioning of the state. Yet, as the case of Syria has shown, completely suppressing religious identity has only been possible through political repression.

The answer to the question of a new model of political integration is perhaps to be found with the Alawites themselves. The Alawites' experience of coping with tenuous security throughout their history, their syncretistic religion incorporating elements from several religious traditions and their historic aptitude for pragmatism qualifies the Alawites as a source for exploring new approaches to political integration. Alawite political preferences have generally been dictated by pragmatic goals of achieving communal security rather than any fundamental ideology or political philosophy. Their politics, therefore, often seem contradictory, such as the apparent centrality of Alawite 'primordial loyalties' to the upholding of a radically secular Ba'thist regime,[4] or Alawite desires for autonomy or to join the diverse Lebanese confessional democracy in 1936, compared with their eventual adoption of a homogenous Arab nationalist ideology.

The Alawite State of 1922–36 was essentially consociational in its design, allocating seats in the representative council proportionate to the various communities; however, the design and operation of the Alawite State was essentially an artificial innovation of the French, who deliberately sought to emphasise sectarian divisions. Whether or not the Alawites would genuinely have preferred secluded autonomy in their territory in north-west Syria is also unclear, as their lack of genuine viable options left them with little choice but to make a pragmatic compromise to commit to the Sunni-dominated Syrian state.

When the more localised Syrian nationalism of the SSNP was terminated, the radical Arab secularism of the Ba'th Party became the best remaining option for Alawites. Consequently, the sect became submerged as a distinct community, which likely reassured their fears of Sunni intolerance. But do Alawites really prefer not being able to assume their religious identity openly? Alawite political preferences seem to be based on three key principles: security, equality and diversity. This was plainly evident from Alawite community leaders. In March 2011, the Alawite Shaykh Muhammad Boz stated:

We don't have any divergence or hatred, we believe in God the merciful who created all mankind. If He wanted He would have created all men Christian or Jews or Alawites ... But God wanted diversity. 'This one is Alawite, this one is Jew, and another one is Christian.' We accept all this and we don't make may difference [between religions].[5]

For the Alawites, diversity is the ideal condition—it is what 'God intended'. This contradicts the principles of Ba'thism, which sought to homogenise citizens into a single Arab polity to the exclusion of all other forms of identity. Further illuminating Alawite perspectives, the Antakya Shaykh 'Ali Yeral articulated his ideal political environment:

Democracy benefits all the people; this means that it benefits the Alawites, the Sunni, the Christians and the Jews ... They will be able to express themselves, they will for example say, 'I am not subscribing to Bashar al-Asad's politics, however, I will not betray my nation [by saying this].' I will not strike and kill when I have a different point of view and you also can have a different point of view.[6]

'Ali Yeral portrayed a pluralist, democratic, political environment with freedom of expression and religious identity. This view also differs from the standard model of Ba'thist conformity to the aspirations of the masses and the unity of the nation. Here, the ideal Alawite political model does not seem to be for a consociational system, but rather a system that enshrines strict equality in citizenship—an understandable priority for the long-discriminated against community. Alawites do not necessarily desire an ethno-religiously based state either. With regard to the possibility of another state along the lines of the Alawite State of 1922–36, Shaykh 'Ali Yeral said, 'We don't want and we don't think about dividing Syria ... Let it be one united country ... I don't think Syria will be divided, for example, Latakia and its suburbs for the Alawites [and] the east of Syria for the Sunnis.'[7]

This view was echoed by the Alawite opposition activist and member of the Syrian National Council, Monzer Makhouz, 'I cannot deny that some lunatics want to have an independent Alawite state, but they are very few, and they don't realize that such a plan will not only destroy Syria but also the Alawites themselves.'[8]

In July 2014, leading Alawite opposition figure Issa Ibrahim, a lawyer and the grandson of Shaykh Saleh al-'Ali, along with Hiedar al-Hassan, a young Alawite political science student from Damascus University, composed a detailed description of what a post-Asad Syrian political system could look like.[9] The key features followed the common formula of a democratic republican political system. They proposed that, most importantly from Alawite perspectives, the political system should reflect the diversity of the Syrian people without resorting to a sectarian power-sharing model, and it should not discriminate in any way on ethnic or sectarian grounds in matters of legal or civil status. This of course has been a historic disadvantage for Alawites for many centuries under Sunni Islamic law. Moreover, they suggest that the state should clearly separate the political and religious realms of public and private life (see appendix for the full document). These latter points could be the most difficult issues to reconcile in future negotiations.

Religion and religious identity is an integral aspect of Middle East culture, and it will always be that way. Consideration must therefore be given to how it can be accommodated within a new political paradigm. In seeking a solution to end the cycle of fear in the Levant, the answer is unlikely to be a consociational, power-sharing arrangement that could reify political–sectarian identities, a radically secular regime that represses any suggestion of sectarian identity or balkanisation into ethno-religiously based polities, but rather a truly pluralist state that openly recognises diverse identities in the context of equal citizenship. Instead of disguising and suppressing identity, as per the tradition of taqiyya or Ba'thism, differences could be highlighted within the framework of a diverse, overlapping mosaic of citizenship; a type of eclectic cosmopolitanism[10] that more fully reflects the essential pluralism of the Levant, or as the Alawite poet Adonis put it, a 'multilayered crucible of identities'.[11] The outcome of the conflict in Syria is far from certain, and the type of political and social system that will emerge from the ruins of the Syrian state is even more so. Most important in the aftermath of the war will be setting forth on an open and honest collective reckoning with sectarianism and the cycle of fear among communities, in a way that has not been possible or attempted before.[12]

APPENDIX

Statement of Mr Issa Ibrahim and Mr Hiedar Al-Hassan, 'Common Vision towards what we Consider a Solution in Syria', July 2014, Beirut and Antakya.

1. The Syrian society is diverse and rich in ethnic, religious and cultural aspects, and has multiple political visions. Generally it contains two sections: one conservative and traditional, and the other vividly aspiring towards national and humanitarian horizons. If we take these observations into account we can understand the nature of the political system needed to project this social structure. We believe that a political republican system based upon a constitution can legitimately reflect the aspirations of these components and Syrian diversity. A constitution based on the principal of separation of judiciary, legislative and executive powers, with a law above them all.

2. It is important for such a diverse society with a combination of traditional and modernising tendencies to have a political system that takes these issues into account, so we suggest the formation of a House of Senates in which each component of the Syrian society is represented by one member. Such members should be drawn from those men or women with significant social, economic and religious status. The duty of this House is to consider the general interests of the Syrian society, foreign policies and relations with other countries. And a House of Representatives whose members are directly elected by the Syrian people, and deals with the detailed procedures, suggests laws and approves them. The superiority in the political system should be largely given to the Parliament as an overall institution.

3. Due to the bad reputation of the presidency and its dictatorial attitudes, the position of the president of the republic should have little authority, mainly in supervising, directing and welfare of institutions. The position of prime minister, or counsellor, should have wider authority, and should be under the supervision of the Parliament and the Senates in decisions that may affect the sovereignty of the state or its general internal politics or foreign affairs.

4. The Supreme Judicial Council should be elected as one member from each province by direct election by the people from those who qualify to take such a position.

5. The state and its institutions, including the army, should be neutral away from religion and politics, respecting freedom of belief, faith, and political activities according to a modern law to organise political parties.

[This is regarding the general view of the future, but we can start by implementing the 1950 constitution in the transition period, which should not last more than one or two years to start building a modern democratic national state.]

6. Implementation of educational policy that respects Syria's religious, ethnic and political diversity without preferential tendency. Some of the subjects taught at elementary and middle schools should be supervised by joint review by researchers who represent the components of the Syrian society, such as history.

7. Cancellation of the Ministry of Information after the transition period. Freedom of speech should be respected, and can only be controlled by the general law.

8. Formation of civil society institutes and groups should be allowed and licensed according to the law and civil management authority.

9. For transitional justice, courts should be held to judge criminal accountability of whomever committed crimes against the Syrian society. The exact format should be left to the representatives of Syrian political powers.

10. Implementation of an economic policy that takes the diversity of the Syrian society into account, so that the state will carry on balanced social justice.

11. Regarding the army, it should be under the control of the Ministry of Defence, represented by the cabinet and a civil minister to implement the internal policy of the ministry, with a chief of staff who is subject to the legal hierarchy without sectarian or ethnic preference. The army should not be used except in case of emergency within or outside the state in agreement between the minister of defence and the prime minister, and approval of both the Senates and the House of Representatives within one month of that decision.

We don't believe the solution to the Syrian crisis can be achieved by division of the country or sectarian shares. The solution in Syria as we see it, and as seen by others who share this vision, is to establish a modern democratic national state.

Regarding the current vision of the opposition, in order for it to become a national stand; meaning to share nationality and citizenship, without indicating special preferences, we believe certain steps should be taken, such as:

1. The opposition must appreciate the Syrian ethnic and religious diversity and deal with it accordingly in all fairness without any preferential treatment except between a criminal and a citizen, without any consideration of ethnic or sectarian background. But only consider the actual criminal act and its dangers and consequences.

2. The opposition should build confidence and trust with fellow Alawite citizens, since they are not all one bloc behind the Asad regime. There are discrepancies in interests and objectively different real visions and aspirations between the sect and the Asad dynasty. These interests and aspirations are shared with the rest of the Syrians.

3. Not to use religion in political work under any reason or circumstances, because that may fragment what is already fragmented within every sect and religion in Syria, and would spoil politics as a science and art, and spoil religion as a faith and a belief.

4. The opposition should balance between the internal Syrian interests and the necessities of regional and international conflicts, realising that Syria is the heart of the Old World. This understanding will lead to the adoption of balanced politics based upon mutual interests and cooperation with the conflicting regional and international powers.

5. Unification of the authority receiving assistance from all countries. Such authority must be under the control of the opposition and should be monitored. Assistance and support must be on the basis of mutual interests not on loyalty.

Issa Ibrahim and Hiedar al-Hassan
Translated from the Arabic by Dr Amer Chaikouni
July 2014

NOTES

INTRODUCTION

1. The Alawites are sometimes referred to as Nusayris. Their original name has been given as 'al-Numayriyya', reflecting the eponym of the sect, Ibn Nusayr's membership of the Banū Numayr tribe in ninth-century Iraq. Ibn Nusayr's full name was Abū Shuʿayb Muhammad Ibn Nusayr al 'Abdī al-Bakrī al-Numayri, the early name of the sect therefore relates to him but also to his tribal affiliation, i.e. Ibn Nusayr *al-Numayri* (from the Numayr tribe). From the tenth century, the group became known as al-Nusayriyya. This name change reflected a shift away from a tribal identity to a sectarian identity focused on the person of Muhammad ibn Nusayr. In the nineteenth century European travellers and missionaries used the term, 'Ansayrii', which is likely a condensed form of al-Nusayriyya. The group retained this name in reference to themselves up until the 1920s when they were officially declared as Alawites during the French Mandate. This latest name change shifted the sect away from a heterodox religious identity towards a more orthodox association with Shi'a Islam. The name 'Alawite' refers generally to adherents of the first Imam 'Ali ibn Abi Talib. Today the group prefers to be known as Alawites and assert that the name Nusayri is only used pejoratively by opponents who wish to discredit them. This point was made clear during three interviews by this author with Alawite religious leaders in Mar. 2011. Alawites hold 'Ali ibn Abi Talib as a central figure in their religion, thus it is logical for the group to be referred to as Alawites. In Arabic, an Alawite is called an *'Alawi*, and the group would be *al-'Alawiyyun*; however, as this research is composed in English, Alawite remains the appropriate name to use here. See Matti Moosa, *Extremist Shiites: The Ghulat Sects*, New York: Syracuse University Press, 1988, p. 262; Yaron Friedman, *The Nuṣayrī-'Alawīs: An Introduction to the Religion, History and Identity of the Leading Minority in Syria*, Leiden: Brill, 2010, pp. 6–7; Xavier de Planhol, *Minorités En Islam, Géographie Politique et Sociale*, Paris: Flammarion, 1997, p. 84.

2. It is important to note that there is a significant difference between the Arab Alawites of the Levant and the Turkish Alevis of Anatolia in terms of ethnicity, culture and religion.

See Tord Olsson, E. Ozdalga and C. Raudvere (eds), *Alevi Identity: Cultural, Religious and Social Perspectives*, Nov. 1996, Swedish Research Institute in Istanbul, Transactions, 1998, vol. 8.

3. Alawite shaykh (anonymous), interview with the author, 28 Mar. 2011, Antakya, Turkey.

4. Alawite shaykh (anonymous), interview with the author, 28 Mar. 2011, Antakya, Turkey.

5. Christa Salamandra, 'Sectarianism in Syria: Anthropological Reflections', *Middle East Critique*, 22, 3 (2013), p. 303.

6. Ibn Khaldun, *The Muqaddimah: An Introduction to History*, trans. Franz Rosenthal, abridged N.J. Dawood, London: Routledge & Kegan Paul, 1967, pp. 123–263.

7. Allen Fromherz, *Ibn Khaldun, Life and Times*, Edinburgh: Edinburgh University Press, 2010, p. 1.

8. Ibid. p. 3.

9. The seminal work of Michel Seurat first identified and examined the concept of 'asabiyya in relation to the Asad regime and its hold on the Alawite community. He died in a Beirut prison in 1986, one year after being kidnapped by Shi'ite militia. Michel Seurat, *Syrie: L'État De Barbarie*, Paris: Presses Universitaires de France, 2012.

10. Yves Lacoste, *Ibn Khaldun: The Birth of History and the Past of Third World*, London: Verso, 1984, pp. 106–7.

11. Khaldun, *The Muqaddimah*, p. 283.

12. Shaykh Nasīr Eskiocak, interview with the author, Antakya, 29 Mar. 2011.

13. For example, Daniel Pipes described it as 'like an untouchable becoming maharajah in India or a Jew becoming Tsar in Russia'. Daniel Pipes, *Greater Syria: The History of an Ambition*, New York: Oxford University Press, 1990, p. 175.

14. Khaldun, *The Muqaddimah*, pp. 123–263.

15. N.J. Dawood, 'Introduction', in Khaldun, *The Muqaddimah*, p. xi.

16. Khaldun, *The Muqaddimah*, p. 123; Lacoste, *Ibn Khaldun*, p. 100.

17. Fuad Khuri has noted and explained this gap in Ibn Khaldun's theories as due to his personal beliefs and historical context. Fuad Khuri, *Imams and Emirs: State, Religion and Sects in Islam*, London: Saqi Books, 1990, pp. 54–5.

18. Barry Posen, 'The Security Dilemma and Ethnic Conflict', in M. Brown (ed.), *Ethnic Conflict and International Security*, Princeton, NJ: Princeton University Press, 1993.

19. Volker Perthes, *The Political Economy of Syria under Asad*, London: I.B. Tauris, 1995, p. 185.

20. It is impossible to determine exact population figures for the Alawites as there is not any recent census data on sect in Syria, Lebanon or Turkey. This rough figure is arrived at by combining estimations of the Turkish, Syrian and Lebanese Arab Alawites. The Alawite population of the Turkish provinces of Adana and Mersin was estimated at between 247,000 and 329,000 in 2000 by G. Prozchazka-Eisl and S. Prozchazka, *The Plain of Saints and Prophets: The Nusayri–Alawi Community of Cilicia (Southern Turkey) and its Sacred Places*, Wiesbaden: Harrassowitz Verlag, 2010, p. 59; Alawite informants in Antakya estimated the population of their community in the Hatay region in 2011 as approxi-

mately 500,000; the Lebanese Alawites number between 70,000 and 120,000; and the Syrian Alawite population is estimated at approximately 3,000,000; see n. 21, below.

21. There has not been a Syrian census containing sectarian information since 1960. Demographer Onn Winckler argues, however, that the Syrian Alawite population is possibly much higher than the usual estimate of 12 per cent, see: Onn Winckler, *Arab Political Demography: Population Growth, Labor Migration and Natalist Policies*, 2nd edn, Eastbourne: Sussex Academic Press, 2009, p. 34; see also Yahya Sadowski, 'The Evolution of Political Identity in Syria', in S. Telhamy and M. Barnett (eds), *Identity and Foreign Policy in the Middle East*, London: Cornell University Press, 2002, p. 144.

22. Peter Gubser, 'Minorities in Power: The Alawites of Syria', in R.D. McLaurin, *The Political Role of Minority Groups in The Middle East*, New York: Praeger, 1979, pp. 30–1; Khuri, *Imams and Emirs*, p. 55. De Planhol, *Minorités En Islam*, p. 87.

23. See Gitta Yaffe and Uriel Dann, 'Suleiman al-Murshid: Beginnings of an Alawi Leader', *Middle Eastern Studies*, 29, 4 (Oct. 1993), pp. 624–40.

24. See Moosa, *Extremist Shiites*, 1988.

25. That the Alawites strongly consider themselves part of the Shi'a tradition was reinforced in interviews with three separate Alawite shaykhs conducted in Antakya, Turkey, in Mar. 2011; see also Friedman, *The Nuṣayrī-ʿAlawīs*.

26. Alawites believe ʿAli ibn Abi Talib to be the closest reflection of the divinity of God on earth. This is however a complex issue. The Alawite concept of divinity is very abstract and, as Yaron Friedman suggests, is reflective of Neoplatonic thought. See Friedman, *The Nuṣayrī-ʿAlawīs*, pp. 72–3.

27. The Alawites vehemently deny this accusation of extremism and make a comparison to the Christian elevation of Jesus to divine status; Shaykh Nasīr Eskiocak, interview with the author, Antakya, 29 Mar. 2011. The most comprehensive study yet published on Alawite religion is: Meir M. Bar-Asher and Aryeh Kofksy, *The Nuṣayrī-ʿAlawī Religion: An Enquiry into its Theology and Liturgy*, Leiden: Brill, 2002.

28. These features of Alawite religion were confirmed to the author in interviews with Alawite shaykhs in Antakya in Mar. 2011.

29. A thorough study of these aspects of Alawite religious customs was conducted by Prochazka-Eisl and Prozchazka, *The Plain of Saints and Prophets*.

30. The main works include René Dussaud, *Histoire et Religion des Nosairies*, Paris: Bouillon, 1900; Samuel Lyde, *The Asian Mystery Illustrated in the History, Religion, and Present State of the Ansaireeh or Nusairis of Syria*, London: Longman, Green, Longman & Roberts, 1860; Bar-Asher and Kofksy, *The Nuṣayrī-ʿAlawī Religion*; Friedman, *The Nuṣayrī-ʿAlawīs*; see also chapters in Moosa, *Extremist Shiites*; Khuri, *Imams and Emirs*; T. Olsson (ed.), *Alevi Identity: Cultural, Religious and Social Perspectives*, Papers Read at a Conference Held at the Swedish Institute in Istanbul, Nov. 1996, Swedish Research Institute in Istanbul Transactions, vol. 8, 1998.

31. This point is well noted by Olsson, *Alevi Identity*, p. 176.

32. Interview with the author, Antakya, Turkey, 28 Mar. 2011.

33. See, for example, Bar-Asher and Kofksy, *The Nusayrī–'Alawī Religion*.
34. See Table 1, p. 00, 'No Tribe/Unknown'.
35. Gubser, 'Minorities in Power', p. 19; Hanna Batatu, *Syria's Peasantry, the Descendants of its Lesser Rural Notables and their Politics*, Princeton, NJ: Princeton University Press, 1999, pp. 12, 188.
36. De Planhol, *Minorités en Islam*, pp. 87–9.
37. The most comprehensive study on the political and economic preferences of Syria's rural peasantry, including the Alawites, is Batatu, *Syria's Peasantry*, pp. 3–191; Khuri, *Imams and Emirs*, p. 75; on Alawite ideology see also Radwan Ziadeh, *Power and Policy in Syria*, London: I.B. Tauris, 2011, p. 16; Moshe Maoz and Ilan Pappe (eds), *Middle Eastern Politics and Ideas: A History from Within*, London: Tauris, 1997, p. 220.
38. Flynt Leverett, *Inheriting Syria: Bashar's Trial by Fire*, Washington, DC: Brookings Institution Press, 2005, pp. 62–3.
39. Torstein Worren suggests that the fact that many Alawites know very little about their own religion actually buttresses their sectarian identity relative to other communities, T. Worren, 'Fear and Resistance', Master's Thesis, 2007; see also Gubser, 'Minorities in Power', p. 22.

1. ORIGINS

1. Diffuse minorities have no core territory and are distributed among a majority. Compact minorities have a core territory where they are a majority within a larger polity. See: Gabriel Ben-Dor, 'Minorities in the Middle East: Theory and Practice', in O. Bengio and G. Ben-Dor (eds), *Minorities and the State in the Arab World*, Boulder: Lynne Rienner, 1999, pp. 1–20.
2. David Waines, 'The Third Century Internal Crisis of the Abbasids', *Journal of the Economic and Social History of the Orient*, 20, 3 (Oct. 1977), pp. 282–306.
3. Xavier de Planhol, *Minorités en Islam, Géographie Politique et Sociale*, France: Flammarion, 1997, p. 84.
4. Yaron Friedman, *The Nuṣayrī–'Alawīs: An Introduction to the Religion, History and Identity of the Leading Minority in Syria*, Leiden: Brill, 2010, pp. 6–7.
5. Kais M. Firro, 'The 'Alawīs in Modern Syria: From Nuṣayrīya to Islam via 'Alawīya', *Der Islam*, 82, 1 (2005), p. 1; Matti Moosa, *Extremist Shiites: The Ghulat Sects*, New York: Syracuse University Press, 1988, p. 259; Meir M. Bar-Asher and Aryeh Kofsky, 'Dogma and Ritual in Kitab al-Ma'Aref by the Nusayri Theologian Abu Said Maymun b. Al-Qasim al-Tabarani (d.426/1034–35)', *Arabica*, LII, 1 (2005), p. 54.
6. Friedman, *The Nuṣayrī–'Alawīs*, p. 6.
7. Ibid.
8. J.P. Berkey, *The Formation Of Islam, Religion and Society in the Near East, 600–1800*, Cambridge: Cambridge University Press, 2003, p. 83.
9. Moosa, *Extremist Shiites*, p. XV.

10. Berkey, *The Formation Of Islam*, p. 95.
11. Ibid. p. 89; Friedman, *The Nuṣayrī-'Alawīs*, p. 223.
12. Berkey, *The Formation Of Islam*, p. 133.
13. Friedman, *The Nuṣayrī-'Alawīs*, pp. 6–7; this political association became important for the Alawites when its leadership shifted to Syria in the tenth century.
14. Shaykh Nasīr Eskiocak, interview with the author.
15. Friedman, *The Nuṣayrī-'Alawīs*, pp. 6–7.
16. Ibid.
17. Bar-Asher and Kofsky, 'Dogma and Ritual in Kitab al-Ma'Aref', p. 54.
18. Friedman, *The Nuṣayrī-'Alawīs*, p. 9.
19. Clifford Edmund Bosworth, *Encyclopaedia of Islam*, Supplement, vol. 12, Leiden: Brill, 1980, p. 94.
20. Friedman, *The Nuṣayrī-'Alawīs*, p. 11.
21. Ibid. p. 8; Friedman used the term excommunication to describe Ibn Nusayr's punishment.
22. Shaykh Nasīr Eskiocak, interview with the author, Antakya, Turkey, 29 Mar. 2011.
23. Firro, 'The 'Alawīs in Modern Syria', p. 1; Moosa, *Extremist Shiites*, p. 259.
24. Friedman, *The Nuṣayrī-'Alawīs*, pp. 16–20; Bar-Asher and Kofsky, 'Dogma and Ritual in Kitab al-Ma'Aref', p. 57.
25. Yaron Friedman, 'Al-Husayn Ibn Hamdan al-Khasibi: A Historical Biography of the Nusayri-Alawite Sect,' *Studia Islamica*, 2001, 93, pp. 97–8.
26. Friedman, *The Nuṣayrī-'Alawīs*, pp. 22–3.
27. For example see Moosa, *Extremist Shiites*, p. 265.
28. Friedman, *The Nuṣayrī-'Alawīs*, p. 35.
29. Meir M. Bar-Asher, 'The Iranian Component of the Nusayrī Religion', *Iran*, 4 (2003), p. 222.
30. Hanna Batatu, *Syria's Peasantry, the Descendants of its Lesser Rural Notables and their Politics*, Princeton, NJ: Princeton University Press, 1999, pp. 105, 223.
31. By the start of the eleventh century, enmity towards Sunni Islam would become an official part of Alawite religious discourse. Bar-Asher and Kofsky, 'Dogma and Ritual in Kitab al-Ma'Aref', p. 62.
32. Friedman, *The Nuṣayrī*, p. 23, n. 72.
33. Moosa, *Extremist Shiites*, p. 134.
34. Friedman, *The Nuṣayrī-'Alawīs*, p. 33.
35. After the 960s, the Hamdanids essentially ruled as a tributary buffer state for the benefit of the Byzantine Empire and were probably not in a position to impose religious policy effectively across northern Syria anyway.
36. Shaykh Nasīr Eskiocak, interview with the author.
37. William Harris, *The Levant: A Fractured Mosaic*, Princeton: Markus Wiener, 2003, p. 197.
38. Friedman, *The Nuṣayrī-'Alawīs*, p. 33; Yaron Friedman, 'al-Husayn Ibn Hamdan al-Khasibi: A Historical Biography of the Nusayrî-Alawite Sect', *Studia Islamica*, 93 (2001); this was confirmed in interviews with the Shaykhs 'Ali Yeral and Nasīr Eskiocak.

39. De Planhol, *Minorités En Islam*, p. 85; Friedman, *The Nuṣayrī-'Alawīs*, pp. 38–9; Stefan Winter, *The Shiites of Lebanon under Ottoman Rule, 1516–1788*, Cambridge: Cambridge University Press, 2010, p. 61.

40. Harris, *The Levant*, p. 60.

41. Ibid.

42. Friedman, *The Nuṣayrī-'Alawīs*, p. 34.

43. Ibid. p. 41.

44. Harris, *The Levant*, p. 64.

45. Friedman, *The Nuṣayrī-'Alawīs*, p. 41.

46. Bar-Asher and Kofsky, 'Dogma and Ritual in Kitab al-Ma'Aref', p. 43; Friedman, *The Nuṣayrī-Alawīs*, p. 41.

47. Bar-Asher and Kofsky, 'Dogma and Ritual in Kitab al-Ma'Aref,'. pp. 43–65; Friedman, *The Nuṣayrī-'Alawīs*, p. 40.

48. Firro, 'The 'Alawīs in Modern Syria', p. 3.

49. See, for example, Harris, *The Levant*, p. 65 and Firro, 'The 'Alawīs in Modern Syria', p. 3.

50. Bar-Asher and Kofsky, 'Dogma and Ritual in Kitab al-Ma'Aref', p. 45; Tripoli was ruled at this time by the Twelver Shi'a 'Amarrids.

51. Friedman, *The Nuṣayrī-'Alawīs*, p. 42.

52. Ibid. p. 48.

53. Ibid.

54. De Planhol, *Minoritès en Islam*, p. 85

55. Harris, *The Levant*, p. 67.

56. Bar-Asher and Kofsky, 'Dogma and Ritual in Kitab al-Ma'Aref', p. 62.

57. Xavier de Planhol, *The World of Islam*, Ithaca, NY: Cornell University Press, 1959.

58. De Planhol, *Minorités en Islam*, p. 84.

59. The incline on the eastern edge of the Jabal al-Sahiliyah is particularly precipitous. See also Colbert Held, *Middle East Patterns: Places, Peoples, and Politics*, Third Edition, Boulder: Westview Press, 2000, p. 242, for a description of the geography of the Jabal al-Sahiliyah.

60. On the Ismailis see ibid. p. 85; On the Armenians see Harris, *The Levant*, p. 100.

61. De Planhol, *Minoritès en Islam*, p. 84.

62. Ibid.

63. Harris, *The Levant*, p. 49.

64. Ibid. p. 53.

65. Berkey, *The Formation Of Islam*, pp. 117–18.

66. Batatu, *Syria's Peasantry*, p. 105.

67. Robert Browning, *The Byzantine Empire*, Washington, DC: The Catholic University of America Press, 1992, pp. 112–116

68. Batatu, *Syria's Peasantry*, p. 103.

69. Friedman, *The Nuṣayrī-'Alawīs*, p. 37.

70. Heinz Halm, p. 159, cited in Harris, *The Levant*, p. 65.

71. Friedman, *The Nuṣayrī-'Alawīs*, p. 38.

72. H. Smith-Williams, *Historians' History*, vol. VIII, London: The Times, 1909, p. 351.

73. See Harris, *The Levant*, Map 6, p. 59 and Map 7, p. 75, for an illustration of this comparison.

74. De Planhol, *Minorités en Islam*, p. 85

75. Friedman, *The Nuṣayrī-'Alawis*, p. 42

76. Ibid. p. 47, and Moosa, *Extremist Shiites*, pp. 267–9.

77. De Planhol, *Minorités en Islam*, p. 87

78. Yvette Talhamy suggests that it was the lack of 'distinctive religious or secular leadership' which prevented the Alawites from achieving solidarity, but it is likely that an additional reason was the physical characteristics of the Jabal al-Sahiliyah. See Yvette Talhamy, 'The Nusayri Leader Isma'il Khayr Bey and the Ottomans (1854–58)', *Middle Eastern Studies*, 44, 6 (Nov. 2008), p. 895.

79. The Jabal al-Sahiliyah stretches from the Homs Gap near Qala'at al-Hosn (Krac de Chevalier) in the south to a point near Jisr al-Shugur. The range has borne many names; in antiquity it was called Ukomo (Black). The Romans referred to them as Bargylus, and the Arabs following from the ancient Syrians, referred to them as Jabal al-Lukam (Black Mountains). From the eleventh century and the emergence of the Nusayri faith among the local population the range was referred to as the Jabal al-Nusayriyya after the sect who inhabited it. Alternately the mountains have been named Jabal 'Ansariyya, another name for the sect. The name was changed to the Jabal al 'Alawi (or 'Alawiyya) when the Nusayri sect changed their name around the beginning of the twentieth century. Most recently the Syrian government has changed the official toponym to Jabal al-Sahiliyah (The Coastal Mountains). This most recent name change is synonymous with regime efforts to down-play sectarian identities. The official Syrian Ministry of Tourism map neglects to name the mountains at all, referring to them simply as scenic 'green mountains'. In the absence of any absolute certainty about the correct name for the ranges, and the fact that the only obvious constant has been their geographic position, perhaps the most appropriate name to use is Jabal al-Sahiliyah. See, Samuel Lyde, *The Asian Mystery Illustrated in the History, Religion, and Present State of the Ansaireeh or Nusairis of Syria*, London: Longman, Green, Longman & Roberts, 1860, p. 5; Moosa, *Extremist Shiites*, p. 256; Held, *Middle East Patterns*, p. 242; Syrian Ministry of Tourism Map, 'The Syrian Coast,' Salhani, est. Damascus, 2008.

80. Robert F. Mahfouda and James N. Beck, 'Petrographic/Geochemical Studies of Primary and Alteration–Weathering Minerals in Garnetiferous Ultramafic Xenoliths–Basanite, Tartous Province, NW Syria', *Microchemical Journal*, 78 (2004), p. 115.

81. De Planhol, *Minorités En Islam*, p. 83.

82. Mahfouda and Beck, 'Petrographic/Geochemical Studies', p. 116.

83. De Planhol, *Minorités En Islam*, p. 83.

84. Hanna Batatu, 'Some Observations on the Social Roots of Syria's Ruling, Military Group and the Causes for its Dominance', *Middle East Journal*, 35, 3 (Summer 1981), pp. 334–5.

85. De Planhol, *Minorités En Islam*, p. 84.

86. Jacque Weulersse, *Paysans de Syrie et du Proche-Orient*, Paris: Gallimard, 1946, p. 272.

87. Yves Lacoste, *Ibn Khaldun: The Birth of History and the Past of Third World*, London: Verso, 1984, p. 106.

88. De Planhol, *Minorités En Islam*, p. 86; Harris, *The Levant*, p. 15.

89. Harris, *The Levant*, pp. 16–17.

90. Moosa, *Extremist Shiites*, p. 269.

91. For example see Freya Stark's observations in her article 'Castles of Syria', *The Geographical Magazine*, 10 (Dec. 1939), p. 96.

92. Berkey, *The Formation Of Islam*, p. 251.

93. Devin, J. Stewart, 'The *Maqāmāt* of Ahmad b. Abī Bakr b. Ahmad al-Rāzī al-Hanafī and the Ideology of the Counter-Crusade in Twelfth-century Syria', *Middle Eastern Literatures*, 11, 2 (Aug. 2008).

94. Ibid. p. 224.

95. Ibid. p. 217.

96. Ibid.

97. Harris, *The Levant*, pp. 9–10.

98. Stewart, 'The *Maqāmāt*', p. 227; Harris, *The Levant*, p. 15.

99. Lutz Weiderhold, 'Blasphemy against the Prophet Muhammad and His Companions (Sabb al-Rasūl, Sabb al-Sahābah): The Introduction of the Topic into Shāfi 'ī Legal Literature and its Relevance for Legal Practice under Mamluk Rule', *Journal of Semitic Studies*, XLII, 1(1997), p. 65.

100. 'Iranians Land in Syria to Fight alongside PLO', *The Times*, London, 19 Dec. 1979.

101. H. Smith-Williams, *Historians' History*, vol. VIII, London: The Times, 1909, p. 382.

102. Harris, *The Levant*, Map 8, p. 83.

103. Friedman, *The Nuṣayrī-'Alawīs*, p. 52; Moosa, *Extremist Shiites*, p. 270.

104. Friedman, *The Nuṣayrī-'Alawīs*, p. 52.

105. Shaykh Nasīr Eskiocak, interview with the author, Antakya, 29 Mar. 2011.

106. As'ad Ahmad 'Ali, *Ma'rifat Allah wa-'l-Makzun al-Sinjari*, Beirut, 1972, pp. 343–6, cited in Friedman, *The Numan—'Alawīs*, pp. 52–3.

107. Ibid. p. 51.

108. Manuscript of a meeting between Alawite Mystics, al-Saigh and al-Jisri, MS Paris 1450, fol. 176b–179a; Cat: Massignon item 38, cited in Friedman, *The Nuṣayrī-'Alawīs*, p. 35, n. 127.

109. Friedman, *The Nuṣayrī-'Alawīs*, pp. 55–6.

110. Moosa, *Extremist Shiites*, p. 270.

111. Friedman, *The Nu Nuan-'Alawīs*, p. 53.

112. Shaykh 'Ali Yeral, interview with the author, Antakya, Turkey, 28 Mar. 2011.

113. Friedman, *The Nu Nuan-'Alawīs*, p. 53.

114. On the battle of 'Ayn Jālūt see: Reuven Amitai, (ed.) *The Mongols in Islamic Lands: Studies in the History of the Ilkhanate*, Aldershot: Ashgate Valorium, 2007, pp. 119–50.

115. Berkey, *The Formation Of Islam*, p. 191.
116. Stewart, 'The *Maqāmāt*', p. 224.
117. See Bernard Lewis, 'Saladin and the Assassins', *Bulletin of the School of Oriental and African Studies*, 15, 2 (1953), pp. 239–45.
118. Stewart, 'The *Maqāmāt*', p. 220.
119. De Planhol, *Minorités En Islam* p. 87.
120. Fuad Khuri, *Imams and Emirs: State, Religion and Sects in Islam*, London: Saqi Books, 1990, p. 74.
121. D. Power and N. Standen, 'Frontiers in Question: Eurasian Borderlands c.700–1700', in Reuven Amitai (ed.), *The Mongols in Islamic Lands*, pp. 134–40.
122. Harris, *The Levant*, p. 98; Sato Tsugitaka, *State & Rural Society in Medieval Islam*, Leiden: Brill, 1997, p. 172.
123. Harris, *The Levant*, p. 98.
124. Power and Standen, 'Frontiers in Question', p. 142.
125. Ibid. pp. 141–2.
126. Tsugitaka, *State & Rural Society*, p. 175.
127. Ibid. p. 170.
128. *Nuwayri*, XXX, fol. 108; 'Iqd al-Juman, fol. 329r; Subh, XIII, 35, cited in Tsugitaka, *State & Rural*, p. 173.
129. Tsugitaka, *State & Rural Society*, p. 173.
130. Ibn Battuta, I, p. 177, cited in Tsugitaka, *State & Rural Society*, p. 172.
131. Tsugitaka, *State & Rural Society*, pp. 171–172; Lutz Weiderhold speaks of a similar edict in 1310 by the Mamluk Sultan al-Nasīr for the construction of mosques in the Alawite villages around Tripoli, see 'Blasphemy against the Prophet Muhammad', p. 66.
132. Tsugitaka, *State & Rural Society*, p. 174.
133. Berkey, *The Formation of Islam*, p. 191, incorrectly dates the revolt as 1317, Tsugitaka provides evidence for its occurrence in Feb. 1318, see Tsugitaka, *State & Rural Society*, pp. 163–4.
134. Friedman, *The Nuṣayrī-'Alawīs*, p. 58; Tsugitaka, *State & Rural Society*, p. 164.
135. Friedman, *The Nuṣayrī-'Alawīs*, pp. 59–60.
136. Tsugitaka, *State & Rural Society*, pp. 163–7.
137. Ibid. p. 167; the exact extent of the area that this group claimed sovereignty over is unclear.
138. Ibid. pp. 167–9, cites Ibn Kathir, XIV, p. 83.
139. Ibid. p. 175.
140. Friedman, *The Nuṣayrī-'Alawīs*, p. 56.
141. Ibn Battuta, *Tuhfat al-nuzzar*, p. 292, cited in Friedman, *The Nuṣayrī-'Alawīs*, p. 2; Daniel Pipes, 'The Alawi Capture of Power in Syria', *Middle Eastern Studies*, 25, 4 (Oct. 1989), p. 436.
142. Friedman, *The Nuṣayrī-'Alawīs*, p. 62.
143. See Reuven Amitai, (ed.) *The Mongols in Islamic Lands*, pp. 359–90.

144. Friedman, *The Nuṣayrī-ʿAlawīs*, p. 62.

145. Sarah K. Raphael, *Climate and Political Climate: Environmental Disasters in the Medieval Levant*, Leiden: Brill, 2013, pp. 73–90. Philip Jenkins, *The Lost History of Christianity*, New York: HarperCollins, 2008, pp. 135–6.

146. Yaron Friedman, 'Ibn Taymiyya's Fatwa against the Nusayri-Alawi Sect', *Der Islam*, 85, 2 (2005), p. 350.

147. Yvette Talhamy, 'The Fatwas and the Nusayri/Alawis of Syria', *Middle Eastern Studies*, 46, 2 (2010), pp. 178–9.

148. Ibid. p. 179; see also Donald Little, 'The Historical and Historiographical Significance of the Detention of Ibn Taymiyya', *International Journal of Middle East Studies*, 4 (1973), pp. 311–27.

149. Talhamy, 'The Fatwas', pp. 180–1; Winter, *The Shiites*, p. 63.

150. Tsugitaka, *State & Rural Society*, pp. 175–6; Talhamy, 'The Fatwas', p. 180.

151. Talhamy, 'The Fatwas', p. 177.

152. Ibid. p. 179.

153. Ibid. p. 180.

154. Friedman, 'Ibn Taymiyya's Fatwa', p. 349.

155. Talhamy, 'The Fatwas', p. 178.

156. Nibras Kazimi, 'The Perfect Enemy', *New York Sun*, 1 June 2007, http://www.nysun.com/opinion/perfect-enemy/55690/

157. Harris, *The Levant*, p. 100.

158. See ibid. p. 99 for an explanation of the Mamluks' new geopolitical concerns.

159. Moosa, *Extremist Shiites*, p. 273.

160. Allen Fromherz, *Ibn Khaldun, Life and Times*, Edinburgh: Edinburgh University Press, 2010, p. 1.

161. Khuri, *Imams and Emirs*, p. 74.

162. De Planhol, *Minorités En Islam*, p. 89.

163. Albert Hourani, *The Emergence of the Modern Middle East*, London: Macmillan, 1981, pp. 19–35.

164. Colin Imber, *The Ottoman Empire 1300–1650*, Basingstoke and New York: Palgrave-Macmillan, 2002, p. 216.

165. Ibid. p. 48.

166. Moosa, *Extremist Shiites*, p. 275.

167. Ibid. p. 275; M.G. Al-Tawil, *T'arikh al-ʿAlawiyyun*, 4th edn, Beirut: Dar al-Andalus, 1981, pp. 394–5, cited in Talhamy, 'The Nusayri Leader', p. 895; see also Talhamy, 'The Fatwas', pp. 181–2; Pipes, 'The Alawi', p. 436.

168. Moosa, *Extremist Shiites*, p. 275.

169. Ibid.

170. J.C. Russell, 'Late Medieval Balkan and Asia Minor Population', *Journal of the Economic and Social History of the Orient*, 3, 3 (1960), p. 268, n. 5.

171. Stefan Winter commented on the 'informal' Ottoman toleration afforded to heterodox Shi'ite groups like the Alawites, see Winter, *The Shiites*, p. 18.

172. Henry Maundrell, *A Journey from Aleppo to Jerusalem in 1697*, Beirut: Kyats, 1963, pp. 16–17.

173. Harris, *The Levant*, pp. 107–8.

174. Stefan Winter, 'The Nusayris before the Tanzimat in the Eyes of Ottoman Provincial Administrators 1804–1834', in T. Philip and C. Schumann (eds), *From the Syrian Land to the States of Syria and Lebanon*, Beirut: Orient-Institute, 2004, p. 109; Winter also mentioned how the Alawites around Safita, in the southern part of the Jabal al-Sahili-yah, came under the jurisdiction of the Shi'ite Hamadas from Lebanon. See Winter, *The Shiites*, p. 80.

175. It seems that these Alawite transgressions against Ottoman authority went largely unpunished, see Winter, *The Shiites*, pp. 106, 113.

176. Louvain, 'Revue d'Etudes Turques', no. 17, in R. Murphey (ed.), *Studies on Ottoman Society and Culture, 16th–18th Centuries*, Aldershot: Ashgate, 2007, pp. XIV, 205.

177. Ibid. pp. XIV, 207.

178. Ibid. pp. XIV, 208.

179. Frederick Walpole, *The Ansayrii (or Assassins) with Travels in the Further East in 1850–51*, Part 1, London: Richard Bentley, 1851, p. 45; see p. 368, for a description of Alawite tobacco production in 1850–1.

180. Louvain, 'Revue d'Etudes Turques', pp. XIV, 212; I visited Suwaydiyya in Turkey (now called Samandağ) in Mar. 2011, and was surprised to find that approximately 90 per cent of the city is Alawite.

181. Ibid. pp. XIV, 213.

182. Jacques Weulersse, 1940, pp. 324–5, cited in De Planhol, *Minorités En Islam*, p. 89.

183. 'Syria Issues Tough New Law against Killer Tobacco', Middle East Online, Damascus, 6 Dec. 2009, IRIN, http://www.middle-east-online.com/english/?id=36089

184. Talhamy, 'The Nusayri Leader', p. 896.

185. Dick Douwes, *The Ottomans in Syria: A History of Justice and Oppression*, London: I.B. Tauris, 2000, p. 142; See also Bernard Lewis, 'Ottoman Land Tenure and Taxation in Syria', *Studia Islamica*, 50 (1979), p. 121; Winter, 'The Nusayris', p. 106, mentions another discriminatory tax, the *mīrī*.

186. Douwes, *The Ottomans in Syria*, p. 80.

187. Ibid. pp. 142–3.

188. Ibn Jibrail al-Qila'i, *Zajaliyyat*, vol. 1, Beirut: Dar Lahad Khatar, 1982, p. 138.

189. Ibid. vol. 2, p. 501.

190. Winter, 'The Nusayris', p. 108; Samuel Lyde provides details about what could possibly be the same event except the Frenchman is recorded as a Captain Boutin, who was robbed and murdered by bandits at 'Arab al-Mulk', south of Jablah in the Kalbiyya district, see Samuel Lyde, *The Asian Mystery Illustrated in the History, Religion, and Present State of the Ansaireeh or Nusairis of Syria*, London: Longman, Green, Longman & Roberts, 1860, pp. 194–5.

191. تاريخ ولاية سليمان باشا العادل ١٨١٩-١٨٠٤ (History of the Province of Suleyman Pasha al-'Adel, 1804–19), Ibrahim al-'Awra, trans. Leon Goldsmith and Jean-Luc Payan, 2010.

192. Winter, 'The Nusayris', p. 106.

193. G. Prochazka-Eisl and S. Prozchazka, *The Plain of Saints and Prophets: The Nusayri-Alawi Community of Cilicia (Southern Turkey) and its Sacred Places*, Wiesbaden: Harrassowitz Verlag, 2010, pp. 56–7; see also, Winter, 'The Nusayris', p. 104.

194. Lyde, *The Asian Mystery*, p. 196.

195. Ibn Khaldun, *The Muqaddimah: An Introduction to History*, trans. Franz Rosenthal, abridged N.J. Dawood, London: Routledge & Kegan Paul, 1967, p. 152.

196. Harris, *The Levant*, p. 112; this is very likely the same person as the 'Saqar al-Mahfouz' noted by Ibn Jibrail, *Zajaliyyat*, vol. 2, p. 501.

197. Douwes, *The Ottomans in Syria*, p. 70 and n. 22, p. 70.

198. Talhamy, 'The Fatwas', p. 183; Lyde, *The Asian Mystery*, p. 196.

199. Winter, 'The Nusayris', p. 102.

200. Ibid.

2. INTEGRATION

1. M. Abir, 'Modernisation, Reaction and Muhammad Ali's "Empire"', *Middle Eastern Studies*, 13, 3 (1977), pp. 295–313.

2. Yvette Talhamy, 'The Nusayri and Druze Minorities in Syria in the Nineteenth Century: The Revolt against the Egyptian Occupation as a Case Study', *Middle Eastern Studies*, 48, 6 (Nov. 2012), p. 974.

3. Stefan Winter, 'The Nusayris before the Tanzimat in the Eyes of Ottoman Provincial Administrators 1804–1834', in T. Philip and C. Schumann (eds), *From the Syrian Land to the States of Syria and Lebanon*, Beirut: Orient-Institute, 2004, p. 105.

4. Frederick Walpole, *The Ansayrii (or Assassins) with Travels in the Further East in 1850–51*, Part 3 London: Richard Bentley, 1851, p. 165.

5. Yvette Talhamy, 'The Nusayri Leader Isma'il Khayr Bey and the Ottomans (1854–58)', *Middle Eastern Studies*, 44, 6 (2008), p. 896.

6. Walpole, *The Ansayrii*, Part 3.

7. Yvette Talhamy, 'The Fatwas and the Nusayri/Alawis of Syria', *Middle Eastern Studies*, 46, 2 (2010), p. 183.

8. Ibid. p. 183.

9. Christians and non-Muslims were exempt from the *nizam* (military service), having to pay a tax instead. See Walpole, *The Ansayrii*, p. 186.

10. Roger Owen, *The Middle East in the World Economy 1800–1914*, London and New York: Methuen, 1981, p. 77.

11. Dick Douwes, *The Ottomans in Syria: A History of Justice and Oppression*, London: I.B. Tauris, 2000, p. 197.

12. De Planhol, *Minorités En Islam*, p. 87.

13. William Harris, *Lebanon: A History 600–2011*, New York: Oxford University Press, 2012, p. 139; S.J. Shaw and E.K. Shaw, *History of the Ottoman Empire and Modern Turkey*, Cambridge: Cambridge University Press, 1977, p. 57.

14. Talhamy, 'The Nusayri Leader', p. 896.

15. Walpole, *The Ansayrii*, p. 353.

16. Talhamy, 'The Nusayri Leader', p. 897; the name *al-Sinjari* suggests that Ismail Khayr Bey was possibly a descendant of al-Makzun or one of his followers from Sinjar.

17. Ibid. p. 898; assuming that the Alawites constituted around 70 per cent of the rural peasants in the Jabal in the early nineteenth century, and taking into account populations in the north, this figure suggests that the 'Alawite population was now somewhere around 100,000.

18. Ibid. pp. 898–900.

19. Reverend Henry H. Jessup, *Fifty-Three Years in Syria*, London: Fleming H. Revell, 1910, p. 152.

20. Ibid. p. 152; cited also in Talhamy, 'The Fatwas', p. 902.

21. Talhamy, 'The Nusayri Leader', p. 905.

22. Jessup, *Fifty-Three Years*, p. 152.

23. Talhamy, 'The Nusayri Leader', p. 903.

24. Jessup, *Fifty-Three Years*, p. 152; Yvette Talhamy, 'The Nusayri Leader', p. 904.

25. Talhamy, 'The Nusayri Leader', p. 906.

26. Samuel Lyde, *The Asian Mystery Illustrated in the History, Religion, and Present State of the Ansaireeh or Nusairis of Syria*, London: Longman, Green, Longman & Roberts, 1860, p. 209.

27. Winter, 'The Nusayris', p. 111.

28. Ibid. p. 111.

29. Walpole, *The Ansayrii*, Part 1, p. 157.

30. Winter, 'The Nusayris', pp. 110–11.

31. Talhamy, 'The Nusayri Leader', p. 898.

32. Winter, 'The Nusayris', p. 112.

33. De Planhol, *Minorités En Islam*, pp. 89–91; Hanna Batatu, *Syria's Peasantry: The Descendants of its Lesser Rural Notables and their Politics*, Princeton, NJ: Princeton University Press, 1999, p. 41; this claim has, however, since been challenged by scholars such as Stefan Winter (2015, forthcoming).

34. Jessup, *Fifty-Three Years*, p. 379.

35. Ibid. pp. 255, 261, 263.

36. See in particular, Bar-Asher and Kofksy, *The Nusayri-ʿAlawī Religion: An Enquiry into its Theology and Liturgy*, Leiden: Brill, 2002.

37. Yvette Talhamy, 'American Protestant Missionary Activity among the Nusayris (Alawis) in Syria in the Nineteenth Century', *Middle Eastern Studies*, 47, 2 (2011), p. 224.

38. Edward E. Salisbury, 'First Ripe Fruit, Disclosing the Mysteries of the Nusairian Religion', *Journal of the American Oriental Society*, 8 (1866), pp. 227–308.

39. Jessup, *Fifty-Three Years*, pp. 261–2.

40. Ibid. pp. 263–4.

41. J.P. Fetcher, *Notes From Nineveh*, Philadelphia: Lea & Blanchard, 1850, p. 313.

42. Talhamy, 'American Protestant Missionary Activity', pp. 215–36.

43. The British formed an alliance with the Druze to balance the French influence among the Maronites, see: Shakeeb Salih, 'The British–Druze Connection and the Druze Rising of 1896 in the Hawran', *Middle East Studies*, 13, 2 (May 1977), pp. 251–7.

44. Talhamy, 'American Protestant Missionary Activity', p. 217.

45. K. Salibi and Y. Khoury, *The Missionary Herald: Reports from Ottoman Syria 1819–1870*, vol. 2, Amman: Royal Institute for Inter-Faith Studies, 1995, p. 65, cited in Talhamy, 'American Protestant Missionary Activity', p. 221.

46. Talhamy, 'American Protestant Missionary Activity', p. 224.

47. Jessup, *Fifty-Three Years*, p. 436.

48. Ibid. Appendix I, pp. 797–800.

49. According to Jessup, out of 650 sworn conversions among the Alawites (and some Greek Orthodox) in 1861–76, only twelve remained actively Protestant, see Jessup, *Fifty-Three Years*, p. 351; Talhamy, 'American Protestant Missionary Activity', p. 224.

50. Talhamy, 'American Protestant Missionary Activity', p. 226.

51. Apart from religious shaykhs the majority of Alawites were illiterate in the nineteenth century, see ibid. p. 221.

52. Jessup, *Fifty-Three Years*, p. 436; the schools were subsequently reopened following Western diplomatic pressure on the Ottoman authorities, who continued to look for ways to stem missionary work among the Alawites, Talhamy, 'American Protestant Missionary Activity', pp. 228–32.

53. Winter, 'The Nusayris', p. 112; Talhamy, 'American Protestant Missionary Activity', p. 230.

54. Talhamy, 'American Protestant Missionary Activity', p. 232.

55. According to information transmitted to the author by his grandson, Issa Ibrahim, the well-known Alawite Shaykh Saleh al-Ali engaged in small-scale guerrilla warfare against Ottoman forces during the course of World War I.

56. Christopher Andrew and A.S. Kanya-Forstner, *The Climax of French Imperial Expansion 1914–1924*, London: Thames & Hudson, 1981, p. 107.

57. Allied naval blockades also played a part in preventing food supplies reaching Mount Lebanon, see G. Agoston and B. Masters, *Encyclopaedia of the Ottoman Empire*, New York: Infobase, 2009, p. 330.

58. According to Stephen Longrigg, *Syria and Lebanon under French Mandate*, London: Oxford University Press, 1958, p. 47, the local population generally ignored the Ottoman call to jihad.

59. Yigal Sheffy, *British Military Intelligence in the Palestine Campaign, 1914–1918*, London: Frank Cass, 1998, p. 80.

60. Andrew and Kanya-Forstner, *The Climax*, pp. 108–110.

61. Longrigg, *Syria and Lebanon*, pp. 8–9.

62. Keith Watenpaugh, *Being Modern in the Middle East: Revolution, Nationalism, Colonialism and the Arab Middle Class*, Princeton, NJ: Princeton University Press, 2006, p. 138.

63. 'The King–Crane Commission Report'—Confidential Appendix, Henry C. King and

Charles R. Crane—28 Aug. 1919. V. 55, No. 27, 2nd Section, 2 Dec. 1922, I. II. 2. 'Wishes of the People'.

64. Longrigg, *Syria and Lebanon*, pp. 80, 121–2.
65. Matti Moosa, *Extremist Shiites: The Ghulat Sects*, New York: Syracuse University Press, 1988, p. 283, suggests that Saleh al-'Ali only agreed to peace with the French if the Syrian seacoast was added to the Syrian state; Longrigg, *Syria and Lebanon*, p. 95, suggests that arms and propaganda from Damascus were sent to Saleh al-'Ali.
66. Phillip Khoury, *Syria and the French Mandate: The Politics of Arab Nationalism 1920–1945*, London: I.B. Tauris, 1987, pp. 99–102; Daniel Pipes, 'The Alawi Capture of Power in Syria', *Middle Eastern Studies*, 25, 4 (Oct. 1989), p. 438.
67. Issa Ibrahim, email correspondence with the author (trans. Amer Chaikouni), July 2014. See also Moosa, *Extremist Shiites*, pp. 282–3.
68. Shaykh Nasīr Eskiocak, interview with the author, Antakya, 29 Mar. 2011.
69. Walpole, *The Ansayrii*, p. 370.
70. Longrigg, *Syria and Lebanon*, p. 113.
71. See Martin Thomas, *Empires of Intelligence*, Berkeley: University of California Press, 2008, p. 159, for a summary of the French 'Moroccan Formula' in Syria.
72. Martin Thomas, 'Crisis Management in Colonial States: Intelligence and Counter-Insurgency in Morocco and Syria after the First World War', *Intelligence and National Security*, 21, 5 (2006), p. 706; Longrigg, *Syria and Lebanon*, pp. 117, 207.
73. Edmund Burke III, 'A Comparative View of French Native Policy in Morocco and Syria, 1912–1925', *Middle East Studies*, 9, 1 (1973), p. 175.
74. William Harris, *The Levant: A Fractured Mosaic*, Princeton: Markus Wiener, 2003, pp. 125–6.
75. Longrigg, *Syria and Lebanon*, p. 125; Khoury, *Syria*, p. 138.
76. *League of Nations Official Journal* (Sep. 1930), Article 1, p. 1124.
77. De Planhol, *Minorités En Islam*, p. 377.
78. *League of Nations Official Journal*, 95th Session of the Council, Annex 1629 'The Mandate' 24 July 1922 (Jan. 1937), Article 8, p. 47.
79. E.J. Brill, *First Encyclopaedia of Islam 1913–1936*, Leiden: Brill (1927; 1993).
80. Ibid.
81. Ibid.; French figures from 1936 put the Alawites as 69, the Sunnis 17 and the Christians 14 per cent of the Alawite State: Longrigg, *Syria and Lebanon*, p. 207, n. 1.
82. The longest-standing governor was M. Schoeffler, who was governor of the Alawite territory from 1927 to 1935, Longrigg, *Syria and Lebanon*, p. 209.
83. De Planhol, *Minorités En Islam*, p. 378. Longrigg, *Syria and Lebanon*, p. 210.
84. Arend Lijphart, *Thinking about Democracy*, Oxon: Routledge, 2008, p. 279.
85. De Planhol, *Minorités En Islam*, p. 378. Longrigg, *Syria and Lebanon*, p. 210.
86. Ibid.
87. Tourists to the region, including the Lebanon, Alawite hills and the Amanus ranges reached 36,000 per annum in 1939. See Longrigg, *Syria and Lebanon*, p. 285, n. 1.

88. Patrick Seale, *Asad of Syria: The Struggle for the Middle East*, London: I.B. Tauris, 1988, p. 57.

89. Barry Posen, 'The Security Dilemma and Ethnic Conflict', in M. Brown (ed.), *Ethnic Conflict and International Security*, Princeton, NJ: Princeton University Press, 1993, p. 103

90. Gitta Yaffe and Uriel Dann, 'Suleiman al-Murshid: Beginnings of an Alawi Leader', *Middle Eastern Studies*, 29, 4 (Oct. 1993), pp. 624–40.

91. Ibid.

92. Ibid. p. 625.

93. Eyal Zisser, 'The 'Alawis, Lords of Syria', in Ofra Bengio and Gabriel Ben-Dor (eds), *Minorities and the State in the Arab World*, Boulder and London: Lynne Rienner Publishers, 1999, p. 143, n. 10.

94. Yaffe and Dann, 'Suleiman al-Murshid', p. 630.

95. Itamar Rabinovitch, *The View From Damascus: State, Political Community and Foreign Relations in Twentieth-Century Syria*, Edgware: Valentine Mitchell, 2008, p. 85.

96. Yaffe and Dann, 'Suleiman al-Murshid', pp. 624–40.

97. Shaykh 'Ali Yeral, interview with the author, Antakya, 28 Mar. 2011.

98. *League of Nations Official Journal* (Sep. 1930), p. 1124, 'Decree of the High Commissioner of the French Republic', no. 3113.

99. Khoury, *Syria*, p. 59.

100. *League of Nations Official Journal* (Sep. 1930), Article 11, p. 1125.

101. Ibid. Article 18, p. 1126.

102. De Planhol, *Minorités En Islam*, p. 378.

103. 'Letter from the French Government to the Secretary General of the League of Nations, Paris, June 11th, 1930', *League of Nations Official Journal* (Sep. 1930), Article 18, p. 1100.

104. *League of Nations Official Journal*, 95th Session of the Council, Annex 1629 'The Mandate', 24 July 1922 (Jan. 1937), Article 13, p. 48.

105. The text and intention of the Mandate mirrored very closely the wording of the King–Crane Commission Report of 1919 which also referred to 'religious liberty' and the 'success of the new Arab State'. Note that it refers to a State singular, not plural. See: 'The King-Crane Commission Report'—Confidential Appendix, Henry C. King and Charles R. Crane—28 Aug. 1919. V. 55, No. 27, 2nd Section, 2 Dec. 1922, III. 6.

106. See N.E. Bou-Nacklie, 'Les Troupes Spéciales: Religious and Ethnic Recruitment, 1916–46', *International Journal of Middle East Studies*, 25, 4 (1993), pp. 545–660.

107. Bou-Nacklie, 'Les Troupes Spéciales,' p. 649; Khoury, *Syria*, p. 630.

108. Ibid. pp. 648–50.

109. Ibid. p. 651; In 1930 the Troupes Spéciales numbered 9,500 but by 1935 numbered 14,000, see Longrigg, *Syria*, p. 269.

110. Ibid. p. 656.

111. Jennifer Dueck, *Educational Conquest: Schools as a Sphere of Politics in French Mandate*

Syria, 1936–1946, Oxford: Oxford University Press, 2006, p. 443; Gitta Yaffe-Schatzmann, 'Alawi Separatists and Unionists: The Events of 25 February 1936', *Middle Eastern Studies*, 31, 1 (Jan. 1995), pp. 29–30.

112. *League of Nations Official Journal*, 104th Session of the Council, Annex 1742 (Feb. 1939), p. 162.

113. Yaffe-Schatzmann, 'Alawi Separatists', p. 30.

114. *League of Nations Official Journal*, 93rd and 94th Sessions of the Council, Annex 1622 (Nov. 1936), p. 1354.

115. Moosa, *Extremist Shiites*, pp. 287–8.

116. Joseph Brewda and Linda de Hoyos, 'The Anglo-French Patrons of Syria's Hafez al-Assad', *Executive Intelligence Review*, 23, 45 (8 Nov. 1996), p. 25.

117. Longrigg, *Syria*, p. 130; Moosa, *Extremist Shiites*, pp. 290–1, cites Archives du Ministère, Paris, E. 412.2, file 393, 8 and file 493, 7.

118. Yaffe-Schatzmann, 'Alawi Separatists', p. 30; according to Yaffe-Schatzmann, Ayubi's Alawite origins were mentioned in the 'Rogues Gallery' by Consul Hole to Rendel, Damascus, 15 July 1932, cites FO 371 16088.

119. Ibid. pp. 35–6

120. Peter Shambrook, *French Imperialism in Syria, 1927–1936*, Reading: Ithaca, 1998, p. 223.

121. Yaffe-Schatzmann, 'Alawi Separatists', p. 35.

122. Paulo Boneschi, "Une fatwà du Grande Mufti de Jérusalem Muhammad Amin al-Husayni sur les Alawites," *Revue de l'histoire des religions* 122(1), July–August 1940, pp. 42–54; Talhamy, 'The Fatwas', pp. 185–6

123. Talhamy, 'The Fatwas', p. 185.

124. *League of Nations Official Journal*, 104th Session of the Council, Annex 1742 (Feb. 1939), p. 162; Longrigg, *Syria*, p. 244.

125. *League of Nations Official Journal*, 104th Session of the Council, Annex 1742 (Feb. 1939), A. 'Observations of the Administration of Certain Territories under Mandate', pp. 161–2; Longrigg, *Syria*, p. 236.

126. James A. Melki, 'Syria and State Department 1937–47', *Middle Eastern Studies*, 33, 1 (Jan. 1997), p. 93.

127. N.E. Bou-Nacklie, 'The 1941 Invasion of Syria and Lebanon: The Role of the Local Paramilitary', *Middle Eastern Studies*, 30, 3 (July 1994), pp. 520–1.

128. Ibid. p. 520.

129. Melki, 'Syria and State Department', pp. 96–7.

130. Götz Nordbruch, *Nazism in Syria and Lebanon*, Oxon: Routledge, 2009, p. 141.

131. Longrigg, *Syria*, p. 348.

132. Onn Winckler, *Arab Political Demography: Population Growth, Labor Migration and Natalist Policies*, 2nd edn, Eastbourne: Sussex Academic Press, 2009, p. 34.

133. Salma Mardem-Bey, *Syria's Quest for Independence 1939–1945*, Beirut: Ithaca, 1994, p. xxiv.

134. Radwan Ziadeh, *Power and Policy in Syria*, London: I.B. Tauris, 2011, p. 16.

135. Hanna Batatu, 'Some Observations on the Social Roots of Syria's Ruling, Military Group and the Causes for its Dominance', *Middle East Journal*, 35, 3 (1981), pp. 341–2.

136. Patrick Seale, *Asad of Syria: The Struggle for the Middle East*, Berkeley: University of California Press, 1989, p. 38.

137. Batatu, 'Some Observations', p. 341.

138. Bou-Nacklie, 'Les Troupes Spéciales', p. 652; see also N.E. Bou-Nacklie, 'The Avenantaires: Syrian Mercenaries in French Africa', *Middle Eastern Studies*, 27, 4 (Oct. 1991), pp. 654–67.

139. Bou-Nacklie, 'The Avenantaires', pp. 654, 665, n. 2.

140. Amos Perlmutter, 'From Obscurity to Rule: The Syrian Army and the Ba'th Party', *The Western Political Quarterly*, 22, 4 (Dec. 1969), p. 830, n. 6.

141. Bou-Nacklie, 'Les Troupes Spéciales', pp. 654–5.

142. Perlmutter, 'From Obscurity', p. 830, n. 6.

143. Batatu, 'Some Observations', p. 342; Batatu, *Syria's Peasantry*, p. 158; Eliezer Be'eri, *Army Officers in Arab Politics and Society*, New York: Praeger Publishers, 1969, p. 336.

144. James A. Melki, 'Syria and State Department', p. 102.

145. Ibid. pp. 102–3.

146. This is not to say that the Turkish military has not been involved in Turkish politics; however, in terms of consistently passing power back to civilian politicians, the Turkish military stands in contrast with the Syrian armed forces.

147. Perlmutter, 'From Obscurity', p. 830.

148. Yaffe and Dann, 'Suleiman al-Murshid', p. 638; see also: Longrigg, *Syria*, p. 344, for a description of Suleiman al-Murshid's demise.

149. Mahmud Faksh, 'The Alawi Community of Syria: A New Dominant Political Force', *Middle Eastern Studies*, 20, 2 (Apr. 1984), p. 139.

150. As observed by this researcher during field work in 2009 and 2011, Alawites still conduct dual lives: waged employment in the city and small-scale agriculture in their villages in the Jabal al-Sahiliyah.

151. Seale, *Asad of Syria*, p. 66.

152. According to the 1933 census, in 1933 there were 54,200 Arab Alawites in the Alexandretta region, compared to 20,400 Sunni Arabs and 70,800 (mainly Sunni) Turks, cited in Longrigg, *Syria*, p. 238, n. 2.

153. See Keith D. Watenpaugh, 'Creating Phantoms: Zaki al-Arsuzi, the Alexandretta Crisis, and Formation of Modern Arab Nationalism in Syria', *International Journal of Middle East Studies*, 28 (1996), pp. 363–89.

154. Shaykh Nasīr Eskiocak, interview with the author, Antakya, 29 Mar. 2011. The shaykh also mentioned two other prominent individuals who moved to Syria at this time: Hasan Jabara, who would be part of Hosni Zaim's government in Syria, and the Shaykh Nasr al-Din Seifa.

155. Nabil M. Kaylani, 'The Rise of the Syrian Ba'th, 1940–1958: Political Success, Party Failure', *International Journal of Middle East Studies*, 3, 1 (Jan. 1972), pp. 3–4.

156. Gordon H. Torrey, 'The Ba'th: Ideology and Practice', *Middle East Journal*, 23, 4 (Autumn, 1969), p. 445.

157. Seale, *Asad of Syria*, p. 89.

158. Michael van Dusen, 'Political Integration and Regionalism in Syria', *Middle East Journal*, 26, 2 (Spring 1972), p. 133.

159. Ibid.

160. Seale, *Asad of Syria*, p. 34; ibid. p. 27.

161. The Sunni officer Amin Hafiz's inability to recognise the 'machinations of his minority subordinates' is a good example of this; Martin Seymour calls this a 'Caesar–Brutus syndrome', see M. Seymour, 'The Dynamics of Power in Syria since the Break with Egypt', *Middle Eastern Studies*, 6, 1 (Jan. 1970), p. 37.

162. Pipes, 'The Alawi Capture of Power' in Syria', p. 441.

163. Watenpaugh, *Being Modern*, p. 299; Seymour, 'The Dynamics', p. 43.

164. Jordi Tejel, *Syria's Kurds: History, Politics and Society*, Oxon: Routledge, 2009, pp. 46–9.

165. Ibid. p. 46.

166. Van Dusen, 'Political Integration', p. 132.

167. On 23 Aug. 1962 Syria was first proclaimed 'The Syrian Arab Republic' and an ensuing special census stripped 120,000 Kurds of their Syrian citizenship, Tejel, *Syria's Kurds*, p. 50; On the SSNP, see Daniel Pipes, 'Radical Politics and the Syrian Social Nationalist Party', *International Journal of Middle East Studies*, 20, 3 (Aug. 1988), pp. 303–24.

168. See Torrey, 'The Ba'th', pp. 445–70; Ulrike Freitag, 'Historical Correctness: The Ba'th Party in Syria', *Middle Eastern Studies*, 35, 1 (Jan. 1999), pp. 1–16; Nabil, 'The Rise', pp. 3–23; Malcolm Kerr, 'Hafiz Asad and the Changing Patterns of Syrian Politics', *International Journal*, 28, 3 (Summer 1973), pp. 689–706; Perlmutter, 'From Obscurity', pp. 827–45.

169. Talhamy, 'The Fatwas', p. 187.

170. Ibid.

171. Batatu, 'Some Observations', p. 341.

172. Seymour, 'The Dynamics', p. 39.

173. For examples of Egyptian agricultural schemes in the Alawite territory see Nevill Barbour, 'Impressions of the United Arab Republic', *International Affairs*, 36, 1 (Jan. 1960), p. 28.

174. Torrey, 'The Ba'th', pp. 457–8.

175. Itamar Rabinovich, *Syria Under the Ba'th, 1963–66: The Army–Party Symbiosis*, Jerusalem: Israel Universities Press, 1972, pp. 24–5.

176. Seymour, 'The Dynamics', p. 39.

177. Annie Laurent, 'Syrie–Liban: faux frères jumeaux', *Politique Ètrangère*, 48 (1983), p. 598; Moosa, *Extremist Shiites*, pp. 301–2.

178. Seymour, 'The Dynamics', p. 39.

179. Leon Goldsmith, 'Unearthing the Alawites: The Political Geography of the Alawite Community of Syria', Dunedin, Honours Dissertation, University of Otago, New Zealand, 2007, p. 43.

180. Nikolaos van Dam, *The Struggle for Power in Syria*, 2nd edn, London: I.B. Tauris, 1996, p. 175, n. 69.

181. Seymour, 'The Dynamics', p. 39; Batatu, 'Some Observations', p. 341.

182. Seale, *Asad of Syria*, p. 64.

183. Kerr, 'Hafiz Asad', p. 693; Tejel, *Syria's Kurds*, p. 134.

184. Winckler, *Arab Political Demography*, 2009, p. 34.

185. Ibid.

186. Seale, *Asad of Syria*, p. 68.

187. Ibid.

188. Seymour, 'The Dynamics', pp. 35–6.

189. Kerr, 'Hafiz Asad', p. 694; Seymour, 'The Dynamics', p. 37.

190. 'A study of the composition of Syrian army units in 1964 discloses that the proportion of Alawites in individual brigades ran from 20 percent to as much as 100 percent.' Seymour, 'The Dynamics', p. 40.

191. Issa Ibrahim, email correspondence with the author, July 2014.

192. Ibid.

193. Batatu, 'Some Observations', p. 344.

194. Rural Sunnis could also be included in Batatu's definition; however, rural-based religious minorities were even more reliant on each other based on their sectarian insecurity.

195. T. Olsson, E. Ozdalga and C. Raudvere (eds), *Alevi Identity: Cultural, Religious and Social Perspectives*, Papers Read at a Conference Held at the Swedish Institute in Istanbul, Nov. 1996, Swedish Research Institute in Istanbul, Transactions, vol. 8, 1998, p. 181.

196. Extract from a translation of *al-Taqrir al-Watha'iqi li-Azmat al-Hizb* (The Documentary Report on the Party's Crisis), pp. 88–93, Appendix B. Nikolaos van Dam, *The Struggle for Power in Syria*, New York: St Martin's Press, 1979, p. 110.

197. Ibid. p. 113.

198. Nikolaos van Dam, *The Struggle for Power in Syria*, 2nd edn, London: I.B. Tauris, 1996, p. 139.

199. Torrey, 'The Ba'th', p. 468; the final insult to the founders of the Ba'ath Party perhaps came when Michel Aflaq's memorial in Baghdad was converted into a shopping mall for US soldiers, Reuters, Baghdad, 20 Sep. 2009, 'Aflaq, Symbol of Iraq and Syria's Shared Past', http://blogs.reuters.com/global/2009/09/20/aflaq-symbol-of-iraq-and-syrias-shared-past/

200. Seymour, 'The Dynamics', p. 40.

201. Nikolaos van Dam, *The Struggle for Power in Syria*, 2nd edn, London: I.B Tauris, 1996, pp. 62–74.

202. Daniel Pipes, *Greater Syria: The History of an Ambition*, New York: Oxford University Press, 1990, p. 160.

203. Van Dam. *The Struggle for Power in Syria: Politics and Society under Asad and the Ba'th Party*, 4th edn, New York: I.B. Tauris, 2011, p. 175, n. 69.

204. Seale, *Asad of Syria*, p. 63.

205. Ibid. p. 63.

206. His father was the commissioner of the Banyas district and his grandfather was one of the tribal leaders of the Haddadin tribal confederation, Nikolaos van Dam, *The Struggle for Power in Syria*, 2nd edn, London: I.B. Tauris, 1996, p. 175, n. 69.

207. Seale, *Asad of Syria*, p. 63.

208. Seymour, 'The Dynamics', pp. 41–2; Massimiliano Trentin, 'Modernization as State Building: The Two Germanies in Syria, 1963–1972', *Diplomatic History*, 33, 3 (June 2009), p. 493.

209. For example, see Eliezer Be'eri, *Army Officers in Arab Politics and Society*, New York: Praeger, 1969, p. 160.

210. Kerr, 'Hafiz Asad', pp. 694–5; Trentin, 'Modernization', pp. 492–3; Seymour, 'The Dynamics', p. 39.

211. Kerr, 'Hafiz Asad', p. 696.

212. See Hanna Batatu, 'Syria's Muslim Brethren', *MERIP Reports*, 110, Syria's Troubles (Nov.–Dec. 1982), p. 19; Trentin, 'Modernization', p. 494; Torrey, 'The Ba'th', pp. 445–70, p. 469.

213. Kerr, 'Hafiz Asad', pp. 698–9.

214. Tejel, *Syria's Kurds*, p. 58.

3. APOGEE AND DECLINE

1. See, for example, Mahmud A. Faksh, 'The Alawi Community of Syria: A New Dominant Political Force', *Middle Eastern Studies*, 20, 2 (Apr. 1984), pp. 133–53.

2. I. Rabinovitch, *The View from Damascus*, Edgware and Portland: Valentine Mitchell, 2008, p. 227.

3. Jordi Tejel, *Syria's Kurds: History, Politics and Society*, Oxon: Routledge, 2009, p. 64.

4. Raymond Hinnebusch, *Authoritarian Power and State Formation in Ba'athist Syria: Army, Party, and Peasant*, Boulder: Westview, 1990.

5. Keith Watenpaugh, *Being Modern in the Middle East: Revolution, Nationalism, Colonialism and the Arab Middle Class*, Princeton, NJ: Princeton University Press, 2006, p. 300.

6. Tejel, *Syria's Kurds*, p. 58.

7. Andrew Rathnell used the term 'keystone' to describe the importance of the Syrian Intelligence Services (Mukhabarat) to the Asad regime, see A. Rathnell, 'Syria's Intelligence Services: Origins and Development', *The Journal of Conflict Studies*, 16, 2 (1996).

8. Ibn Khaldun, *The Muqaddimah: An Introduction to History*, trans. Franz Rosenthal, abridged N.J. Dawood, London: Routledge & Kegan Paul, 1967, p. 146.

9. Tejel, *Syria's Kurds*, p. 83, suggests that the Syrian regime became 'capable of shaping the whole Syrian society'; Sylvia Chiffoleau said that it was time for Syrian society to 'emerge unified and cleansed of its ethnic denominational, social, and clannish blemishes'. Sylvia Chiffoleau (ed.), 'La Syrie au quotidian: Cultures et pratiques du changement,' *Revue des mondes musulmans et de la Méditerranée* (REMMM), nos 115–116, p. 10.

10. Patrick Seale, *Asad of Syria: The Struggle for the Middle East*, London: I.B. Tauris, 1988, p. 317.

11. D. Gubser, 'Minorities in Power: The Alawites of Syria', in R.D. Mclaurin (ed.), *The Political Role of Minority Groups in the Middle East*, New York: Greenwood, 1979, pp. 17–18.

12. Onn Winckler, *Arab Political Demography: Population Growth, Labor Migration and Natalist Policies*, 2nd edn, Eastbourne: Sussex Academic Press, 2009, p. 34.

13. Ibid. pp. 33–4.

14. Tord Olsson, 'The Gnosis of Mountaineers and Townspeople: The Religion of the Syrian Alawites, or the Nusairis', in T. Olsson (ed.), *Alevi Identity: Cultural, Religious and Social Perspectives*, Papers Read at a Conference Held at the Swedish Institute in Istanbul, Nov. 1996, Swedish Research Institute in Istanbul, Transactions, vol. 8, 1998, p. 168.

15. Winckler, *Arab Political Demography*, p. 62.

16. Hanna Batatu, 'Some Observations on the Social Roots of Syria's Ruling, Military Group and the Causes for its Dominance', *Middle East Journal*, 35, 3 (Summer 1981), p. 332.

17. Christa Salamandra, 'Consuming Damascus: Public Culture and the Construction of Social Identity', in W. Armbrust (ed.), *Mass Mediations: New Approaches to Popular Culture in the Middle East and Beyond*, Berkeley: University of California Press, 2000, pp. 329–36.

18. Edward R.F. Sheehan, 'How Kissinger Did It: Step by Step in the Middle East', *Foreign Policy*, 22 (Spring 1976), p. 42.

19. Nikolaos van Dam, *The Struggle for Power in Syria*, London: I.B. Tauris, 1996, pp. 137–8.

20. Daniel Pipes poses this question and suggests that sect is the most important element in Syrian politics; see D. Pipes, 'The Alawi Capture of Power in Syria', *Middle Eastern Studies*, 25, 4 (Oct. 1989), p. 446.

21. Abd al-Halim Khaddam, interview with the author, Paris, Sep. 2009.

22. Khaldun, *The Muqaddimah*, p. 146

23. Judge Detlev Mehlis commented on the 'statesman-like' qualities of Abd al-Halim Khaddam: interview with the author, Dunedin, May 2009.

24. Seale, *Asad of Syria*, p. 286.

25. Hanna Batatu, *Syria's Peasantry: The Descendants of its Lesser Rural Notables and their Politics*, Princeton, NJ: Princeton University Press, 1999, p. 237.

26. This is of course an exaggeration designed to make a point about the political volatility which existed prior to Hafiz al-Asad's capture of power in 1970.

27. Shaykh Nasīr Eskiocak, interview with the author, Antakya, 29 Mar. 2011.

28. Radwan Ziadeh, *Power and Policy in Syria*, New York: I.B. Tauris, 2011, pp. 139–40.

29. 'Syria Say Charter Wins 97.6 Percent of Vote', *New York Times*, 14 Mar. 1973.

30. 'Militant Syrian Leader: Nureddin al-Atassi', *New York Times*, 23 Sep. 1970.

31. Yvette Talhamy, 'The Fatwas and the Nusayri/Alawis of Syria', *Middle Eastern Studies*, 46, 2 (2010), p. 189.

32. Alasdair Drysdale, 'The Asad Regime and Its Troubles', *MERIP Reports*, 110, Syria's Troubles (Nov.–Dec. 1982), p. 8.

33. Juan de Onis, 'Religious Freedom in Charter Said to Stir Syrian Disorders', *New York Times*, 25 Feb. 1973.

34. *New York Times*, 14 Mar. 1973; 'Syrian Arab Republic Constitution', adopted 13 Mar. 1973: Chapter 1 Article 3(1): 'The Religion of the President of the Republic has to be Islam'.

35. Ziadeh, *Power and Policy*, p. 140.

36. Interview with the author.

37. Abd al-Halim Khaddam, interview with the author, Paris, Sep. 2009.

38. E. Sivan and M. Friedman, *Religious Radicalism and Politics in the Middle East*, Albany: State University of New York Press, 1990, p. 97; Talhamy, 'The Fatwas', p. 188.

39. Talhamy, 'The Fatwas', p. 188.

40. Ibid.

41. Ibid.

42. Sivan and Friedman, *Religious Radicalism*, p. 97.

43. Batatu, *Syria's Peasantry*, p. 20.

44. Talhamy, 'The Fatwas', p. 190.

45. Naomi Weinberger, *Syrian Intervention in Lebanon*, New York: Oxford University Press, 1986, p. 104.

46. Kamal Dib, *Warlords and Merchants*, Reading: Ithaca, 2004, p. 251.

47. Weinberger, *Syrian Intervention*, pp. 102–3.

48. Although Hafiz al-Asad began remedying this situation by moderating Syrian foreign policy, see: 'New Syrian Chief Realigns Party', *New York Times*, 17 Nov. 1970.

49. Weinberger, *Syrian Intervention*, p. 188. The Damascus Agreement was negotiated in February 1976 and outlined a constitutional restructuring of the Lebanese political system, which became a blueprint for Syria's 'special relationship' with Lebanon and the Taef Accord of 1989.

50. Ibid. pp. 197, 205, 207, 209.

51. Reuvan Avi-Ran, *The Syrian Involvement in Lebanon Since 1975*, Boulder: Westview Press, 1991, p. 184, n. 57; Tony Badran suggests that al-Sadr's ties to the Syrians and his deteriorating relations with the Palestinians cost him his life, see: 'Lebanon's Militia Wars', in B. Rubin (ed.), *Conflict and Insurgency in the Contemporary Middle East*, Oxon: Routledge, 2009, p. 172.

52. Abd al-Halim Khaddam suggested that Hafiz al-Asad's son, Bashar, 'grew up in a very non-religious environment', interview with this author. Also, Shaykh 'Ali Yeral explained that Hafiz al-Asad was not particularly knowledgeable in the Alawite religion, interview with this author, Antakya, 28 Mar. 2011.

53. Riad Yazbeck, 'Return of the Pink Panthers?' *Mideast Monitor*, 3, 2 (Aug. 2008); Talhamy, 'The Fatwas', pp. 189–90.

54. Yazbeck, 'Return'; Talhamy, 'The Fatwas', pp. 189–90.

55. Elie Salem, interview with this author, Balamand, 16 Mar. 2011; Salem is a former Lebanese foreign minister and academic who is currently president of Balamand University in Lebanon.

56. Yazbeck, 'Return'.

57. Olsson, The Gnosis, p. 180; see also Batatu, Syria's Peasantry, p. 20.

58. Yazbeck, 'Return'; Talhamy, 'The Fatwas', pp. 189–90.

59. Tejel, Syria's Kurds, p. 58.

60. Batatu, Syria's Peasantry, p. 299.

61. Norvelle DeAtkine, 'The Arab as Insurgent and Counterinsurgent', in Rubin, Conflict and Insurgency, p. 32.

62. Weinberger, Syrian Intervention, p. 81.

63. Avi-Ran, The Syrian Involvement, p. 7.

64. The Times, London, 23 June 1980.

65. 'Lebanese Christian Plea to Syria', The Times, 31 May 1976; C.L. Sulzberger, 'Shifting Levantine Patterns', New York Times, 26 June 1976.

66. Drysdale, 'The Asad Regime', pp. 4–5; 'President Assad of Syria Faces Disquiet at Home as Troops are Stretched across 300 Miles', The Times, London, 16 June 1976; Seale, Asad of Syria, pp. 283, 286.

67. Batatu, Syria's Peasantry, p. 300.

68. Ibid. p. 297.

69. Avi-Ran, The Syrian Involvement, p. 7.

70. New York Times, 26 June 1976.

71. Eric Pace, 'Adroit Syrian President, Hafiz al-Asad', New York Times, 10 May 1977.

72. For a discussion of the origins and ideology of the Syrian Muslim Brothers see: Itzchak Weismann, 'Sa'id Hawwa: The Making of a Radical Muslim Thinker in Modern Syria', Middle Eastern Studies, 29, 4 (Oct. 1993), pp. 601–23; see also, Seale, Asad of Syria, p. 322.

73. Weinberger, Syrian Intervention, p. 79.

74. Ibid. p. 79.

75. Book Review, Journal of Church and State, 26, 3 (1984), p. 548.

76. Umar F. Abdallah, The Islamic Struggle in Syria, Berkeley: Mizan Press, 1983, pp. 48, 211; also cited in Rabinovitch, The View, pp. 229–30.

77. James F. Clarity, 'Reporters Notebook: Syrians are Served News in Confusing Portions, Well Spiced by Rumors', New York Times, 10 Oct. 1976.

78. New York Times, 10 Oct. 1976.

79. 'Syria on Edge over College Murder', The Times, London, 3 Mar. 1977; New York Times, 10 July 1977; see also Seale, Asad of Syria, p. 317, for an extensive list of victims; Raphaël Lefèvre, Ashes of Hama: The Muslim Brotherhood in Syria, London: Hurst, 2013, p. 227.

80. New York Times, 10 July 1977; see also Seale, Asad of Syria, p. 321.

81. Avi-Ran, The Syrian Involvement, p. 198.

82. New York Times, 10 July 1977.

83. *The Times*, London, 3 Mar. 1977.

84. Farid al-Khazen, 'Kamal Jumblatt, the Uncrowned Druze Prince of the Left', *Middle Eastern Studies*, 24, 2 (Apr. 1988), p. 183; *New York Times*, 17 Mar. 1977.

85. Ibid.

86. حرب اللبنان (The Lebanon War), Documentary, Al-Jazeera, 2001.

87. Ibid.; see also Seale, *Asad of Syria*, pp. 288–9.

88. Ibid.

89. *New York Times*, 17 Mar. 1977.

90. Nikolaos van Dam suggests a figure of thirty-two, Nikolaos van Dam, *The Struggle for Power in Syria*, 2nd edn, London: I.B. Tauris, 1996, p. 91, while other sources give sixty as the casualty figure, *Journal of Church and State*, 21 (1979), p. 602; *New York Times*, 4 Sep. 1979; Seale, *Asad of Syria*, p. 316. Alawite sources give a larger figure of 100.

91. Nikolaos van Dam, *The Struggle for Power in Syria*, 2nd edn, London: I.B. Tauris, 1996, p. 91.

92. Marvine Howe, 'Moslem Extremists in Syria trying to Destabilise Government with Terrorist Attacks', *New York Times*, 20 Aug. 1979.

93. '3 More Alawites Slain in Syria', *New York Times*, 23 Sep. 1979.

94. See, for example, *New York Times*, 20 Aug. 1979.

95. Seale, *Asad of Syria*, pp. 323–4.

96. *New York Times*, 20 Aug. 1979.

97. 'CIA Accused of Fomenting Internal Disorder in Syria', *The Times*, London, 14 Mar. 1980; 'Assad's Star Fades in City where he was a Hero', *New York Times*, 3 Apr. 1980.

98. Christopher Wren, 'Political Killers in Syria Taking 2 to 3 Lives a Week', *New York Times*, 28 Oct. 1979.

99. *New York Times*, 14 Oct. 1979.

100. A report in the *New York Times*, 4 Sep. 1979 suggested zero casualties from sectarian fighting, whereas another report, *New York Times*, 14 Oct. 1979 reported forty dead from the rioting.

101. 'Syria Said to Send Army Troops to Latakia to Put Down Rioting', *New York Times*, 4 Sep. 1979; *Journal of Church and State*, 22 (1980), pp. 183–4.

102. *New York Times*, 4 Sep. 1979.

103. *New York Times*, 28 Oct. 1979.

104. Marvine Howe, *New York Times*, 20 Aug. 1979, cites diplomatic sources in Damascus.

105. Batatu, *Syria's Peasantry*, p. 271.

106. *New York Times*, 14 Oct. 1979.

107. Asad began by replacing six governors, see: 'Crisis Reportedly Defused by Show of Force', *New York Times*, 13 Apr. 1980; 'Technocrats Conspicuous in Syria's New Cabinet', *The Times*, London, 17 Jan. 1980.

108. John F. Kifner, 'Strains in Damascus Testing Assad Rule', *New York Times*, 28 Oct. 1979.

109. Robert Fisk, 'Sectarian Tensions over Alawite Dominance Could Lead to Outbreak of Civil War in Syria', *The Times*, London, 2 Apr. 1980; Stanley F. Reed, 'Dateline Syria: Fin de Règime?' *Foreign Policy*, 39 (Summer 1980), pp. 176–90.

110. 'Inflation and Corruption Threaten the Baathist Regime in Syria', *The Times*, London, 28 Mar. 1980.

111. *The Times*, London, 28 Mar. 1980.

112. Howe, 'Assad's Star Fades'.

113. *New York Times*, 3 Apr. 1980.

114. Robert Fisk, 'Disturbing Change of Style in Syria', *The Times*, London, 2 Apr. 1980.

115. Marvine Howe, *New York Times*, 3 Apr. 1980.

116. Stanley F. Reed, 'Dateline Syria: Fin de Règime?' *Foreign Policy*, 39 (Summer 1980), p. 176; 'Syrian Leader Eases Unrest and Strikes', *New York Times*, 13 Apr. 1980; see also Stanley Reed, 'Little Brother and The Brotherhood', *The Nation*, 16 May 1981, p. 592.

117. *New York Times*, 13 Apr. 1980; Reed, 'Dateline Syria', p. 176.

118. Reed, 'Dateline Syria', p. 177.

119. G. Michaud and J. Paul, 'The Importance of Bodyguards', *MERIP Reports*, 110, Syria's Troubles (Nov.–Dec. 1982), p. 30; Reed, 'Little Brother', p. 592.

120. Reed, 'Dateline Syria' p. 179.

121. Batatu, *Syria's Peasantry*, p. 269.

122. Reed, 'Little Brother', p. 592.

123. G. Michaud and J. Paul, 'The Importance of Bodyguards', p. 29.

124. Fuad Khuri suggests that Hafiz al-Asad may be elevated in Alawite folklore alongside their greatest historical figures, see: Fuad Khuri, *Imams and Emirs: State, Religion and Sects in Islam*, London: Saqi Books, 1990, p. 201.

125. Nikolaos van Dam, *The Struggle for Power in Syria*, 2nd edn, London: I.B. Tauris, 1996, pp. 105–6.

126. Michaud and Paul, 'The Importance of Bodyguards', p. 30; Nikolaos van Dam, *The Struggle for Power in Syria*, 2nd edn, London: I.B. Tauris, 1996, pp. 105–6.

127. *New York Times*, 13 Apr. 1980; *The Times*, London, 17 Jan. 1980.

128. 'Syria Denounces U.S. as Mastermind of Plot to Remove his Regime', *New York Times*, 9 Mar. 1980.

129. 'Syria to Arm Peasants in Fight against "Killers"', *The Times*, London, 11 Mar. 1980.

130. 'Syria Outlaws Muslim Brotherhood', *The Times*, London, 9 July 1980.

131. 'Chief of Muslim Militants Shot Dead in Syria', *The Times*, London, 18 Aug. 1980.

132. Transcript of an interview with Salah al-Din al-Bitar, *MERIP Reports*, 110, Syria's Troubles (1982), pp. 21–3.

133. Cited in Batatu, *Syria's Peasantry*, p. 229.

134. 'Former Syrian Premier is Slain at Paris Office by Unknown Gunman', *New York Times*, 22 July 1980; *The Times*, London, 22 July 1980.

135. 'Syria Agrees to Unite with Libya', *The Times*, London, 3 Sep. 1980.

136. The Soviet invasion of Afghanistan, widely condemned in the Islamic world, caused a dilemma for Asad because he could not criticise his key ally, see *New York Times*, 9 Mar. 1980.

137. 'Syria Signs Military and Political Pact with Moscow', *The Times*, London, 9 Oct. 1980.

138. 'Hunting of Muslim Brotherhood Reveals its Strength', *The Times*, London, 25 Oct. 1980.

139. 'Amman Report of Mass Shootings Denied by Syria', *The Times*, London, 3 Jan. 1981.

140. 'Banned Muslim Brotherhood Lose 7 in Syria', *The Times*, London, 30 Dec. 1980.

141. *The Times*, London, 28 Feb. 1981.

142. John Kifner, 'Envoy Catches Syria at a Very Bad Time', *New York Times*, 6 Dec. 1981; *The Times*, London, 1 Dec. 1981; *New York Times*, 29 May 1982.

143. See, for example, Omar Ilsley, 'Syria: Hama Massacre', in H. Adam (ed.), *Hushed Voices: Unacknowledged Atrocities of the 20th Century*, Highclere: Berkshire Academic Press, 2011; Itzchak Weismann, 'Sa'id Hawwa: The Making of a Radical Muslim Thinker in Modern Syria', *Middle Eastern Studies*, 29, 4 (Oct. 1993).

144. *New York Times*, 29 May 1982.

145. 'Syria Said to Raze Part of Rebel City', *New York Times*, 21 Feb. 1982.

146. *New York Times*, 29 May 1982.

147. *New York Times*, 14 Feb. 1982.

148. 'Syria Pulls a Tiger's Tail', *New York Times*, 14 Feb. 1982.

149. 'Syrian Troops are Said to Battle Rebels Encircled in Central City', *The Times*, London, 16 Feb. 1982; *New York Times*, 12 Feb. 1982.

150. *New York Times*, 14 Feb. 1982.

151. *New York Times*, 21 June 1983.

152. 'Asad Said to be in Control Despite Rebel Uprising', *New York Times*, 14 Feb. 1982.

153. Jubin Goodarzi, *Syria and Iran: Diplomatic Alliance and Power Politics in the Middle East*, London: Tauris, 2006, pp. 54, 61; *New York Times*, 12 Nov. 1985.

154. Shaykh Nasīr Eskiocak, interview with this author, Antakya, 28 Mar. 2011.

155. 'Rebels Hold Out on Island in Hama', *The Times*, London, 15 Feb. 1982; 'Hama Rebels Crushed, Say Syrians', *The Times*, London, 16 Feb. 1982.

156. *New York Times*, 24 Mar. 1982.

157. 'Syrian Rebellion Simmers Down but Tensions Endure', *New York Times*, 24 Mar. 1982.

158. Seale, *Asad of Syria*, p. 333.

159. *New York Times*, 14 Feb. 1982.

160. Tejel, *Syria's Kurds*, p. 67.

161. Tejel suggests that Hafiz al-Asad maintained a 'functional alliance with the Kurds' which he utilised increasingly during the internal struggle of 1976–82, see ibid. p. 62.

162. This view is reflected in the definition of Hafiz al-Asad provided by Shaykh Nasīr Eskiocak on p. 89 above, when he said that he ruled with 'equality'.

163. This figure is derived from population records of the city of Hama between 1979 and 1983, see Onn Winckler, *Demographic Developments and Population Policies in Ba'thist Syria*, Brighton and Portland: Sussex Academic Press, 1999, p. 72.

164. 'Syria Says US Exaggerated Unrest in Hama', *The Times*, London, 12 Feb. 1982.

165. 'Syria Says "Times" Man Lied', *The Times*, London, 14 Feb. 1982.

166. *The Times*, London, 15 Feb. 1982.

167. 'Syrian Press Denounces Brotherhood', *The Times*, London, 17 Feb. 1982.

168. DeAtkine, 'The Arab as Insurgent'.

169. Suleiman al-Khalidi, 'Survivors of Syria's Hama Massacre Watch and Hope', Reuters, 7 July 2011, http://www.reuters.com/article/2011/07/07/us-syria-hama-idUSTRE7 665R620110707

170. Rula Amin, 'Syrian Opposition Figure Triggers Debate', Al-Jazeera, 11 July 2011 http:// www.aljazeera.com/video/middleeast/2011/07/201171111013603226.html; Reporters without Borders website: http://en.rsf.org/middle-east-north-africa-journalists-targeted-by-23–03–2011,39852.html (accessed 11 July 2011).

171. Y. Sadowski, 'The Evolution of Political Identity in Syria', in S. Telhami and M. Barnett, *Identity and Foreign Policy in the Middle East*, Ithaca and London: Cornell University Press, 2002, p. 138.

172. Anonymous conversation with the author.

173. Khaldun, *The Muqaddimah*, p. 146.

174. *New York Times*, 10 Oct. 1976.

175. Batatu, *Syria's Peasantry*, pp. 63–6; De Planhol, *Minorités En Islam* pp. 89–91.

176. Ibid. p. 66.

177. Batatu, *Syria's Peasantry*, p. 69; in 1960 Nevill Barbour noted that the roads into the Jabal al-Sahiliyah were little more than rough dirt tracks, see 'Impressions of the United Arab Republic', *International Affairs*, 36, 1 (Jan. 1960), p. 28.

178. William Harris, *Lebanon: A History, 600–2011*, New York: Oxford University Press, 2012.

179. Batatu, *Syria's Peasantry*, p. 71.

180. See Steven Heydemann, *Networks of Privilege in the Middle East: The Politics of Economic Reform Revisited*, Basingstoke and New York: Palgrave Macmillan, 2004.

181. Tejel, *Syria's Kurds*, p. 68.

182. Anthony Shadid, 'Death of Syrian Minister leaves Sect adrift in Time of Strife', *Washington Post*, 31 Oct. 2005.

183. John Kifner, 'Syrian Success Story: A Hated Minority Sect becomes the Ruling Class', *New York Times*, 26 Dec. 1986.

184. Harris, *Lebanon*.

185. *New York Times*, 26 Dec. 1982.

186. Throughout this work careful attention to the maintenance of complete anonymity has been taken. The names of specific villages are thus not given in order to protect the identities of those who provided information.

187. Olsson, 'The Gnosis', p. 182.

188. Seale, *Asad of Syria*, p. 11.

189. Winckler, *Demographic Developments*, pp. 62, 72, Table 3.4, main sources cited include: Great Britain Naval Intelligence Division, *Syria*, 1943; *The Middle East and North Africa*, 1953–65/6; UN Demographic Yearbook 1963–94.

190. Winckler, *Demographic Developments*, p. 72.

191. Ibid.
192. Ibid. For these statistics Winckler cites estimates from the UN Demographic Yearbooks (1981, p. 279; 1984, p. 272).
193. 'War of Succession', *New York Times*, 17 May 1984.
194. Ramadan is the month of fasting and religious celebration for Muslims.
195. Philip Jenkins, *The Lost History of Christianity*, New York: HarperCollins, 2008, pp. 132–8.
196. Tartous: population 52,589 (1981 census), primarily Alawites and Christians; Suwayda: 43,414 (1981 census); Zahle: 54, 129 (2010, est.) data source: *World Gazetteer*, 'Syria'; according to local residents Suweydiya is 90 per cent Alawite.
197. For example, the district of Nozha in Homs has been primarily Alawite since the 1980s.
198. 'Kassioun, Syria', *The Times*, London, 5 Sep. 1980.
199. David Rain, 'Damascus: A Geographical Field Note', *Geographical Review*, 99, 1 (Jan. 2009), p. 102.
200. Ibid.
201. Yves Lacoste, *Ibn Khaldun: The Birth of History and the Past of Third World*, London: Verso, 1984, p. 100.
202. Khaldun, *The Muqaddimah*, p. 109.
203. Paul Rivlin, *Arab Economies in the Twenty-First Century*, New York: Cambridge University Press, 2009, p. 240.
204. On Hafiz al-Asad's aspiration for strategic parity with Israel see: Eyal Zisser, *Asad's Legacy*, London: Hurst, 2001, p. 13.
205. Winckler, *Arab Political Demography*, p. 407.
206. Ibid. p. 191.
207. In 1974 Hafiz al-Asad established the 'Syrian Family Planning Association' as a voluntary non-government organisation, ibid. p. 191.
208. Monique Cardinal, 'Religious Education in Syria: Unity and Difference', *British Journal of Religious Education*, 31, 2 (2009), pp. 97–8.
209. Torstein Schiøtz Worren, 'Fear and Resistance: The Construction of Alawi Identity in Syria', Master's Thesis, Department of Sociology and Human Geography, University of Oslo, Feb. 2007.
210. The Druze share this characteristic.
211. Cited in Batatu, *Syria's Peasantry*, p. 20.
212. Drysdale, 'The Asad Regime', p. 247.
213. Batatu, *Syria's Peasantry*, pp. 232–3.
214. Abd al-Halim Khaddam, interview with this author, Paris, 16 Sep. 2009.
215. Seale, *Asad of Syria*, p. 425.
216. *New York Times*, 6 Mar. 1984; Drysdale, 'The Asad Regime', p. 247; Seale, *Asad of Syria*, p. 427; Batatu, *Syria's Peasantry*, p. 234.
217. Batatu, *Syria's Peasantry*, p. 234.
218. *New York Times*, 6 Mar. 1984; Drysdale, 'The Asad Regime', p. 249; Batatu, *Syria's Peasantry*, p. 234.

219. Jubin Goodarzi, *Syria and Iran: Diplomatic Alliance and Power Politics in the Middle East*, London: Tauris, 2006, pp. 110–11; ironically at this moment of Asad dynasty weakness the Lebanese President Amin Gemayal travelled to Damascus in early Mar. to restore normal relations with Syria, *New York Times*, 6 Mar. 1984; the major cause of poor Lebanese–Syrian relations was the assassination of Lebanon's president elect, Bashir Gemayal, in Beirut on 14 Sep. 1982, in all likelihood by Syrian proxies, Seale, *Asad of Syria*, p. 420; Goodarzi, *Syria and Iran*, p. 75.

220. Shaykh 'Ali Yeral, interview, 28 Mar. 2011, Antakya

221. Drysdale, 'The Asad Regime', p. 249; 'War of Succession', *New York Times*, 17 May 1984.

222. It is possible that Hafiz al-Asad, in his poor health, considered preparing a return to previous arrangements whereby a Sunni figurehead would assume the presidency while Alawite military officials controlled real power behind the scenes.

223. Drysdale, 'The Asad Regime', p. 250

224. *New York Times*, 17 May 1984; Drysdale, 'The Asad Regime', p. 250; Seale, *Asad of Syria*, p. 432.

225. Cited in Batatu, *Syria's Peasantry*, p. 236.

226. Seale, *Asad of Syria*, p. 433.

227. Batatu, *Syria's Peasantry*, p. 236; Eyal Zisser, 'The Syrian Army: Between the Domestic and External Fronts', *MERIA*, 5, 1 (Mar. 2001), p. 5.

228. Drysdale, 'The Asad Regime', p. 250.

229. 'Assad's Brother Exiled "Forever," Syrian Declares', *New York Times*, 12 Sep. 1984.

230. *New York Times*, 12 Sep. 1984.

231. Batatu, *Syria's Peasantry*, p. 236.

232. James Quinlivan, 'Coup-Proofing: Its Practice and Consequences in the Middle East', *International Security*, 24, 2 (Autumn 1999), p. 148.

233. For example, '[t]alking to supporters in a lunch at the Damascus Sheraton, [Rifa'at al-Asad] said he favoured a more liberal economic policy ...' *New York Times*, 17 May 1984.

234. Drysdale, 'The Asad Regime', p. 255.

235. Batatu, *Syria's Peasantry*, Appendix.

236. Ibid. p. 252.

237. Goodarzi, *Syria and Iran*, p. 6.

238. Ibid. p. 18.

239. These Alawite preferences were reinforced by the Alawite Shaykhs 'Ali Yeral and Nasīr Eskiocak in 2011.

240. Drysdale, 'The Asad Regime', pp. 247–8

241. Seale, *Asad of Syria*, p. 319

242. A noteworthy exception to this general tendency of Alawites was the al-Murtada Association founded by Hafiz al-Asad's brother Jamil in 1981. They espoused right-wing Alawite nationalism and even tried to 'Alawise' (convert) rural Beduins. Hafiz al-Asad

closed it down in 1983. See Nikolaos van Dam, *The Struggle for Power in Syria: Politics and Society under Asad and the Ba'th Party*, 4th edn, New York: I.B. Tauris, 2011, p. 122.

243. Khaldun, *Muqaddimah*, p. 146.

244. Goodarzi, *Syria and Iran*, p. 16.

245. Ibid. p. 25.

246. Lacoste, *Ibn Khaldun*, pp. 107–8.

247. Goodarzi, *Syria and Iran*, pp. 149–50.

248. Ibid. pp. 155–6.

249. Ibid. pp. 201–2; this was possibly done in retaliation for their kidnapping of a pro-Syrian Christian politician, Michel Samaha, by Hizballah.

250. Ibid. p. 203.

251. Ibid. p. 271.

252. Interview with the author, 16 Sep. 2009, Paris.

253. Shaykh 'Ali Yeral, interview with this author, Antakya, 28 Mar. 2011.

254. Khaldun, *The Muqaddimah*, p. 146.

255. Abd al-Halim Khaddam, interview with the author.

256. Risa Brooks, *Political–Military Relations and the Stability of Arab Regimes*, Adelphi Paper no. 324, New York: Oxford University Press, 1998, p. 57. For some commentary on the personal characteristics of Bashar al-Asad and the circumstances of his becoming heir to the Asad dynasty, see also Don Belt, 'Shadowland', *National Geographic*, Nov. 2009

257. Volker Perthes, *The Political Economy of Syria under Asad*, London: I.B. Tauris, 1995, p. 269.

258. 'Salah Jadid, 63, Leader of Syria Deposed and Imprisoned by Asad', *New York Times*, 24 Aug. 1993.

259. Paul Kingston, O. Haklai and N. Hasemi, 'Entering the 21st Century—The Middle East', *International Journal*, 55 (1999–2000), p. 652.

260. Shmuel Bar, 'Bashar's Syria: The Regime and its Strategic Worldview', *Comparative Strategy*, 25 (2006), p. 369.

261. For example see Shaykh 'Ali 'Aziz al-Ibrahim, *The Alawites and the Shi'a*, Beirut: 1992; also three books were published by the son of Alawite Shaykh 'Abd al-Rahman al-Khayr, see: Ulrike Freitag, 'In Search of "Historical Correctness": The Ba'th Party in Syria', *Middle Eastern Studies*, 35, 1 (Jan. 1999), pp. 12–13.

262. Shaykh Muhammad Boz, interview with this author, Antakya, 28 Mar. 2011.

263. Ziadeh, *Power and Policy*, p. 39.

264. Ibid. p. 37; Heba El Laithy and Khalid Abu-Ismail, 'Poverty in Syria: 1996–2004,' United Nations Development Programme, June 2005, p. 11

265. Ibid. p. 43.

266. Khaldun, *The Muqaddimah*, p. 149.

4. RAPID DESCENT

1. *New York Times*, 12 June 2000.
2. Abd al-Halim Khaddam, interview with the author, Paris, Sep. 2009.
3. Ibid.
4. The day after his father's death, Bashar was named commander of Syria's armed forces and he was promoted from colonel to lieutenant-general, and the Regional Command of the Ba'ath Party nominated him for the Syrian presidency, *New York Times*, 12 June 2000.
5. Susan Sachs, 'Assad Patronage Puts a Small Sect on Top in Syria', *New York Times*, 22 June 2000.
6. Ibn Khaldun, *The Muqaddimah: An Introduction to History*, trans. Franz Rosenthal, abridged N.J. Dawood, London: Routledge & Kegan Paul, 1967, p. 146.
7. 'Leaders of Syria Building Support for Son of Assad', *New York Times*, 12 June 2000; *The Economist*, 15 June 2000.
8. Hugh Pope, 'Assad's Death Worries Most-Favoured Sect', *Wall Street Journal*, 14 June 2000.
9. Ibid.
10. Pope, 'Assad's Death'.
11. 'A New Hurdle to Peace', *New York Times*, 11 June 2000.
12. Eyal Zisser, 'The Syrian Army on the Domestic and External Fronts', in B. Rubin and T. Keaney (eds), *Armed Forces in the Middle East: Politics and Strategy*, Oxon: Frank Cass, 2002; former Syrian vice-president Abd al-Halim Khaddam suggested a figure of 95 per cent, interview with the author.
13. Paul Kingston, O. Haklai and N. Hasemi, 'Entering the 21st Century—The Middle East', *International Journal*, 55 (1999–2000), p. 652; Radwan Ziadeh, *Power and Policy in Syria*, London: I.B. Tauris, 2011, p. 41.
14. Zisser, 'The Syrian Army', p. 120.
15. Ibid. p. 115.
16. 'Bashar's World', *The Economist*, 15 June 2000.
17. Cited in Thomas Friedman, 'Three Movies and a Funeral', *New York Times*, 16 June 2000; on Bushra al-Asad's important role in the Asad family see, Mohamad Daoud, 'Dossier: Bushra Assad', *Mid-East Monitor*, 1, 3 (Sep.–Oct. 2006).
18. Jane Perlez, 'Allbright Finds Syria's New Leader Willing to Pursue Talks', *New York Times*, 14 June 2000.
19. *The Economist*, 15 June 2000; *New York Times*, 22 June 2000; Kingston, Haklai and Hasemi, 'Entering', p. 652.
20. Susan Sachs, 'Exiled Relative Issues Challenge to Syria's Heir to Power', *New York Times*, 13 June 2000.
21. Zisser, 'The Syrian Army', p. 2.
22. Ariel I. Ahram, 'Iraq and Syria: The Dilemma of Dynasty', *Middle East Quarterly*, 9, 2 (2002), p. 42.

23. Susan Sachs, 'Syrians See in the Heir Possibility of Progress', *New York Times*, 11 June 2000.

24. Gary Gambill, 'The Lion in Winter: Bashar Assad's Self-Destruction', *Mideast Monitor*, 1, 1 (Feb. 2006).

25. 'Is Syria Really Changing?' *The Economist*, 16 Nov. 2000.

26. On the Damascus Spring see: Ziadeh, *Power and Policy*, pp. 61–75.

27. *The Economist*, 16 Nov. 2000.

28. See for example, Carsten Wieland, *Syria at Bay: Secularism, Islamism, and Pax Americana*, London: Hurst, 2006.

29. Neil Farquhar, 'Syria is Forced to Adapt to a New Power Next Door', *New York Times*, 22 Apr. 2003.

30. This impression is gained from the transcript of an interview with Bashar al-Asad by Don Belt, see, 'Shadowland', *National Geographic*, Nov. 2009.

31. Khaldun, *Muqaddimah*, p. 149.

32. *New York Times*, 22 June 2000, cites Al-Jazeera.

33. Shaykh 'Ali Yeral, interview with the author, Antakya, 28 Mar. 2011.

34. Shmuel Bar, 'Bashar's Syria: The Regime and its Strategic Worldview', *Comparative Strategy*, 25 (2006), pp. 353–445, p. 380.

35. Ibid. p. 380.

36. Neil Farquhar, 'Syria is Forced to Adapt to a New Power Next Door', *New York Times*, 22 Apr. 2003.

37. Shaykh 'Ali Yeral, interview with the author, Antakya, 28 Mar. 2011.

38. Sachs, 'Syrians'.

39. Perlez, 'Allbright'.

40. Ibid.

41. Jane Perlez, 'Syria's New Cabinet is Overshadowed by Old Realities', *New York Times*, 21 Jan. 2002.

42. Andrew England, '"Damascus Spring" Fades from Memory', *Financial Times*, 13 Sep. 2008.

43. Riad Seif publicly stated that the contract 'would cost the Syrian public billions of dollars in lost revenue', Perlez, 'Syria's New Cabinet'.

44. Abd al-Halim Khaddam, interview with the author.

45. Khaldun, *The Muqaddimah*, p. 146.

46. UN Security Council, UNSC/6878 Press Release, 'Security Council Endorses Secretary General's Conclusion on Israeli Withdrawal from Lebanon as of 16 June', 18 June 2000.

47. See Marwan Iskander, *Rafiq Hariri and the Fate of Lebanon*, London: Saqi, 2006.

48. Neil Farquhar, 'Syria, Long Ruthlessly Secular Sees Fervent Islamic Resurgence', *New York Times*, 24 Oct. 2003.

49. Farquhar, 'Syria is Forced to Adapt'.

50. Syrian state television aired a documentary about Islamic architecture during this event; however, satellite television, widely available in Syria by 2003, provided many Syrians with images of the dramatic events in Iraq in Mar./Apr. 2003. See Volker Perthes, *Syria*

under Bashar al-Asad: Modernisation and the Limits of Change, Adelphi Paper 366, New York: Oxford University Press, 2004, p. 50.

51. *New York Times*, 22 Apr. 2003.

52. Lucy Ashton, 'Syria's Retreat from Lebanon Emboldens Islamist Opposition', *Financial Times*, 6 May 2005.

53. Carsten Wieland, *Syria—A Decade of Lost Chances: Repression and Revolution from Damascus Spring to Arab Spring*, Seattle: Cune Press, 2012, pp. 176–80.

54. *New York Times*, 24 Oct. 2003.

55. Al-Ghassi's usefulness was both rhetorical and material, for example in 2003 he reportedly provided financial assistance to resistance forces in Iraq, see aired confession on Al-Fayhaa Televison, Iraq/UAE, 14 Jan. 2005, translated by *Memri*, Special Dispatch no. 849.

56. *New York Times*, 24 Oct. 2003.

57. Farquhar, 'Syria, Long Ruthlessly Secular'.

58. Combating Terrorism Center, West Point, 'Al-Qaida's Foreign Fighters in Iraq', p. 20, Accessed 9 Apr. 2013. https://www.ctc.usma.edu/posts/al-qaidas-foreign-fighters-in-iraq-a-first-look-at-the-sinjar-records; 'Asharq Al-Awsat Talks to Paul Bremer (Part Two)', *Ash-Sharq al-Awsat*, London, 15 May 2009.

59. Michael J. Totten, 'Killing a Crocodile', *Commentary Magazine*, 4 Nov. 2008.

60. Although, as Michael Young has argued, the United States may never have really contemplated military intervention in Syria, Michael Young, 'The Canard of Regime Change in Syria', *Daily Star*, Beirut, 16 Dec. 2010.

61. Omar Amiralay was active during the 'Damascus Spring' and a signatory to the Declaration of 99, demanding the lifting of emergency laws, freeing of political prisoners, independent political parties and civil society in Syria, see: 'Statement by 99 Syrian Intellectuals', *Al-Hayat*, London, 27 Sep. 2000.

62. Neil Farquhar, 'Hussein's Fall Leads Syrians to Test Government Limits', *New York Times*, 20 Mar. 2004; see 'Influential Syrian Film-Maker Amilray Dies', Reuters, Damascus, 5 Feb. 2011.

63. Neil Farquhar, 'Hussein's Fall Leads Syrians to Test Government Limits', *New York Times*, 20 Mar. 2004.

64. 'Exile Seeks to Muster Opposition to Syrian Regime', *Financial Times*, 28 Sep. 2004.

65. Jordi Tejel, *Syria's Kurds: History, Politics and Society*, Oxon: Routledge, 2009, pp. 115–16.

66. *New York Times*, 20 Mar. 2004.

67. Ibid.

68. Tejel, *Syria's Kurds*, pp. 130–1.

69. Ibid. p. 117; see also Julie Gauthier, 'The 2004 Events in al-Qamishli: Has the Kurdish Question Erupted in Syria?' in Fred Lawson (ed.), *Demystifying Syria*, London: Saqi, 2009, pp. 105–19.

70. Ibid.

71. Tejel, *Syria's Kurds*, pp. 130–1.

72. Bar, 'Bashar's Syria', p. 444.

73. *New York Times*, 20 Mar. 2004.

74. Neil Farquhar, 'Gains by Kin in Iraq Inflame Kurds' Anger at Syria', *New York Times*, 24 Mar. 2004.

75. In 2004 Syria's new intelligence chief in Lebanon, Rustom Ghazali, allegedly made threats against Rafiq al-Hariri and his children, see Iskander, *Rafiq Hariri*, p. 56; on the growing resentment by Lebanese of Syrian economic extortion, see pp. 89–90.

76. *Financial Times*, 24 Mar. 2005.

77. UNIIIC, 'Report of the International Independent Investigation Commission', Detlev Mehlis, Beirut, 19 Oct. 2005, document available at: http://www.un.org/news/dh/docs/mehlisreport.pdf (accessed 28 July 2011).

78. UN Security Council, S/RES/1559 (2004) 04–49892 (E), adopted by the Security Council, 2 Sep. 2004.

79. Ibid.

80. UNIIIC, 'Report of the International Independent Investigation Commission', Detlev Mehlis, Beirut, 19 Oct. 2005, document available at: http://www.un.org/news/dh/docs/mehlisreport.pdf (accessed 28 July 2011).

81. Roula Khalaf, 'International Pressure has Forced Damascus to Contemplate a Humbling Retreat', *Financial Times*, 24 Mar. 2005.

82. 'Lebanon and Syria: Who Will Blink First?' *Economist*, 31 Mar. 2005.

83. *Financial Times*, 24 Mar. 2005; *Naharnet*, Beirut, 23 Mar. 2005; *Economist*, 31 Mar. 2005.

84. William Harris, 'Lebanon's Day in Court', *Foreign Affairs*, 30 June 2011, http://www.foreignaffairs.com/articles/67971/william-harris/lebanons-day-in-court; see also 'Mandate and Jurisdiction', Special Tribunal for Lebanon, official website, http://www.stl-tsl.org/section/AbouttheSTL

85. *Financial Times*, 24 Mar. 2005. '14 March' was the date when a massive demonstration, involving over a million people, was staged in Beirut demanding an end to Syria's role in Lebanon.

86. 'Syria under Bashar Assad, One of the Last Survivors of a Dying Breed', *Economist*, 16 June 2005.

87. 'Last Syrian Soldiers Depart Lebanon', *The Washington Post*, 27 Apr. 2005. This is an old Arabic tradition that believes that turning up a stone or breaking a water-jar behind the back of any disliked person will prevent his or her return.

88. UN Security Council, S/RES/1595 (2005), 05–29998(E), 7 Apr. 2005.

89. 'Profile: UN Investigator of Hariri Killing a "Tenacious Terrier"', Lebanon Wire, 21 Oct. 2005, http://www.lebanonwire.com/1005/05102130AFP.asp; see also John Follain, *Jackal*, New York: Arcade, 1998, pp. 237–8.

90. Joshua Landis, 'Confessional Violence: Alawites Attack Ismaili Stores in Qadmous', Syria Comment, 28 July 2005, http://faculty-staff.ou.edu/L/Joshua.M.Landis-1/syriablog/2005/07/alawi-ismaili-confrontation-in-qadmous.htm

91. Anthony Shadid 'Death of Syrian Minister Leaves a Sect Adrift in a Time of Strife', *Washington Post*, 31 Oct. 2005.

92. 'No Immunity for Assad over Hariri Murder', Ya Libnan, Beirut, 10 Apr. 2008, http://yalibnan.com/site/archives/2008/04/no_immunity_for.php

93. Ian Black, 'US Reassures Lebanon as it Woos Syria', *Guardian*, London, 16 May 2007.

94. Reuters, 20 May 2007, http://www.alertnet.org/thenews/newsdesk/L20130134.htm

95. 'Syria Distances Itself from Islamists in Lebanon', *Khaleej Times*, 22 May 2007; 'Syria Says UN Hariri Tribunal May Destabilize Lebanon', Xinhua, 31 May 2007, http://english.people.com.cn/200705/31/eng20070531_379577.html; 'Free Shiite Movement Accuses Syria of North Lebanon Violence', Ya Libnan, 20 May 2007, http://yalibnan.com/site/archives/2007/05/free_shiite_mov_3.php; 'Syria Admits Lebanon Turmoil is Linked to UN Vote on Tribunal', Ya Libnan, 22 May 2007, http://yalibnan.com/site/archives/2007/05/syria_admits_le_1.php; 'Jumblatt: Lebanon's Fatah al Islam was Made in Syria', Ya Libnan, 28 May 2007, 'http://yalibnan.com/site/archives/2007/05/jumblatt_lebano_4.php; Scott MacLeod, 'Lebanon's PM: Syria is Threatening my Country', *Time*, 31 May 2007; 'Eid Discovered the Link between Fatah al Islam & Syria', Ya Libnan, Beirut, 26 Jan. 2008, http://yalibnan.com/site/archives/2008/01/eid_discovered.php; Olivier Guitta, 'Planning an Invasion of Lebanon?' *Middle East Times*, Cairo, 11 Nov. 2008.

96. 'Report: Fatah al-Islam Linked to Bashar Assad's Brother-in-Law', Naharnet, Beirut, 18 July 2007, http://www.naharnet.com/domino/tn/NewsDesk.nsf/0/1928E602F2D4AEE4C225731C004D856F?OpenDocument

97. Abu Kais, 'Is the "Opposition" Running Out of Cash?' Agravox, France, 11 July 2007, http://www.agoravox.com/article.php3?id_article=6425

98. Chapter 7, Article 42 of the UN Charter states: 'Should the Security Council consider that [non-violent] measures provided for in Article 41 would be inadequate or have proved to be inadequate, it may take such action by air, sea, or land forces as may be necessary to maintain or restore international peace and security', available at: http://www.un.org/en/documents/charter/chapter7.shtml (accessed 10 Aug. 2008).

99. United Nations, 'Note of the Secretary-General's Meeting with his Excellency President Bashar al-Assad of Syria, Held at the Palace in Damascus on 24 April, 2007'.

100. Shaykh 'Ali Yeral, interview with the author, 28 Mar. 2011, Antakya, Turkey.

101. UN Security Council, S/RES/1757 (2007), 07–36357 (E), adopted 30 May 2007.

102. 'Syria Rushes to Applaud Army Seizure of Nahr al-Bared', Naharnet, Beirut, 2 Sep. 2007, http://www.naharnet.com/domino/tn/newsdesk.nsf/0/0A946680A859277DC225734A0069C8BC?OpenDocument

103. 'International Tribunal for Lebanon Killings Reaches Start-Up Phase—UN Report', UN News Centre, 18 Mar. 2008, http://www.un.org/apps/news/story.asp?NewsID=26021&Cr=leban&Cr1=tribunal

104. 'Intruders Strike Home of Judge Tied to Hariri Court—Again', *Daily Star*, Beirut, 23 Apr. 2008.

105. 'Syria: Reveal Fate of Hariri-Case Detainee', Human Rights Watch, 23 June 2009; 'Hariri Witness Held for Four Years Without Charge in Syria', Amnesty International, 20 July 2009, http://www.amnesty.org/en/news-and-updates/news/hariri-witness-held-four-years-without-charge-syria-20090720

106. Omar Bashir is accused by the ICC of numerous counts of crimes against humanity, war crimes and genocide against civilians in Darfur in the period after 2003. ICC website, http://www.icc-cpi.int/en_menus/icc/situations%20and%20cases/situations/situation%20icc%200205/Pages/situation%20icc-0205.aspx

107. See: 'A Middle Way for Justice in Sudan', *The Economist*, 11 Dec. 2008.

108. *Al-Thawra*, Damascus, 6 Mar. 2009, trans. Memri, available at http://www.thememriblog.org/blog_personal/en/14406.htm

109. 'Mehlis: Hariri Murder Probe "Appears to Have Lost Momentum"', Naharnet, Beirut, 28 Jan. 2008, http://www.naharnet.com/domino/tn/NewsDesk.nsf/0/1F59882360B36387C22573DE00356E57?OpenDocument

110. Detlev Mehlis, interview with this author, 12 May 2009, Dunedin.

111. Neil MacDonald, 'CBC Investigation: Who Killed Lebanon's Rafik Hariri?' CBC News, Canada, 21 Nov. 2010; see also: 'Indictment and its Confirmation Made Public', Special Tribunal for Lebanon, Leidschendam, 17 Aug. 2011, available at: http://www.stl-tsl.org/en/media/press-releases/17-08-2011-indictment-and-its-confirmation-decision-made-public

112. Lucy Ashton, 'Syria's Retreat from Lebanon Emboldens Islamist Opposition', *Financial Times*, 6 May 2005.

113. *Financial Times*, 6 May 2005.

114. Michael Slackman, 'Fearing an Iraq in a Post-Asad Syria', *New York Times*, 6 Nov. 2005; in 2005, Daniel Byman raised the possibility of a coup by one of the 'Alawite Barons', see: Daniel L. Byman, 'The Implications of Leadership Change in the Arab World', *Political Science Quarterly*, 120, 1 (2005).

115. See Batatu, *Syria's Peasantry*, p. 223.

116. Gary C. Gambill, 'Why Did Kanaan Die?' *The National Post*, Toronto, 17 Oct. 2005, available at: Mideast Monitor, http://www.mideastmonitor.org/gambill/051017.htm

117. Esther Pan, 'Syria's Leaders', Council on Foreign Relations, 10 Mar. 2006; although Shihabi was 'rehabilitated' shortly afterwards, his career was effectively terminated in 1998.

118. Abd al-Halim Khaddam, interview with the author.

119. Gary C. Gambill, 'Dossier: Abd al-Halim Khaddam', *Mideast Monitor*, 1, 1 (Feb. 2006).

120. Ibid.

121. 'Ghazi Kanaan Shoots Himself Dead Ahead of U.N. Report on Hariri's Murder', Naharnet, Beirut, 12 Oct. 2005, available at: http://old.naharnet.com/domino/tn/NewsDesk.nsf/getstory?openform&0433802B18F56720C2257098003F78DD

122. See, for example, Joshua Landis, 'Ghazi Kanaan—the Most Senior Alawi—Suicide? Or Was it Murder?' SyriaComment.com, available at: http://faculty-staff.ou.edu/L/Joshua.M.Landis-1/syriablog/2005/10/ghazi-kanaan-most-senior-alawi-suicide.htm

123. Mohamad Daoud, 'Dossier: Bushra Assad', *Mideast Monitor*, 1, 3 (Sep.–Oct. 2006).

124. See Gary Gambill (ed.), 'Dossier: Rami Makhlouf', *Mideast Monitor*, 3, 1 (Jan.–Mar. 2008).

125. Bar, 'Bashar's Syria', pp. 28, 44; see also: US House of International Relations Committee, HIRC, 2004, 'Syria' Documents 2 and 6.

126. Abd al-Halim Khaddam, interview with the author.

127. Kim Ghattas, 'Syria's Minority Alawites Fear for Future', BBC, London, 22 Nov. 2005.

128. Anthony Shadid, 'Death of a Syrian Minister Leaves a Sect Adrift in Time of Strife', *The Washington Post*, 31 Oct. 2005.

129. Naharnet, Beirut, 10 Nov. 2006.

130. A member of the Kana'an family showed little affection for the Asads during a conversation with the author in Latakia in 2011.

131. Khaldun, *The Muqaddimah*, p. 146.

132. Gary C. Gambill, 'Dossier: Abd al-Halim Khaddam', *Mideast Monitor*, 1, 1 (Feb. 2006).

133. Reuters, 17 Mar. 2006.

134. 'Exiled Syrian Opposition Pledges to Protect Alawite Minority', *Financial Times*, 5 June 2006.

135. Al-Jazeera, broadcast 17 Aug. 2006, cited in 'The Bayanouni–Khaddam Link-Up: Is the Opposition Real Now?' Syria Comment, http://faculty-staff.ou.edu/L/Joshua.M.Landis-1/syriablog/2006/03/bayanouni-khaddam-link-up-_114264946582158617.htm

136. Paulo Boneschi, "Une fatwà du Grande Mufti de Jérusalem Muhammad Amin al-Husayni sur les Alawites," *Revue de l'histoire des religions* 122(1), July–August 1940, pp. 42–54; Yvette Talhamy, 'The Fatwas and the Nusayri/Alawis of Syria', *Middle Eastern Studies*, 46, 2 (2010), pp. 185–6.

137. This type of political shift, due to new political realities, can also perhaps explain the realignment of Walid Jumblat and the Lebanese Druze.

138. Abd al-Halim Khaddam, interview with the author.

139. Anonymous informant, Aug. 2009.

140. Anthony Shadid, *Washington Post*, 31 Oct. 2005.

141. UN Security Council, S/RES/1686 (2006), 06–39006 (E), 15 June 2006.

142. UN Security Council, S/RES/1701 (2006), 06–46503 (E), 11 Aug. 2006.

143. For an analysis of the conduct of this conflict see, S. Biddle and J.A. Friedman, *The 2006 Lebanon Campaign*, Carlisle, PA: Strategic Studies Institute, United States Army War College, Sep. 2008.

144. *Ha'aretz*, Israel, 7 June 2007.

145. Esther Pan, 'Syria, Iran, and the Mideast Conflict', Council on Foreign Relations, 18 July 2006, http://www.cfr.org/iran/syria-iran-mideast-conflict/p11122 (accessed 1 Sep. 2011).

146. Abd al-Halim Khaddam, interview with the author.

147. For a full discussion of the personality cult of Hafiz al-Asad, see: Lisa Wedeen, *Ambiguities of Domination*, Chicago and London: University of Chicago Press, 1999.

148. Khaldun, *The Muqaddimah*, p. 146.

149. Wieland, *Syria—A Decade of Lost Chances*, p. 73.

150. Paul Rivlin, 'The Socio-Economic Crisis in Syria', *Iqtisadi*, 1, 3 (June 2011), p. 3.

151. National Salvation Front (NSF) website, available at: http://www.free-syria.com/en/ (accessed 2 Oct. 2009).

152. Fiscal operations are actions taken by the government to implement budgetary policies, such as revenue and expenditure measures, as well as issuance of public debt instruments and public debt management. Taken from: 'Glossary of Statistical Terms', OECD, available at: http://stats.oecd.org/glossary/detail.asp?ID=4470

153. IMF Country Report no. 07/288, Aug. 2007, p. 33; figures are shown in 2007 exchange rates.

154. Matthew Levitt, 'Global Anti-Terrorism Financing Group Challenged by Syria's Application', Washington Institute for Near East Policy, Policy Watch, no. 1238, 31 May 2007, http://www.washingtoninstitute.org/templateC05.php?CID=2609; see also: 'International Narcotics Control Strategy Report', vol. II, 'Money Laundering and Financial Crimes', US Department of State, pp. 364–7.

155. Abd al-Halim Khaddam, interview with the author.

156. IMF Country Report, no. 10/86, 'Syrian Arab Republic: 2009 Article IV Consultation—Staff Report; and Public information Notice', Mar. 2010, p. 10.

157. Ibid. p. 8.

158. World Bank Data, 'Syrian Arab Republic', http://data.worldbank.org/country/syrian-arab-republic (accessed 12 Apr. 2012).

159. *Washington Post*, 31 Oct. 2005.

160. Ibid.

161. The taxi driver who took this author to Qurdaha assumed the reason for travelling there was to purchase alcohol.

162. Christa Salamandra, 'Consuming Damascus: Public Culture and the Construction of Social Identity', in W. Armbrust (ed.), *Mass Mediations: New Approaches to Popular Culture in the Middle East and Beyond*, Berkeley: University of California Press, 2000, pp. 182–202.

163. Ibid. p. 191.

164. Ibid. pp. 188–9.

165. *Washington Post*, 31 Oct. 2005.

166. Ibid.

167. UNDP Report, 'The Impact of the World Economic Downturn on Syrian Economy, Inequality and Poverty', 2 Nov. 2009, p. 27; 'Syria: Harvest Hit by Poor Weather, Inefficient Farming Practices', Reuters, Damascus, 5 July 2007.

168. Yves Lacoste, *Ibn Khaldun: The Birth of History and the Past of Third World*, London: Verso, 1984, pp. 113–14.

169. Raphael Lefevre, 'Power Struggles among the Alawites in Lebanon', Carnegie Endowment for International Peace, 1 Jan. 2014, www.carnegie endowment.org (accessed 14 Apr. 2014).

170. *New York Times*, 21 June 1982; although, similarly to the Syrian Alawites, they retained links back to their rural villages.

171. '3 Syrians Killed in Ambush in Lebanon', *New York Times*, 21 June 1982.

172. The ADP has also been known unofficially as the 'Pink Panthers' owing to the colour of their militia uniforms.

173. *New York Times*, 21 June 1982.

174. Riad Yazbeck, 'Return of the Pink Panthers', *Mideast Monitor*, 3, 2 (Aug. 2008).

175. The son of the murdered Rafiq al-Hariri.

176. Naharnet, Beirut, 7 Sep. 2008.

177. Nicholas Blandford, 'Lebanese Sects Aim to End Clashes', Christian Science Monitor, 12 Sep. 2008.

178. 'Lebanon Car Bomb Kills 19 at Mosque', *New York Times*, 6 Aug. 1983.

179. Rami G. Khoury, 'Tripoli Distils Mideastern Complexities', *Daily Star*, Beirut, 18 Aug. 2008.

180. Robert Worth, 'Up North, Hothouse of Tension in Lebanon', *New York Times*, 15 Oct. 2008.

181. 'Accord Signed to End North Lebanon Bloodshed', AFP, France, 8 Sep. 2008, http://afp.google.com/article/ALeqM5jnKXdReKZOXG75K7qn84NYVLp7UA

182. 'Lebanon Fears an Invasion as Syrian Troops Mass', *The Australian*, Sydney, 25 Sep. 2008.

183. Naharnet, Beirut, 9 Sep. 2008.

184. Michael Young, 'Syria Pushes the Envelope in the North', *Daily Star*, Beirut, 25 Sep. 2008.

185. Interview with Kuwaiti newspaper, *Al-Rai*, cited in Naharnet, Beirut, 9 Sep. 2008.

186. Tripoli has also been an arena for inter-Alawite rivalry. In the 1970s and early 1980s, Rifa'at al-Asad played a major role as patron of the ADP and its militia, the Arab Red Knights (ARK) or 'Pink Panthers'. After his fall from grace in Damascus and departure into exile in 1984, Rifa'at maintained a presence in Jabal Mohsen. The kidnapping and possible transfer to Syria of an affiliate of Rifa'at al-Asad, Nawar 'Abboud, in Tripoli on 25 Dec. 2008, showed that Rifa'at al-Asad continues to maintain a presence in Tripoli, see: 'Lebanon: Investigate Syrian Opposition Figure's Fate', Human Rights Watch, 25 Mar. 2009.

187. Asher Kaufman, 'Let Sleeping Dogs Lie', *Middle East Journal*, 63, 4 (Autumn 2009), p. 541.

188. Ibid., p. 556; *Jerusalem Post*, 19 July 2009.

189. Andrew Tabler, 'Solomon's Baby in the Middle East', *Foreign Policy*, 6 Sep. 2010, http://www.foreignpolicy.com/article/2010/02/02/solomons_baby_in_the_middle_east

190. 'An Entity of Problematic Identity, Al-Ghajar: Three States in Dispute Over One Village', *Monday Morning Magazine*, Beirut, Issue no. 1968, 13 Sep. 2010.

191. 'Ghajar Residents Refuse to Become Part of Lebanon', Naharnet, Beirut, 22 July 2009, http://www.naharnet.com/domino/tn/NewsDesk.nsf/0/5B388C171F3FFFC1C22575FB002CFA02?OpenDocumen; see also: 'Ghajar Leaders: Divide Would Kill Us', *Jerusalem Post*, 22 July 2009.

5. REVOLUTION

1. Khaldun, *The Muqaddimah*, p. 149.
2. Abd al-Halim Khaddam, interview with the author, 16 Sep. 2009, Paris.
3. 'Lebanon Tribunal High on Agenda of Iran FM & Syria's Assad', Ya Libnan, Beirut, 1 June 2007, http://yalibnan.com/site/archives/2007/06/lebanon_tribuna_2.php
4. 'Lebanese Presidential Election Postponed', Radio Netherlands, 25 Sep. 2007, http://static.rnw.nl/migratie/www.radionetherlands.nl/currentaffairs/lbn070925-redirected. The latest victim was anti-Syrian Member of Parliament, Antoine Ghanem, on 19 Sep. 2007, a few days before the elections were slated, *Daily Star*, Beirut, 20 Sep. 2007.
5. 'Meet Michel Suleiman, Lebanon's Next President', Ya Libnan, Beirut, 21 May 2008, http://yalibnan.com/site/archives/2008/05/meet_michel_sul.php
6. Rodger Shanahan, *Hizbullah: Walking the Lebanese Tightrope*, Sydney: Lowy Institute for International Policy, July 2008.
7. Glenn Kessler, 'Rice Cautions Israel on Syria', *Washington Post*, 30 May 2007, http://www.washingtonpost.com/wp-dyn/content/article/2007/05/29/AR2007052901808.html; 'New French FM Says Paris will Continue to Snub Syria', *Ha'aretz*, Israel, 25 May 2007.
8. Adam Entous, 'Israeli Officials: Syria Seems Serious about Talks', Reuters, 26 May 2007, http://www.alertnet.org/thenews/newsdesk/L26375948.htm; Steven Erlanger, 'For Israel, Reasons to Talk to Syria are Adding Up', *New York Times*, 27 May 2007; 'Senior IDF Officials Urge Olmert to Talk to Assad', Ynet, 3 June 2007, http://www.ynetnews.com/articles/0,7340,L-3407830,00.html
9. 'Reports: Olmert Sent Peace Messages to Syria via Turkey', *Today's Zaman*, Istanbul, 9 June 2007, http://www.todayszaman.com/tz-web/detaylar.do?load=detay&link=113569; 'Turkish Official Denies Mediation in Israel–Syria Secret Talks', *Today's Zaman*, Istanbul, 14 June 2007, http://www.todayszaman.com/tz-web/detaylar.do?load=detay&link=114007; 'Assad: Israel and Syria in Touch via Third Country', *Ha'aretz*, Israel, 19 July 2007.
10. 'White House Hails Sarkozy's Election in France', MSNBC, 7 May 2007, http://www.msnbc.msn.com/id/18535501/ns/politics/
11. Cited in 'US Iran Talks: Is Iran Trying to Inherit Syria in Lebanon?' Ya Libnan, 28 May 2007, http://yalibnan.com/site/archives/2007/05/us_iran_talks_i_1.php
12. 'Italian FM to Visit Syria Monday on Lebanon Issue', Xinhua, China, 4 June 2007, http://english.people.com.cn/200706/04/eng20070604_380537.html; 'Syria Differentiates between Hariri Probe and Tribunal', Xinhua, 6 June 6, 2007, http://english.people.com.cn/200706/06/eng20070606_381283.html
13. 'Syria Ordered its Lebanon Cells to Kill 4 Prominent Lebanese', Ya Libnan, Beirut, 11 June 2007, http://yalibnan.com/site/archives/2007/06/syria_orders_it.php
14. 'An End to Chirac's Pro-Christian Policy?' *Ha'aretz*, Tel Aviv, 15 July 2007.
15. 'France Tells Syria, Iran: Quit Betting on Deal over Lebanon', Ya Libnan, Beirut, 21 July 2007, http://yalibnan.com/site/archives/2007/07/france_tells_sy_1.php

16. 'Spanish FM has "Positive Message" from Syria for Olmert', *Ha'aretz*, Israel, 6 Aug. 2007.

17. Ivan Ureta, *Spain, the EU and the Mediterranean: From 1985 to the Arab Spring*, London: Ashgate, 2015 (forthcoming).

18. 'Washington Declines Comment after Syria Fires on Israeli Planes', AFP, Washington, 6 Sep. 2007, http://afp.google.com/article/ALeqM5iQTC3YIzqSjOB0dNDb2cLZeyg Muw

19. 'Former Syrian VP: "Assad is a Joke"', *Jerusalem Post*, 20 Sep. 2007, http://www.jpost. com/servlet/Satellite?cid=1189411453349&pagename=JPost%2FJPArticle%2FShow Full

20. 'Spanish FM has "Positive Message" from Syria for Olmert', *Ha'aretz*, Israel, 6 Aug. 2007.

21. 'Report: Syria Calling Reserve Forces following Israeli Flyover', Al-Bawaba, Amman, 9 Sep. 2007, http://www.albawaba.com/en/countries/Syria/216657

22. Hazem Khandil, 'The Challenge of Restructuring: Syrian Foreign Policy', in B. Korany and A.E.H. Dessoukip (eds), *The Foreign Policies of Arab States*, Cairo: AUC Press, 2009, p. 428.

23. Ammar Abd al-Hamid, 3 Nov. 2007, http://tharwacommunity.typepad.com/amarji/ 2007/11/index.html; see also 'Rifaat Al-Assad Posters in Syria October–2007', YouTube, http://www.youtube.com/watch?v=X_yyPooueMg&feature=player_embedded

24. Ibid.

25. 'Israel, Syria Acknowledge Indirect Talks in Turkey', CNN, 21 May 2008, http://articles. cnn.com/2008-05-21/world/israel.syria_1_indirect-talks-peace-golan-heights?_s=PM: WORLD

26. 'Deal for Lebanese Factions Leaves Hezbollah Stronger', *New York Times*, 22 May 2008.

27. John Kerry and Chuck Hagel, 'It's Time to Talk to Syria', *Wall Sreet Journal*, 5 June 2008.

28. Judith Miller, 'Obamamania in Damascus', *City Journal*, New York, 19, 14 (3 June 2008).

29. 'Mediterranean Union Launch Summit in Paris', Reuters, 13 July 2008, http://uk.reuters. com/article/2008/07/13/uk-france-mediterranean-idUKL1323466820080713

30. 'Boycott Lifted as France Hosts Syria's President', *The Guardian*, 12 July 2008.

31. For example see: 'Political Master Strokes', Oxford Analytica, UK, 31 July 2008, available at, http://www.oxan.com/worldnextweek/2008–07–31/PoliticalMasterstroke.aspx

32. Khaldun, *The Muqaddimah*, p. 141.

33. 'Turnout in Syria Vote for Assad "Unprecedented"', *Khaleej Times*, UAE, 28 May 2007.

34. 'Assad No Longer Stands in his Father's Shadow', *Ha'aretz*, Israel, 21 June 2009.

35. 'Barry Rubin: Being Nice to Syria will Lead Nowhere', IMRA, 23 May 2007, http:// www.imra.org.il/story.php3?id=34455

36. 'Syria Court Sentences Dissidents for "Speaking False News"', Jurist, Legal News & Research, 14 May 2007, http://jurist.law.pitt.edu/paperchase/2007/05/syria-court-sen-tences-dissidents-for.php; 'Syria: Four More Activists Sentenced to Prison', Human Rights Watch, Reuters, 16 May 2007, http://www.alertnet.org/thenews/newsdesk/HRW/be50 9caa985cc6ca3257a42790d873c0.htm; 'Syria Jails Four More Dissidents', Middle East Online, Damascus, 5 June 2007, http://www.middle-east-online.com/english/?id=20961

37. Abd al-Halim Khaddam, interview with Lee Smith, 'Damascus's Deadly Bargain', *New Republic*, 14 Nov. 2008.

38. Antony T. Sullivan, 'War and Rumors of War: The Levantine Tinderbox', *Middle East Policy*, XV, 1 (Spring 2008), p. 128.

39. Ibid. p. 125; 'Imad Mughniyeh Assassinated in Damascus', *Daily Star*, Beirut, 14 Feb. 2008.

40. Ibid. p. 128.

41. Gary C. Gambill, 'The Mysterious Downfall of Assef Shawkat', *Mideast Monitor*, 3, 2 (Aug. 2008); *IWPR*, Syria Issue 29, London, 3 Oct. 2008. Abd al-Halim Khaddam affirmed his view to this writer in 2009 that Asef Shawkat was taken out of his position of responsibility in 2008.

42. US Embassy Cable, 'SECRET SECTION 01 of 02 DAMASCUS 000541', 3 Aug. 2008 (WikiLeaks).

43. 'Chief Hamas Aide Assassinated in Syria', *The Australian*, Sydney, 17 Sep. 2008.

44. 'Syria Hunts for Damascus Bombers', AFP, France, 27 Sep. 2008; MEMRI, 30 Sep. 2008, http://www.thememriblog.org/blog_personal/en/10176.htm; 'Syrian Car Bomb Kills 17', BBC, London, 27 Sep. 2008; 'Did the Damascus Blast Target Syrian Intelligence Officer Linked to the Hariri Crime?' Naharnet, Beirut, 29 Sep. 2008, http://www.naharnet.com/domino/tn/newsdesk.nsf/0/C59A886E5C185DC5C22574D300609132?OpenDocument; Albert Aji, 'Killer Car Bomb Hits Damascus', *The Times*, London, 27 Sep. 2008.

45. 'Top Syrian Officer among Bomb Victims', *Jerusalem Post*, 28 Sep. 2008.

46. 'Syrian TV Shows Men "Confessing" to Deadly Bomb Attack', AFP, Damascus, 6 Nov. 2008, http://afp.google.com/article/ALeqM5gq6arHHkxl-wuzRVxux2KtF6E5qg

47. See *SANA*, Damascus, 29 Sep. 2008; *Daily Star*, Beirut, 30 Sep. 2008; *Gulf News*, UAE, 1 Oct. 2008.

48. Tony Badran, 'Divided They Stand: The Syrian Opposition', *Mideast Monitor*, 1, 3 (Sep.–Oct. 2006).

49. 'What Could Lie Behind Syria Raid?' BBC, 26 Oct. 2008, http://news.bbc.co.uk/2/hi/middle_east/7692263.stm

50. 'Syrian Culture Minister Extols Resistance', *Al-Ittihad*, UAE, 27 Mar. 2009, trans. Memri, 26 July 2009, no. 2462, http://www.memri.org/bin/latestnews.cgi?ID=SD246209

51. 'Israeli Troops Mobilize as Gaza Assault Widens', Associated Press, 29 Dec. 2008; see also: Associated Press, 18 Jan. 2009.

52. 'Syrian President Whips up Religious Fervour', *Gulf News*, UAE, 18 Jan. 2009; for another example of Bashar al-Asad's rhetoric on Gaza see: 'Syrian President Says Gaza Attacks "Worse than Nazism"', *Adnkronos*, Italy, 16 Jan. 2009, http://www.adnkronos.com/AKI/English/Security/?id=3.0.2916833303

53. 'Syria Profits from Regional Diplomatic Upheaval after Gaza Conflict', VOA, United States, 2 Feb. 2009, http://www.voanews.com/english/2009–02–02-voa39.cfm

54. 'Assad No Longer Stands in his Father's Shadow', *Ha'aretz*, Israel, 21 June 2009.

55. Jonathan Spyer, 'Analysis: Israel's Reluctant Allies', *Jerusalem Post*, 30 Dec. 2008.

56. Ibid.; 'Israel Bombs Gaza in "All-Out War" on Hamas', AFP, 30 Dec. 2008, http://www.google.com/hostednews/afp/article/ALeqM5iFQrIY68kBMfb7ujJHSJrDJAQrJg

57. Abd al-Halim Khaddam was emphatic on this point, interview with the author, 16 Sep. 2009, Paris.

58. 'A New Partner in Syria?' *Washington Post*, 24 Dec. 2008; 'How Did Assad Manage to Gain International Respect?' *Ha'aretz*, Israel, 26 Dec. 2008.

59. 'Hamas Rejects UN Call for Gaza Ceasefire', *Guardian*, 9 Jan. 2008.

60. Ynet, Israel, 8 Jan. 2008, http://www.ynetnews.com/articles/0,7340,L-3652614,00.html. This was more likely a strategic move by the Syrian Muslim Brotherhood than a genuine ideological shift, see: Liad Porat, 'The Syrian Muslim Brotherhood and the Asad Regime', *Middle East Brief*, no. 47, Dec. 2010, Crown Center for Middle East Studies, Brandeis University.

61. 'Syrian Muslim Brotherhood Withdraws from the Opposition National Salvation Front', Ex Oriente Lux, 5 Apr. 2009, http://orientelux.com/?p=31; 'Syrian Opposition Group Collapses', *The National*, Abu Dhabi, 22 Apr. 2009.

62. Roula Khalaf and Anna Fifield, 'An Assured Assad', *Financial Times*, 10 May 2009; 'Arab Public Opinion 2009', *Foreign Policy*, 19 May 2009, http://lynch.Foreignpolicy.com/posts/2009/05/19/arab_public_opinion_in_2009

63. Khaldun, *The Mqaddimah*, pp. 255–6.

64. 'Between 1995 and 2005 the Syrian population increased by 29 percent and the working age population rose by 48 percent', see Paul Rivlin, 'Syria, Lost Potential,' in *Arab Economies in the Twenty-First Century*, Cambridge: Leiden University Press, 2009, pp. 240–65.

65. Søren Schmidt, 'The Developmental Role of the State in the Middle East: Lessons from Syria', in R. Hinnebusch (ed.), *The State and the Political Economy of Reform in Syria*, Fife: St Andrews Papers on Contemporary Syria, p. 33.

66. Philip Jenkins, *The Lost History of Christianity*, New York: HarperCollins, 2008, pp. 135–6.

67. Abd al-Halim Khaddam, interview with the author, Paris, 16 Sep. 2009.

68. See UNDP report 'Impact of the World Economic Downturn on Syrian Economy, Inequality and Poverty', 3 Nov. 2009; also IMF Country Report no. 10/86, March 2010; *Gulf News*, 30 Apr. 2009.

69. Paul Rivlin, 'The Socio-Economic Crisis in Syria', *Iqtisadi*, 1, 3 (June 2011), pp. 3–4.

70. Volker Perthes, *The Political Economy of Syria under Asad*, London: I.B. Tauris, 1995, p. 136.

71. Between 2003 and 2007, oil-related proceeds decreased from 14.7 per cent to 3.8 per cent of GDP, see IMF Report no. 07/288, p. 32.

72. US Energy Information Administration, 'Syria Analysis', available at http://205.254.135.7/countries/cab.cfm?fips=SY; BP Statistical Review of World Energy, June 2011, bp.com/statisticalreview; see also *Syria Today*, Damascus, issue 55, Nov. 2009.

73. Bashar al-Asad's trips to Armenia and Azerbaijan in 2009 were all focused on realising this objective, see: 'Syria's President: "Azerbaijan Gave Consent to Sell 1 Billion Cubic Meters of Gas per Year to Syria at Current Prices"', *APA*, 11 July 2009, http://en.apa.az/news.php?id=104976; 'Al-Assad Begins an Official Visit to Azerbaijan', *SNS*, Damascus, 9 July 2009, http://sns.sy/sns/?path=news/read/2978; 'Syrian President due in Armenia on June 17', *Turkish Weekly*, Istanbul, 16 June 2009.

74. 'Iraq, Syria Agree on Plan to Repair Kirkuk–Banias Oil Line', *Oil & Gas Journal*, Los Angeles, 24 Apr. 2009, http://www.ogj.com/display_article/360224/120/ARTCL/none/Trasp/1/Iraq,-Syria-agree-on-plan-to-repair-Kirkuk-Banias-oil-line/

75. Nimrod Raphaeli, 'The Missed Opportunity of the Iraq–Syria Oil Pipeline: Syria Chooses Terrorism over Long-Term Economic Gains', *Memri*, 18 May 2009, Inquiry and Analysis, no. 515, http://www.memri.org/bin/articles.cgi?Page=archives&Area=ia&ID=IA51509

76. Ibid.

77. Volker Perthes, *Syria under Bashar al-Asad: Modernisation and the Limits of Change*, Adelphi Paper no. 366, New York: Oxford University Press, 2004, p. 66.

78. *Washington Post*, 9 May 2009.

79. See Anja Zorob, 'Trade Liberalization and Adjustment via Regional Integration: The Syrian–European Association Agreement', in R. Hinnebusch (ed.), *Syria and the Euro-Mediterranean Relationship*, Fife: University of St Andrews Centre for Syrian Studies, 2009.

80. 'Syria Raises Doubts about Signing EU Partnership', AFP, France, 14 Oct. 2009, http://www.google.com/hostednews/afp/article/ALeqM5hhTUW9gcG92cTzf9Yn2hEaCZwBLQ; on the EU association agreement Bashar al-Asad said in Nov. 2009: 'the partner has to be a friend and we have never seen this during the latest years', *Cham Press*, Damascus, 13 Nov. 2009, http://www.champress.net/index.php?q=en/Article/view/47949.

81. 'Tough Time Ahead for Returning Syrians', *The National*, UAE, 12 June 2009.

82. 'Arab Countries Should Coordinate Crisis Response, to Avoid Social Backlash', Business Intelligence Middle East, May 17, 2009, http://www.bi-me.com/main.php?id=36359&t=1&c=62&cg=4&mset

83. Paul Rivlin, 'The Socio-Economic Crisis in Syria', *Iqtisadi*, 1, 3 (June 2011), p. 5.

84. Ibid. p. 5.

85. 'Syria Launches Long-Awaited Stock Exchange as Part of Moves to Liberalize Economy', *Daily Star*, Beirut, 11 Mar. 2009.

86. 'Syria Attracts Cash, to Boost Capital Rules', Trade Arabia, 7 July 2009, http://www.tradearabia.com/news/newsdetails.asp?Sn=ECO&artid=164585; 'Syria—Pursuing Partnership with the Private Sector', Global Arab Network, 11 Nov. 2009.

87. *Forbes*, 26 Oct. 2009, http://www.forbes.com/2009/10/23/syria-unctad-trade-business-oxford-analytica.html

88. Schmidt, 'The Developmental Role', p. 33.

89. 'Dardari Defends Syria's Economic Reforms', *Syria Today*, Damascus, issue 56, Dec. 2009.

90. See, for example, 'Opening to Tourism, Syria Flaunts Hidden Treasures', Reuters, 16 July

2009, http://www.reuters.com/article/lifestyleMolt/idUSTRE56G00C20090717?page Number=2&virtualBrandChannel=0

91. 'Income of $ 3.9 Billion from International Tourism in Syria', Syria News Station, Damascus, 15 June 2009, http://sns.sy/sns/?path=news/read/2294b

92. 'Syrian Tourism Grows Fast Amidst Economic Crisis', Xinhua, China, 10 Aug. 2009, http://news.xinhuanet.com/english/2009–08/10/content_11858058.htm

93. 'Turkey, Syria Extend Cooperation to Tourism', *Today's Zaman*, Istanbul, 5 Nov. 2009, http://www.todayszaman.com/tz-web/news-192048–102-turkey-syria-extend-cooper-ation-to-tourism.html

94. 'Syria—Emerging Attractive Tourist Destination', Global Arab Network, London, 1 Sep. 2009, http://www.english.globalarabnetwork.com/200909012498/Travel/syria-emerging-attractive-tourist-destination.html

95. Paul Rivlin, 'The Socio-Economic Crisis in Syria', *Iqtisadi*, 1, 3 (June 2011), p. 6.

96. 'Lebanon–Syria: Wretched conditions for Syrian Workers', IRIN, 14 Apr. 2009, http://www.irinnews.org/Report.aspx?ReportId=83900; the poor living and working conditions of Syrians in Lebanon was confirmed to this writer during a visit to Lebanon in 2011. See also: John Chalcroft, *The Invisible Cage: Syrian Migrant Workers in Lebanon*, Stanford: Stanford University Press, 2009.

97. 'Opposition in Syria Raises its Head', Ynet, Israel, 3 Sep. 2007, http://www.ynetnews.com/articles/0,7340,L-3445000,00.html

98. Ibid.

99. 'Assad Revokes Citizenship of Politician who Visited Knesset', *Ha'aretz*, Israel, 15 Sep. 2007.

100. 'Exiled Syrian Reformer Urges Return of Golan—But Not To Assad', *Ha'aretz*, Israel, 11 June 2007.

101. 'Dutch Foreign Minister, in Syria, Calls for "Bold Steps", *Earth Times*, 23 June 2009, http://www.earthtimes.org/articles/show/274340,dutch-foreign-minister-in-syria-calls-for-bold-steps.html

102. 'Ex-Political Prisoners Remain Outcasts', IWPR, Damascus, 9 Jan. 2009, http://www.iwpr.net/?p=syr&s=f&o=349011&apc_state=henh

103. 'Blackout on July Unrest at Sednaya Amid Reports of More Violence', Human Rights Watch, 27 Jan. 2009, http://www.hrw.org/en/news/2009/01/27/syria-reveal-inmates-conditions

104. 'Syria Accused of Covering Up Deaths of 25 Prisoners', *Telegraph*, UK, 30 Apr. 2009.

105. Ibid.

106. For a full examination of Syria's human rights record under Bashar al-Asad see: 'A Wasted Decade: Human Rights in Syria during Bashar al-Asad's First Ten Years in Power', Human Rights Watch, New York, 2010.

107. E. Piguet and F. Laczko (eds), *People on the Move in a Changing Climate*, Global Migration Issues, 2, Dordrecht: Springer, 2014, p. 122.

108. Paul Rivlin, 'The Socio-Economic Crisis in Syria', p. 4; 'Syria: Drought Exacerbates

Economic Woes', IRIN, Damascus, 4 Mar. 2009, http://www.irinnews.org/Report. aspx?ReportId=83292

109. Cattle Network, 13 May 2009, http://www.cattlenetwork.com/Content.asp?Content ID=314143 (accessed 14 May 2009).

110. *Al-Thawra*, Damascus, August 9, 2009, translated and cited in AFP, France, 9 Aug. 2009, http://www.google.com/hostednews/afp/article/ALeqM5htmizu2w29_9Ovwv4 0osK_6Zxtxw

111. IRIN, Damascus, 4 Mar. 2009.

112. Environment News Service, Latakia, 13 July 2009, http://www.ens-newswire.com/ens/ jul2009/2009-07-13-02.asp (accessed 16 July 2009).

113. '160 Syrian Villages Deserted "Due to Climate Change"', AFP, Paris, 6 June 2009, http://www.google.com/hostednews/afp/article/ALeqM5jXbS8a3ggi Mm4ekludBbmWQMb-HQ; 'Syria: Drought Driving Farmers to the Cities', IRIN, Damascus, 2 Sep. 2009, http://www.irinnews.org/report.aspx?reportid=85963

114. Anonymous conversation with the author.

115. 'Severe Drought Affects 1.3 Million in Syria', Christian Science Monitor, 18 Sep. 2009, http://www.csmonitor.com/World/Middle-East/2009/0918/p06s04-wome.html

116. 'Four Die in Clashes Over Demolitions Near Damascus', *Daily Star*, Beirut, 4 June 2009.

117. Ibid.

118. For example, an explosive device was detonated near the home of Tripoli Alawite leader Rifa'at Eid in Aug. 2009, see: *Adnkronos*, Italy, 13 Aug. 2009, 'Lebanon: Three Injured in Bomb Attack in Northern Port Cist,' http://www.adnkronos.com/AKI/English/ Security/?id=3.0.3653410406; see also: 'Spate of Security Incidents Rattles Lebanon', *Daily Star*, Beirut, 24 Sep. 2009.

119. Sebastian Malo, 'From Bullets to Paint Brushes in Bab al-Tabbaneh', *Daily Star*, Beirut, 22 May 2009.

120. This was especially so after the termination of Rifa'at al-Asad's overt corruption inside Syria.

121. I discussed this point by with numerous Sunni Muslim acquaintances in Syria and the overwhelming consensus was that Alawites were not 'genuine' Muslims. This view is shared by some Shi'ites who consider Alawites extremists (*Ghulat*).

122. 'Syria Issues Tough New Law against Killer Tobacco', IRIN, Damascus, 3 Dec. 2009, http://www.irinnews.org/report.aspx?reportid=87304

123. 'PM Otri Makes an Economic Review at NPF Branches Meeting, Rate of GDP Increased to SYP 1343.2 Billions in 2008', *ChamPress*, Damascus, 9 Dec. 2009, http://www.cham-press.net/index.php?q=en/Article/view/49749

124. Cited in Hassan M. Fattah, 'Assad Grows into Role of Syria's Iron Ruler', *New York Times*, 24 May 2007.

125. 'Licence Obtained for Syria Venture', *Gulf Times*, UAE, 16 May 2007; 'First Bank under Islamic Law Opens in Syria', *Jerusalem Post*, 27 Aug. 2007; see also: 'Syria Eyes $30 bln

Foreign Investments', Reuters, London, 25 June 2009, http://www.reuters.com/article/rbssFinancialServicesAndRealEstateNews/idUSLP22304420090625

126. See: 'Arab Banks Seek Syria Entry as Economy Grows', *Gulf Times*, UAE, 6 June 2007.

127. Rivlin, 'The Socio-Economic Crisis in Syria', p. 6.

128. 'Embrace Democracy: Syria's Top Dissident Urges Assad', *Khaleej Times*, 16 May 2007.

129. 'Syria: Prominent Cleric—Who Supported Iraqi Resistance—Assassinated', *Al-Bawaba*, Amman, 28 Sep. 2007, http://www.albawaba.com/en/countries/Iraq/217288

130. 'Imam Shot Dead at Syrian Mosque', AFP, 28 Sep. 2007, http://afp.google.com/article/ALeqM5gWSgqmyNNAsHkUfeyEOmxhnQs2fg; see also 'Aleppo: Syria's Sleeping, Giant', Al-Jazeera, 23 June 2011.

131. Emmanuel Sivan, 'Arab—Speak Arabic', *Ha'aretz*, Israel, 5 Oct. 2007.

132. Murad Batal al-Shishani, 'Jihadis Turn their Eyes to Syria as a Post Iraq Theater of Operations', *Terrorism Monitor*, VII, 26 (20 Aug. 2009), pp. 3–4.

133. Nibras Kazimi, 'The Perfect Enemy', *New York Sun*, 1 June 2007, http://www.nysun.com/opinion/perfect-enemy/55690/;'Explosion in Syria Kills 15 Soldiers', CTV News, Canada, 26 July 2007, http://www.ctv.ca/servlet/ArticleNews/story/CTVNews/20070726/syria_explosion_070726/20070726?hub=World

134. For example see, *The National*, UAE, 26 September 2008.

135. CTV News, Canada, 26 July 2007.

136. 'Syria Blast "Linked to Chemical Weapons": Report', AFP, London, 19 Sep. 2007, http://afp.google.com/article/ALeqM5iJugIQvDKwkxupz9eULk1ml6OZ4Q

137. Sivan, 'Arab—Speak Arabic'.

138. *Ha'aretz*, Israel, 5 Oct. 2007; see also 'President al-Assad Meets General Federation of Arab Writers Delegation', SANA, Damascus, 5 Nov. 2008, www.sana.sy/eng/142/2008/11/04/199887.htm

139. Shaykh 'Ali Yeral spoke with the author about how Bashar al-Asad moved closer to the Sunnis than his father.

140. In 2005 23 per cent of Syrians were aged fifteen–twenty-four, therefore in 2011 a large proportion of Syria's population would be approximately twenty–thirty-four, see Navtej Dhillon and Tarik Yousef (eds), *Generation in Waiting: The Unfulfilled Promise of Young People in the Middle East*, Washington, DC: Brookings Institution, 2009, p. 189; see also Nader Kabbani and Noura Kamel, 'Youth Exclusion in Syria: Social, Economic, and Institutional Dimensions', Working Paper—The Middle East Youth Initiative, no. 4, Sep. 2007, Wolfensohn Center for Development, Dubai.

141. This impression was gained during the many conversations this author had with young Syrians from all sects, all of whom must remain anonymous.

142. UN Data, 'Percentage of Individuals using the Internet—Syria', available at http://data.un.org/Data.aspx?q=Syria&d=ITU&f=ind1Code%3aI99H%3bcountryCode%3aSYR

143. 'Syria Intensifying Internet Crackdown: Watchdog', *Sydney Morning Herald*, 8 July 2007.

144. Tony Badran, 'Divided They Stand: The Syrian Opposition', *Mideast Monitor*, 1, 3 (Sep.–Oct. 2006).

145. Rula Amin, 'Syrian Opposition Figure Triggers Debate', Al-Jazeera, 11 July 2011.

146. 'U.S. Attacks Syria Sentencing', UPI, Washington, DC, 22 June 2007, http://www.upi.com/Business_News/Security-Industry/2007/06/22/US-attacks-Syria-sentencing/UPI-32291182551387/

147. O. Winter, Memri, 31 July 2007, 'Inquiry and Analysis—No. 378, "Syrian Oppositionists Criticize Oppression of Young People in Syria"', http://www.memri.org/report/en/0/0/0/0/0/0/0/2315.htm

148. 'Syrian Intelligence Training New Recruits in UK, Germany', AINA, Washington, DC, 30 Sep. 2007, http://www.aina.org/news/20070930144804.htm

149. 'Syria: Minister of Defense Says World Lives in "Foggy Stage" after Bush Administration', ISRIA, France, 1 June 2009, http://www.isria.com/pages/1_June_2009_19.htm

150. 'Syria Bans Facebook to Reclaim Golan Heights', Ha'aretz, Israel, 15 Sep. 2009.

151. Syria was listed in the top three most repressive countries for 'bloggers' by CNN, May 2009, 'Myanmar Tops List of Worst Places to be a Blogger', http://edition.cnn.com/2009/TECH/05/04/world.bloggers/

152. Anna Skibinsky, 'Syria's Democracy Activist on Moving toward Peaceful Revolutions', The Epoch Times, 4 Aug. 2009, http://www.theepochtimes.com/n2/content/view/20484/

153. 'Syria to Auction Third Mobile Licence by Q1 2010', TeleGeography, 17 Apr. 2009, http://www.telegeography.com/cu/article.php?article_id=28041&email=html

154. UN Data, 'Mobile-Cellular Subscriptions per 100 Inhabitants', available at http://data.un.org/Data.aspx?q=Syria&d=ITU&f=ind1Code%3aI911%3bcountryCode%3aSYR

155. By 2007 the Chinese telecommunications company, Huawei, had captured a large share of the Syrian market with its cheap handsets, see: Ben Simpfendorfer, The New Silk Road, 2nd edn, Basingstoke: Palgrave Macmillan, 2009, p. 86.

156. Rami Makhlouf acquired 75 per cent of Syriatel in 2000. This was the procurement that Riad Seif opposed and for which he was jailed in 2001. For details of Syriatel, see: Soren Schmidt, 'The Politics of Economic Liberalization in Syria', International Development Studie Occasional Paper no. 25, 2006, p. 239.

157. Khaldun, Muqaddimah, p. 232.

158. See, for example: 'Syria: Has it Won?' The Economist, 26 Nov. 2009; Ayman Abdel Nour, 'Syria's Season of Clout', Gulf News, UAE, 9 Oct. 2009.

159. 'Syrian President's Younger Brother Dies', Press TV, Tehran, 12 Dec. 2009, http://www.presstv.ir/detail.aspx?id=113584&sectionid=351020206

160. 'Former Syrian President Amin Hafez dies at 89', Associated Press, Damascus, 17 Dec. 2009, http://www.google.com/hostednews/ap/article/ALeqM5hi0ikWWKplSnbywIWE1AYfozlE3gD9CL9LU05; with the exception of Abd al-Halim Khaddam's very short caretaker role in 2000.

161. Ibn Khaldun wrote: 'as a rule no dynasty lasts beyond three generations', The Muqaddimah, p. 136.

162. 'Street Seller's Death Sets Off Mass Revolt', The Financial Times, 17 Jan. 2011.

163. See, 'Interview with Syrian President Bashar al-Asad', Wall Street Journal, 31 Jan. 2011.

164. Lisa Wedeen, 'Ideology and Humor in Dark Times: Notes from Syria', *Critical Inquiry*, 39, 4 (Summer 2013), pp. 841–73.

165. Khaldoun Khashanah, 'The Syrian Crisis: A Systemic Framework', *Contemporary Arab Affairs*, 7, 1 (2014), pp. 1–21.

166. Ted Galen Carpenter, 'Tangled Web: The Syrian Civil War and its Implications,' *Mediterranean Quarterly*, 24, 1 (Winter 2013), pp. 1–11.

167. Sham Network, SNN, YouTube, http://www.youtube.com/watch?v=CDuc76Lk9XY (uploaded 13 Sep. 2011).

168. Christa Salamandra, 'Sectarianism in Syria: Anthropological Reflections', *Middle East Critique*, 22, 3 (2013), p. 303.

169. Youtube, uploaded 15 March, 2011 by 'xgotfiveonitx,' http://www.youtube.com/watch?v=2nPpjdv0GiM

170. 'The Squeeze on Asad', *Economist*, anonymous correspondent, 30 June 2011.

171. 'Prominent Alawite Clerics Denounce Assad Regime's "Atrocities"', *Al-Arabiya*, Dubai, 12 Sep. 2011, http://english.alarabiya.net/articles/2011/09/12/166498.html.

172. 'Syrian Opposition Figure Triggers Debate', Rula Amin, Al-Jazeera, 11 July 2011; 'Profiles: Syrian Opposition Figures', Al-Jazeera, 27 June 2011.

173. Sunda Suleiman (Representative of the Syrian Arab Alawite Society), interview by V. Ayhan and O. Orhan, Antalya, Turkey, 'An Interview with Sunda Suleiman', ORSAM, 1 June 2011, 14 Mar. 2014, http://www.orsam.org.tr/en/showOrsamGuest.aspx?ID=182; 'Q&A: Nir Rosen on Syrian Sectarianism', Al Jazeera, 18 Feb. 2012.

174. Ibid.

175. Sunda Suleiman, interview, Orsam, Antalya, Turkey, 1 June 2011

176. Khaled Yacoub Oweis, 'Fearing Stark Future, Syrian Alawites Meet in Cairo', Reuters, 23 Mar. 2013.

177. Leon Goldsmith, 'Crisis and Compromise: A Turning Point for Syria's Alawites?' Global Politics, Aug. 2012, http://global-politics.co.uk/blog/2012/07/31/crisis_compromise_Syria/

178. Oren Kessler, 'Alawite Defections from Syrian Army may be on Rise', *Jerusalem Post*, 8 Mar. 2012.

179. 'Damascus Chaos Strikes Fear in Assad's Alawite Bastion', Reuters, 22 July 2012.

180. Salamandra, 'Sectarianism in Syria'.

181. Nir Rosen, 'Assad's Alawites: The Guardians of the Throne', Al-Jazeera, 10 Oct. 2011.

182. Hanna Batatu, 'Some Observations on the Social Roots of Syria's Ruling, Military Group and the Causes for its Dominance', *Middle East Journal*, 35, 3 (1981), p. 332.

183. Michael Weiss, 'Sectarianism or a Trap by Assad?' *The Weekly Standard*, 22 July 2012.

184. Ibid. pp. 7, 13.

185. Khaled Yacoub Oweis, 'Notables Calm Sectarian Tensions in Syrian City', Reuters, 28 Mar. 2011.

186. Author's observations, Latakia, 25 Mar. 2011

187. Hiedar al-Hassan, email correspondence with the author, July 2014.

188. Jomana Qaddour, 'Unlocking the Alawite Conundrum in Syria,' *The Washington Quarterly*, Vol. 36, No. 4 (December 2013), pp. 67–78.

189. Yassin al-Haj Salih, 'The Syrian Shabiha and Their State', Heinrich Boll Stuftung, Apr. 2012.

190. Aaron Reese, 'Sectarian and Regional Conflict in the Middle East', *Middle East Security Report*, 13, Institute for the Study of War (July 2013), p. 14.

191. Isabel Nassief, "The Campaign for Homs and Aleppo." *Middle East Security Report*, Institute for the Study of War, No. 17 (2014), p. 13; Jonathan Spyer, 'Fragmented Syria', *Middle East Review of International Affairs*, 17, 3 (Fall 2013), p. 11.

192. Charles Lister, 'Dynamic Stalemate: Surveying Syria's Military Landscape', Brookings Doha Center, May 2014, p. 3.

193. Joseph Halliday, 'The Struggle for Syria in 2011', Institute for the Study of War, December 2011, http://www.understandingwar.org/sites/default/files/Struggle_For_Syria.pdf

194. Syrian Arab News Agency, 9 July 2011, http://www.sana.sy/en/

195. Roula Hajjar and Borzou Daragahi, 'Syrian Reports Suggest Divisions in Security Forces', *Los Angeles Times*, 9 June 2011, http://articles.latimes.com/2011/jun/09/world/la-fg-syria-jisr-shughur-20110609

196. Louis Charbonneau, 'Syria Conflict Now a Civil War, U.N. Peacekeeping Chief Says', Reuters, 12 June 2012, http://uk.mobile.reuters.com/article/topNews/idUKBRE85B1FM20120612

197. Mark Fitzpatrick, 'Destroying Syria's Chemical Weapons', *Survival: Global Politics and Strategy*, 55, 6 (2013), pp. 107–14.

198. Charles Lister, 'Dynamic Stalemate', p. 2.

199. 'Syrian President Bashar al-Assad Wins Third Term', BBC Middle East, 5 June 2011, http://www.bbc.com/news/world-middle-east-27706471 (accessed 18 June 2014).

200. See, Aymenn Jawad al-Tamimi, 'The Dawn of the Islamic State of Iraq and ash-Sham', *Current Trends in Islamist Ideology*, 16 (2014).

201. Ali Mamouri, 'Why Islamic State has no Sympathy for Hamas', Al-Monitor, 29 July 2014, http://www.al-monitor.com/pulse/originals/2014/07/islamic-state-fighting-hamas-priority-before-israel.html

202. 'Syrian Alawites Horrified by Rising Death Toll', Al-Monitor, 5 Aug. 2014.

CONCLUSION

1. Volker Perthes (ed.), *Arab Elites: Negotiating the Politics of Change*, Boulder: Lynne Rienner, 2004, p. 110.

2. Arend Lijphart, *Thinking about Democracy*, Oxon: Routledge, 2008, p. 279.

3. Donald L. Horowitz, *Ethnic Groups in Conflict*, Berkeley: University of California Press, 1985, pp. 570–6.

4. Nikolaos van Dam, *The Struggle for Power in Syria: Politics and Society under Asad and the Ba'th Party*, 4th edn, New York: I.B. Tauris, 2011, p. 144.

5. Shaykh Muhammad Boz, interview with the author, 28 Mar., Antakya.

6. Shaykh 'Ali Yeral, interview with author, 28 Mar. 2011, Antakya.

7. Ibid.

8. 'Syrian Alawites Hate Assad: Opposition Figure', *Al-Arabiya*, 20 Dec. 2011.

9. Issa Ibrahim and Hiedar al-Hassan, email correspondence with the author, July 2014. See Appendix for the full document.

10. David Held, *Cosmopolitanism: Ideals and Realities*, Cambridge: Polity Press, 2010.

11. Franck Salameh, 'Adonis, the Syrian Crisis, and the Question of Pluralism in the Levant', *Bustan: The Middle East Book Review*, 3 (2012), p. 36.

12. Christa Salamandra, 'Sectarianism in Syria: Anthropological Reflections', *Middle East Critique*, 22, 3 (Oct. 2013), pp. 305–6.

BIBLIOGRAPHY

Arabic Sources

Al-'Awra, Ibrahim, *Tarikh Waliyat Suleiman Pasha al-'Adil, 1804–1819*, pp. 205–6, trans. Leon Goldsmith and Jean-Luc Payan, 2010.

Al-Ibrahim, 'Ali 'Aziz, *Al-Alawiyyun wa al-Shi'a*, Beirut: 1992.

Al-Qila'i, Ibn Jibrail, *Zajaliyyat*, Beirut: Dar Lahad Khatar, 1982.

Haqqi, Ismail, *Lubnan: Mabahith Ilmiya wa Ijtima'iya*, ed. Fuad Bustani from the 1918 original, 2 vols, Beirut: Manshurat al-Jami'at al-Lubnaniyya, Qism al-Dirasat al-Tarikhiyya, 1970.

Primary Sources—English

BP, 'Statistical Review of World Energy', June 2011.

'Decree of the High Commissioner of the French Republic', *League of Nations Official Journal*, 3113 (Sep. 1930), p. 1124.

IMF Country Report no. 07/288, Aug. 2007.

——— no. 10/86, Mar. 2010.

King, Henry C. and Charles R. Crane, 'Wishes of the People', 'The King–Crane Commission Report—Confidential Appendix—August 28, 1919', vol. 55, no. 27, 2nd Section, 2 Dec. 1922, I. II. 2.

League of Nations Official Journal, 93rd and 94th Sessions of the Council, Annex 1622 (Nov. 1936), p. 1354.

——— 104th Session of the Council, Annex 1742 (Feb. 1939), p. 162.

'Letter from the French Government to the Secretary General of the League of Nations', Paris, 11 June 1930, *League of Nations Official Journal* (Sep. 1930), Article 18, p. 1100.

'"The Mandate" July 24th 1922', *League of Nations Official Journal*, 95th Session of the Council, Annex 1629 (Jan. 1937), Article 8, p. 47.

'Observations of the Administration of Certain Territories under Mandate', *League of Nations Official Journal*, 104th Session of the Council, Annex 1742 (Feb. 1939), A. pp. 161–2.

BIBLIOGRAPHY

UNDP, 'The Impact of the World Economic Downturn on Syrian Economy, Inequality and Poverty', 3 Nov. 2009, available at: http://www.undp.org/content/dam/aplaws/publication/en/publications/poverty-reduction/poverty-website/psia/syria-full-report/The_Impact_of_the_World_Crisis_Revised_Version%20SYRIA.pdf

UNIIIC, 'Report of the International Independent Investigation Commission', Detlev Mehlis, Beirut, 19 Oct. 2005, document available at: http://www.un.org/news/dh/docs/mehlisreport.pdf (accessed 28 July 2009).

United Nations, 'Official U.N. Transcript of the Meeting of U.N. Secretary-General Ban Ki-moon with Bashar al-Asad. Damascus', 24 Apr. 2007.

UN Security Council, S/RES/1559 (2004) 04–49892 (E), adopted 2 Sep. 2004.

———— S/RES/1595 (2005), 05–29998(E), adopted 7 Apr. 2005.

———— S/RES/1686 (2006), 06–39006 (E), adopted 15 June 2006.

———— S/RES/1701 (2006), 06–46503 (E), adopted 11 Aug. 2006.

———— S/RES/1757 (2007), 07–36357 (E), adopted 30 May 2007.

(All UN Security Council Resolutions available at: http://www.un.org/Docs/sc/)

US Embassy Cable, 'SECRET SECTION 01 of 02 DAMASCUS 000541', 3 Aug. 2008 (WikiLeaks), available at, http://www.guardian.co.uk/world/us-embassy-cables-documents/164634 (accessed 12 Aug. 2009).

US Energy Information Administration, 'Syria Analysis', http://205.254.135.7/countries/cab.cfm?fips=SY

World Bank, 'Syrian Arab Republic', http://data.worldbank.org/country/syrian-arab-republic

Personal Interviews

Abd al-Halim Khaddam, 16 Sep. 2009, Paris.
Judge Detlev Mehlis, 12 May 2009, Dunedin.
Professor Elie Salam, 16 Mar. 2011, Balamand.
Shaykh 'Ali Yeral, 28 Mar. 2011, Antakya (in Arabic).
Shaykh Muhammad Boz, 28 Mar. 2011, Antakya (in Arabic).
Shaykh Nasīr Eskiocak, 29 March 2011, Antakya (in Arabic).

Email Consultations

Mr Heidar Al-Hassan (in Arabic)
Mr Issa Ibrahim (grandson of Shaykh Saleh Al-Ali) (in Arabic)

Newspapers, News Websites and Magazines

Agence France-Presse, daily, Paris.
Al-Hayat, daily, London.

BIBLIOGRAPHY

Ash-Sharq al-Awsat, daily, London.

BBC News, UK, news website, http://www.bbc.co.uk/news/

Financial Times, daily, London.

Ha'aretz, daily, Tel Aviv.

Institute of War and Peace Reporting, UK, news website, http://iwpr.net/

Jerusalem Post, daily, Jerusalem.

Los Angeles Times, daily, Los Angeles

Naharnet, Beirut, news website, http://www.naharnet.com

New York Times, daily, New York.

Press TV, Tehran, news website, http://www.presstv.ir/

Syrian Arab News Agency, Damascus, news website, http://www.sana.sy/index_eng.html

Syria Today, monthly, Damascus.

The Daily Star, daily, Beirut.

The Economist, weekly, London.

The Times, daily, London.

Washington Post, daily, Washington, DC.

Xinhua, China, news website, http://www.xinhuanet.com/english2010/

Secondary Sources

Abboud, Samer, 'The Transition Paradigm and the Case of Syria', in R. Hinnebusch (ed.), *Syria's Economy and the Transition Paradigm*, Fife: University of St Andrews Centre for Syrian Studies, 2009.

Abdallah, Umar F., *The Islamic Struggle in Syria*, Berkeley: Mizan Press, 1983.

Abdulghanim, Jasim, *Iraq and Iran: The Crisis Years*, Sydney: Croom Helm, 1984.

Abir, M., 'Modernisation, Reaction and Muhammad Ali's Empire', *Middle Eastern Studies*, 13, 3 (Oct. 1977).

Agoston G. and B. Masters, *Encyclopaedia of the Ottoman Empire*, New York: Infobase, 2009.

Ahmad, Z., *The Epistemology of Ibn Khaldun*, London: Routledge-Curzon, 2003.

Amitai, R., (ed.) *The Mongols in Islamic Lands: Studies in the History of the Ilkhanate*, Aldershot: Ashgate-Valorium, 2007.

Andrew, C. and A.S. Kanya-Forstner, *The Climax of French Imperial Expansion 1914–1924*, London: Thames & Hudson, 1981.

Al-Azmeh, A., *Ibn Khaldun: An Essay in Reinterpretation*, Budapest: Central European Press, 2003.

———— *Ibn Khaldun in Modern Scholarship: A Study in Orientalism*, London: Third World Research Centre, 1981.

Al-Bitar, Salah al-Din, Interview with M. Aulas, trans. M. Hooglund, E. and J. Paul, 'The Major Deviation of the Ba'th is Having Renounced Democracy', *MERIP Reports*, 110, Syria's Troubles (Nov.–Dec. 1982).

Al-Tawīl, Muhammad Amīn Ghālib, *Ta'rīkh al-'Alawiyyīn*, Latakia: 1966.

BIBLIOGRAPHY

Arslanian, Ferdinand, 'Growth in Transition and Syria's Economic Performance', in R. Hinnebusch (ed.) *Syria's Economy and the Transition Paradigm*, Fife: University of St Andrews Centre for Syrian Studies, 2009.

Ashworth, L.M., 'Ibn Khaldun and the Origins of State Politics', in N. Persram (ed.) *Postcolonialism and Political Theory*, Plymouth: Lexington Books, 2007.

Avi-Ran, Reuben, *The Syrian Involvement in Lebanon Since 1975*, Boulder: Westview Press, 1991.

Badran, Tony, 'Divided They Stand: The Syrian Opposition', *Mideast Monitor*, 1, 3 (Sep.-Oct. 2006).

Balanche, Fabrice, *La Région Alaouite et le Pouvoir Syrien*, Paris: Karthala, 2006.

Bar-Asher, Meir M., 'The Iranian Component of the Nusayrī Religion', *Iran*, 4 (2003), pp. 217–27.

Bar-Asher, Meir M. and Aryeh Kofksy, *The Nusayri-'Alawī Religion: An Enquiry into its Theology and Liturgy*, Leiden: Brill, 2002.

Bar, Shmuel, 'Bashar's Syria: The Regime and its Strategic Worldview', *Comparative Strategy*, 25 (2006), pp. 353–445.

Barbour, Nevill, 'Impressions of the United Arab Republic', *International Affairs*, 36, 1 (Jan. 1960), pp. 21–34.

Batatu, Hanna, 'Some Observations on the Social Roots of Syria's Ruling Military Group and the Causes for its Dominance', *Middle East Journal*, 35, 3 (Summer 1981), pp. 331–44.

——— 'Syria's Muslim Brethren', *MERIP Reports*, 110, Syria's Troubles (Nov.–Dec. 1982), pp. 12–20, 34, 36.

——— *Syria's Peasantry: The Descendants of its Lesser Rural Notables and their Politics*, Princeton: Princeton University Press, 1999.

Be'eri, Eliezer, *Army Officers in Arab Politics and Society*, New York: Praeger Publishers, 1969.

Bengio, Ofra, and Gabriel Ben-Dor (eds), *Minorities and the State in the Arab World*, Boulder: Lynne Rienner, 1999.

Berkey, J.P., *The Formation Of Islam: Religion and Society in the Near East, 600–1800*, Cambridge: Cambridge University Press, 2003.

Biddle, S. and J.A. Friedman, *The 2006 Lebanon Campaign and the Future of Warfare: Implications for Army and Defense Policy*, Carlisle, PA: Strategic Studies Institute, 2008.

Boneschi, Paulo, "Une fatwà du Grande Mufti de Jérusalem Muhammad Amin al-Husayni sur les Alawites," *Revue de l'histoire des religions* 122(1), July–August 1940, pp. 42–54.

Bou-Nacklie, N.E., 'The 1941 Invasion of Syria and Lebanon: The Role of the Local Paramilitary', *Middle Eastern Studies*, 30, 3 (July 1994).

——— 'Les Troupes Spéciales: Religious and Ethnic Recruitment, 1916–46', *International Journal of Middle East Studies*, 25, 4 (1993), pp. 545–660.

Bosworth, Clifford E., *Encyclopaedia of Islam*, Supplement, vol. 12, Leiden: Brill, 1980.

Browning, Robert, *The Byzantine Empire*, Washington, DC: The Catholic University of America Press, 1992.

Cardinal, Monique C., 'Religious Education in Syria: Unity and Difference', *British Journal of Religious Education*, 31, 2 (Mar. 2009), pp. 91–101.

BIBLIOGRAPHY

Chalcroft, John, *The Invisible Cage: Syrian Migrant Workers in Lebanon*, Stanford: Stanford University Press, 2009.

Chouet, Alain, 'L'Espace Tribal Des Alaouites à l'Epreuve du Pouvoir: La disintegration par le politiques', *Maghreb-Mashreq*, 147 (1995).

Cohen, S.B., *Geopolitics: The Geography of International Relations*, 2nd edn, Lanham: Rowman & Littlefield Publishers, 2009.

Cox, K.R., M. Low and J. Robinson (eds), *The Sage Handbook of Political Geography*, London: Sage Publications, 2008.

Daalder, Ivo H. and James G. Stavridis, 'NATO's Victory in Libya', *Foreign Affairs*, 91, 2 (Mar./Apr. 2012).

Davis, Eric, 'Pensée 3: A Sectarian Middle East?' *International Journal of Middle East Studies*, 40, 4 (Nov. 2008), pp. 555–8.

De Planhol, Xavier, *Minorités En Islam, Géographie Politique et Sociale*, Paris: Flammarion, 1997.

———— *The World of Islam*, Ithaca, NY: Cornell University Press, 1959.

Dhillon, Navtej and Tarik Yousef (eds), *Generation in Waiting: The Unfulfilled Promise of Young People in the Middle East*, Washington, DC: Brookings Institution, 2009.

Dib, Kamal, *Warlords and Merchants: The Lebanese Business and Political Establishment*, Reading: Ithaca, 2004.

Doğruel, Fulya and Johan Leman, 'Conduct and Counter-conduct on the Southern Border of Turkey: Multicultural Antakya', *Middle Eastern Studies*, 45, 4 (July 2009), pp. 593–610.

Dostal, Jörg Michael, 'The European Union and Economic Reform in Syria', in R. Hinnebusch (ed.), *Syria and the Euro-Mediterranean Relationship*, Fife: University of St Andrews Centre for Syrian Studies, 2009.

Douwes, Dick, *The Ottomans in Syria: A History of Justice and Oppression*, London: I.B. Tauris, 2000.

Drysdale, Alasdair, 'The Asad Regime and Its Troubles', *MERIP Reports*, 110, Syria's Troubles (Nov.–Dec. 1982), pp. 3–11, 36.

———— 'The Syrian Political Elite, 1966–76: A Spatial and Social Analysis', *Middle Eastern Studies*, 17, 1 (1981), pp. 3–31.

Dueck, Jennifer M., *Educational Conquest: Schools as a Sphere of Politics in French Mandate Syria, 1936–1946*, Oxford: Oxford University Press, 2006.

Dussaud, Rene, *Histoire et Religion des Nosairies*, Paris: Bouillon, 1900.

Eid, Abdulrazak, 'The Syrian Regime: The Impossibility of Reformation', Paper Presented at the Hudson Institute, Washington, DC, 26 Mar. 2009.

Eisner, Elliot W., *The Enlightened Eye: Qualitative Inquiry and the Enhancement of Educational Practice*, Upper Saddle River, NJ: Prentice Hall, 1998.

Emadi, H., *Politics of the Dispossessed: Superpowers and Developments in the Middle East*, Westport: Praeger, 2001.

Faksh, Mahmud A., 'The Alawi Community of Syria: A New Dominant Political Force', *Middle Eastern Studies*, 20, 2 (Apr. 1984), pp. 133–53.

BIBLIOGRAPHY

Fearon, James, Kimuli Kasara and David Laitin, 'Ethnic Minority Rule and Civil War Onset', *American Political Science Review*, 101, 1 (Feb. 2007).

Fetcher, Rev. J.P., *Notes from Nineveh, and Travels in Mesopotamia, Assyria, and Syria*, Philadelphia: Lea & Blanchard, 1850.

Firro, Kais M., 'The ʿAlawīs in Modern Syria: From Nusayrīya to Islam via ʿAlawīya', *Der Islam*, 82, 1 (2005), pp. 1–31.

Fox, J., 'Is Islam More Conflict Prone than Other Religions? A Cross-Sectional Study of Ethnoreligious Conflict', *Nationalism & Ethnic Politics*, 6, 2 (Summer 2000), pp. 1–24.

Frank, R.H. and B.S. Bernanke (eds), *Principles of Economics*, 3rd edn, New York: McGraw-Hill Irwin, 2007.

Freitag, Ulrike, 'Historical Correctness: The Baʾth Party in Syria', *Middle Eastern Studies*, 35, 1 (Jan. 1999), pp. 1–16.

Friedman, Yaron, 'Ibn Taymiyyaʾs Fatwa against the Nusayri-Alawi Sect', *Der Islam*, 82, 2 (2005).

——— 'Al-Husayn Ibn Hamdan al-Khasibi: A Historical Biography of the Nusayri-Alawite Sect,' *Studia Islamica*, 93, (2001), pp. 97–8.

——— *The Nusayrī—ʿAlawīs: An Introduction to the Religion, History and Identity of the Leading Minority in Syria*, Leiden: Brill, 2010.

Fromherz, Allen, *Ibn Khaldun, Life and Times*, Edinburgh: Edinburgh University Press, 2010.

Gambill, Gary C., 'The Mysterious Downfall of Assef Shawkat', *Mideast Monitor*, 3, 2 (Aug. 2008).

Gauthier, Julie, 'The 2004 Events in al-Qamishli: Has the Kurdish question Erupted in Syria?' in Fred Lawson (ed.), *Demystifying Syria*, London: Saqi, 2009.

Gellner, E., *Nations and Nationalism*, Oxford: Basil Blackwell, 1983.

George, Alan, *Syria: Neither Bread Nor Freedom*, London and New York: Zed Books, 2003.

Ghadban, Najib, Book Review, *Journal of Arab Affairs*, 10, 2 (31 Oct. 1991).

Ghadry, Farid, 'Syrian Reform: What Lies Beneath', *Middle East Quarterly* (Winter 2005), pp. 61–70.

Goodarzi, Jubin M., *Syria and Iran: Diplomatic Alliance and Power Politics in the Middle East*, London and New York: Tauris, 2006.

Gotlieb, Y., *Self-Determination in the Middle East*, New York: Praeger, 1982.

Hall, J.A. and F. Trentmann (eds), *Civil Society: A Reader in History, Theory and Global Politics*, Basingstoke: Palgrave Macmillan, 2005.

Halliday, F., *Nation and Religion in the Middle East*, Boulder: Lynne Rienner Publishers, 2000

Halm, Heinz, *The Arabs, A Short History*, trans. A. Brown and T. Lampert, Princeton: Markus Wiener, 2007.

Harik, Iliya F., 'The Ethnic Revolution and Political Integration in the Middle East', *International Journal of Middle East Studies*, 3, 3 (July 1972), pp. 303–23.

Harris, William, 'Crisis in the Levant: Lebanon at Risk', *Mediterranean Quarterly*, 18, 2 (16 Aug. 2007), pp. 37–60.

——— *Lebanon: A History, 600–2011*,'New York: Oxford University Press, 2012.

——— *The Levant, A Fractured Mosaic*, Princeton: Markus Wiener, 2003.

BIBLIOGRAPHY

Haugbolle, S., 'Imprisonment, Truth Telling and Historical Memory in Syria', *Mediterranean Politics*, 13, 2 (July 2008), pp. 261–76.

Held, Colbert *Middle East Patterns: Places, Peoples, and Politics*, Third Edition, Boulder: Westview Press, 2000.

Held, David, *Cosmopolitanism: Ideals and Realities*, Cambridge: Polity Press, 2010.

Helfont, Samuel, 'The Muslim Brotherhood and the Emerging "Shia Crescent"', *Orbis*, 53, 2 (Spring 2009), pp. 284–99.

Hinnebusch, Raymond, *Authoritarian Power and State Formation in Ba'athist Syria: Army, Party, and Peasant*, Boulder: Westview, 1990.

Hinnebusch, Raymond and Neil Quilliam, 'Contrary Siblings: Syria, Jordan and the Iraq War', *Cambridge Review of International Affairs*, 19, 3 (Sep. 2006), pp. 513–28.

Horowitz, Donald L., *Ethnic Groups in Conflict*, Berkeley: University of California Press, 1985.

Hourani, Albert, *The Emergence of the Modern Middle East*, London: Macmillan, 1981.

———— 'Islam and the Philosophers of History', *Middle Eastern Studies*, 3, 3 (Apr. 1967), pp. 206–68.

———— 'Middle Eastern Studies Today', *Bulletin (British Society for Middle Eastern Studies)*, 11, 2 (1984), pp. 111–20.

———— *Syria and Lebanon: A Political Essay*, London: Oxford University Press, 1946.

Ilsley, Omar, 'Syria: Hama Massacre', in A. Heribert (ed.), *Hushed Voices: Unacknowledged Atrocities of the 20th Century*, Highclere: Berkshire Academic Press, 2011.

Imber, Colin, *The Ottoman Empire 1300–1650: The Structure of Power*, Basingstoke: Palgrave MacMillan, 2002.

Irwin, Robert, 'Toynbee and Ibn Khaldun', *Middle Eastern Studies*, 33, 3 (July 1997), pp. 461–79.

Iskandar, Marwan, *Rafiq Hariri and the Fate of Lebanon*, London: Saqi, 2006.

Jabar, F.A. and H. Dawood (eds), *Tribes and Power: Nationalism and Ethnicity in the Middle East*, London: Saqi, 2003.

Jenkins, Philip, *The Lost History of Christianity*, New York: HarperCollins, 2008.

Jessup, Reverend Henry H., *Fifty Three Years in Syria*, London: Fleming H. Revell, 1910.

Kanovsky, Eliyahu, 'Will Arab–Israel Peace Bring Prosperity?' *The Middle East Quarterly*, 1, 2 (June 1994).

Kaplan, Robert, 'The Revenge of Geography', *Foreign Policy* (May/June 2009).

Kaylani, Nabil M., 'The Rise of the Syrian Ba'th, 1940–1958: Political Success, Party Failure', *International Journal of Middle East Studies*, 3, 1 (Jan. 1972), pp. 3–23.

Kedar, Mordechai, *Asad in Search of Legitimacy: Message and Rhetoric in the Syrian Press under Hafiz and Bashar*, Brighton: Sussex University Press, 2005.

Kerr, Malcolm, 'Hafiz Asad and the Changing Patterns of Syrian Politics', *International Journal*, 28, 3 (Summer 1973), pp. 689–706.

Khaldun, Ibn, *The Muqaddimah: An Introduction to History*, trans. F. Rosenthal, abr. N.J. Dawood, London: Routledge & Kegan Paul, 1967.

BIBLIOGRAPHY

Khandil, Hazem, 'The Challenge of Restructuring: Syrian Foreign Policy', in B. Korany and A.E.H. Dessoukip (eds), *The Foreign Policies of Arab States*, Cairo: AUC Press, 2009.

Al-Khazen, Farid, 'Kamal Jumblatt, the Uncrowned Druze Prince of the Left', *Middle Eastern Studies*, 24, 2 (Apr. 1988), pp. 178–205.

Khoury, Philip, *Syria and the French Mandate: The Politics of Arab Nationalism, 1920–1945*, London: I.B. Tauris, 1987.

Khuri, Fuad, *Imams and Emirs: State, Religion and Sects in Islam*, London: Saqi Books, 1990.

Lacoste, Yves, *Ibn Khaldun: The Birth of History and the Past of Third World*, London: Verso, 1984.

Lawson, Fred (ed.), *Demystifying Syria*, London: Saqi, 2009.

Lefèvre, Raphaël, *Ashes of Hama: The Muslim Brotherhood in Syria*, London: Hurst, 2013.

Lesch, David, *The New Lion of Damascus: Bashar al-Asad and Modern Syria*, New Haven: Yale University Press, 2005.

———— 'Syrian Arab Republic', in D.E. Long, B. Reich and M. Gasiorowski (eds), *The Government and Politics of the Middle East and North Africa*, 5th edn, Boulder: Westview Press, 2007, pp. 259–91.

Leverett, Flynt, *Inheriting Syria: Bashar's Trial by Fire*, Washington, DC: Brookings Institute Press, 2005.

Lijphart, Arend, *Thinking about Democracy*, Oxon: Routledge, 2008.

Longrigg, Stephen H., *Syria and Lebanon under French Mandate*, London: Oxford University Press, 1958.

Lyde, Rev. Samuel, *The Asian Mystery Illustrated in the History, Religion, and Present State of the Ansaireeh or Nusairis of Syria*, London: Longman, Green, Longman and Roberts, 1860.

Mahdi, Muhsin, *Ibn Khaldun's Philosophy of History*, London: Allen & Unwin, 1957.

Mahfouda, Robert F. and James N. Beck, 'Petrographic/Geochemical Studies of Primary and Alteration-Weathering Minerals in Garnetiferous Ultramafic Xenoliths–Basanite, Tartous Province, NW Syria', *Microchemical Journal*, 78 (2004), pp. 115–26.

Maoz, Moshe, *Syria and Israel: From War to Peace-Making*, New York: Oxford University Press, 1995.

Maoz, Moshe and Ilan Pappe (eds), *Middle Eastern Politics and Ideas: A History from Within*, London: Tauris, 1997.

Mardem-Bey, S., *Syria's Quest for Independence 1939–1945*, Beirut: Ithaca, 1994.

Martin, Kevin W., 'Peasants into Syrians', *International Journal of Middle East Studies*, 41 (2009).

Martines, Lauro, *April Blood: Florence and the Plot against the Medici*, London: Pimlico, 2004.

Masters, B., *Christians and Jews in the Ottoman Arab World, the Roots of Sectarianism*, Cambridge: Cambridge University Press, 2001.

Maundrell, Henry, *A Journey from Aleppo to Jerusalem in 1697*, Beirut: Kyats, 1963.

Mclaurin, R.D. (ed.), *The Political Role of Minority Groups in The Middle East*, New York: Praeger, 1979.

Melander, Erik, 'The Geography of Fear: Regional Ethnic Diversity, the Security Dilemma and Ethnic War', *European Journal of International Relations*, 15, 95 (2009).

BIBLIOGRAPHY

Melki, James A., 'Syria and State Department 1937–47', *Middle Eastern Studies*, 33, 1 (Jan. 1997), pp. 92–106.

Messier, Ronald A., 'The Worlds of Ibn Khaldun: Introduction', *The Journal of North African Studies*, 13, 3 (Sep. 2009).

Michaud, G. and J. Paul, 'The Importance of Bodyguards', *MERIP Reports*, 110, Syria's Troubles (Nov.–Dec. 1982), pp. 29–33.

Migdal, Joel S. (ed.), *Boundaries and Belonging: States and Societies in the Struggle to Shape Identities and Local Practices*, Cambridge: Cambridge University Press, 2004.

Moosa, Matti, *Extremist Shiites: the Ghulat Sects*, New York: Syracuse University Press, 1988.

Murphy, Rhoads, *Studies on Ottoman Society and Culture, 16th–18th Centuries*, Aldershot: Ashgate, 2007.

Nordbruch, Götz, *Nazism in Syria and Lebanon*, Oxon: Routledge, 2009.

Olsson, Tord, 'The Gnosis of Mountaineers and Townspeople: The Religion of the Syrian Alawites, or the Nusairis', in T. Olsson, E. Ozdalga and C. Raudvere (eds), *Alevi Identity: Cultural, Religious and Social Perspectives*, Papers read at a conference Held at the Swedish Institute in Istanbul, Nov. 1996, Swedish Research Institute in Istanbul Transactions, vol. 8, 1998.

Pain, R. and S.J. Smith (eds), *Fear: Geopolitics and Everyday Life*, Aldershot: Ashgate, 2008.

Perlmutter, Amos, 'From Obscurity to Rule: The Syrian Army and the Ba'th Party', *The Western Political Quarterly*, 22, 4 (Dec. 1969), pp. 827–45.

Perthes, Volker, *The Political Economy of Syria under Asad*, London: I.B. Tauris, 1995.

——— 'Syria under Bashar al-Asad: Modernisation and the Limits of Change', Adelphi Papers, 44, 366 (2004).

Perthes, Volker (ed.), *Arab Elites: Negotiating the Politics of Change*, Boulder: Lynne Rienner, 2004.

Philip, T. and C. Schumann (eds), *From the Syrian Land to the States of Syria and Lebanon*, Beirut: Orient-Institute, 2004.

Piguet, E. and F. Laczko (eds), *People on the Move in a Changing Climate*, Global Migration Issues, 2, Dordrecht: Springer Science and Business Media, 2014.

Pipes, Daniel, 'The Alawi Capture of Power in Syria', *Middle Eastern Studies*, 25, 4 (Oct. 1989), pp. 429–50.

——— *Greater Syria: The History of an Ambition*, New York: Oxford University Press, 1990.

Porat, Liad, 'The Syrian Muslim Brotherhood and the Asad Regime', *Middle East Brief*, 47 (Dec. 2010).

Posen, Barry, 'The Security Dilemma and Ethnic Conflict', in M. Brown (ed.), *Ethnic Conflict and International Security*, Princeton: Princeton University Press, 1993.

Prochazka-Eisl, G. and S. Prozchazka, *The Plain of Saints and Prophets: The Nusayri-Alawi Community of Cilicia (Southern Turkey) and its Sacred Places*, Wiesbaden: Harrassowitz Verlag, 2010.

Qaddour, Jomana, 'Unlocking the Alawite Coundrum in Syria', *Washington Quarterly*, 36, 4 (2013), pp. 67–78.

BIBLIOGRAPHY

Quinlivan, James T., 'Coup-Proofing: Its Practice and Consequences in the Middle East', *International Security*, 24, 2 (Autumn 1999), pp. 131–65.

Rabinovich, Itamar, *Syria under the Ba'th, 1963–66: The Army–Party Symbiosis*, Jerusalem: Israel Universities Press, 1972.

——— *The View from Damascus*, Edgware and Portland: Valentine Mitchell, 2008.

Rain, David, 'Damascus: A Geographical Field Note',' *Geographical Review*, 99, 1 (Jan. 2009).

Raphael, Sarah K., *Climate and Political Climate: Environmental Disasters in the Medieval Levant*, Leiden: Brill, 2013.

Reed, Stanley F. III, 'Syria: Fin de Régime?' *Foreign Policy*, 39 (Summer 1980), pp. 176–90.

Reeva, Simon et al., *The Jews of the Middle East and North Africa in Modern Times*, New York: Columbia University Press, 2003.

Rivlin, Paul, *Arab Economies in the Twenty-First Century*, New York: Cambridge University Press, 2009.

——— 'The Socio-Economic Crisis in Syria', *Iqtisadi*, 1, 3 (June 2011), pp. 2–7.

Rubin, Barry (ed.), *Conflict and Insurgency in the Contemporary Middle East*, New York: Routledge, 2009.

Russell, B., *History of Western Philosophy*, London: Unwin University Books, 1946.

Russell, J.C., 'Late Medieval Balkan and Asia Minor Population', *Journal of the Economic and Social History of the Orient*, 3, 3 (1960).

Salamandra, Christa, 'Consuming Damascus: Public Culture and the Construction of Social Identity', in W. Armbrust (ed.), *Mass Mediations, New Approaches to Popular Culture in the Middle East and Beyond*, Berkeley: University of California Press, 2000, pp. 182–202.

——— 'Sectarianism in Syria: Anthropological Reflections', *Middle East Critique*, 22, 3 (Oct. 2013), pp. 305–6.

Salame, Ghassan, '"Strong" and "Weak" States: A Qualified Return to the Muqaddimah', in Ghassan Salame (ed.), *The Foundations of the Arab State*, vol. 1, New York: Croom Helm, 1987.

Salameh, Franck, 'Adonis, the Syrian Crisis, and the Question of Pluralism in the Levant', *Bustan: The Middle East Book Review*, 3 (2012), pp. 36–61.

Salih, Shakeeb, 'The British–Druze Connection and the Druze Rising of 1896 in the Hawran', *Middle East Studies*, 13, 2 (May 1977), pp. 251–7.

Salisbury, Edward E., 'First Ripe Fruit, Disclosing the Mysteries of the Nusairian Religion', *Journal of the American Oriental Society*, 8 (1866), pp. 227–308.

Salzman, Philip C., *Culture and Conflict in the Middle East*, New York: Humanity Books, 2008.

Satloff, Robert, 'U.S.–Syria Relations and the Peace Process', Prepared remarks for delivery at debate with Syrian Ambassador Imad Mustapha, American University, 11 Nov. 2009, Washington Institute for Near East Policy.

Schmidt, Soren, 'The Developmental Role of the State in the Middle East: Lessons from Syria', in R. Hinnebusch (ed.), *The State and the Political Economy of Reform in Syria*, Fife: University of St Andrews Centre for Syrian Studies, 2009.

BIBLIOGRAPHY

——— 'The Politics of Economic Liberalization in Syria', *International Development Studies Occasional Paper*, 25 (2006).

Seale, Patrick, *Asad of Syria: The Struggle for the Middle East*, London: I.B. Tauris, 1988.

Selvik, Kjetil, 'It's the Mentality Stupid: Syria's Turn to the Private Sector', in R. Hinnebusch (ed.), *Changing Regime Discourse and Reform in Syria*, Fife: University of St Andrews Centre for Syrian Studies, 2009.

Seurat, Michel, *Syrie: L'État De Barbarie*, Paris: Presses Universitaires de France, 2012.

Seymour, Martin, 'The Dynamics of Power in Syria since the Break with Egypt', *Middle Eastern Studies*, 6, 1 (Jan. 1970), pp. 35–47.

Shambrook, Peter, *French Imperialism in Syria, 1927–1936*, Reading: Ithaca, 1998.

Sharp, Jeremy M., 'Syria: Background and U.S. Relations', Congressional Research Service, 11 Mar. 2009.

Shaw, S.J. *History of the Ottoman Empire and Modern Turkey*, Cambridge: Cambridge University Press, 1977.

Shaw, S.J. and Shaw, E.K., *History of the Ottoman Empire and Modern Turkey*, vol. II, Cambridge: Cambridge University Press, 1977.

Sheehan, Edward R.F., 'How Kissinger Did It: Step by Step in the Middle East', *Foreign Policy*, 22 (Spring 1976), pp. 3–70.

Simpfendorfer, Ben, *The New Silk Road*, 2nd edn, Basingstoke: Palgrave Macmillan, 2009.

Sindawi, Khalid, 'The Shiite Turn in Syria', *Current Trends in Islamist Ideology*, 8 (23 June 2009).

Slater, David, 'Editorial', *Political Geography*, 23 (2004), pp. 645–6.

Smith, L.V., 'Wilsonian Sovereignty in the Middle East: The King–Crane Commission Report of 1919', in D. Howland and L. White, *The State of Sovereignty*, Bloomington: Indiana University Press, 2009.

Smith-Williams, H. (ed.), *Historians' History of the World*, 25 vols, London: The Times, 1909.

Sottimano, Aurora, 'Ideology and Discourse in the Era of Ba'thist Reforms: Towards an Analysis of Authoritarian Governmentality', in R. Hinnebusch (ed.), *Changing Regime Discourse and Reform in Syria*, Fife: University of St Andrews Centre for Syrian Studies, 2009.

Staniland, Paul, 'Explaining Civil–Military Relations in Complex Political Environments: India and Pakistan in Comparative Perspective', *Security Studies*, 17 (2008), pp. 322–62.

Stewart, Devin J., 'The *Maqāmāt* of Ahmad b. Abī Bakr b. Ahmad al-Rāzī al-Hanafī and the Ideology of the Counter-Crusade in Twelfth-century Syria', *Middle Eastern Literatures*, 11, 2 (Aug. 2008).

Sullivan, Antony T., 'War and Rumors of War: The Levantine Tinderbox', *Middle East Policy*, XV, 1 (Spring 2008).

Talhamy, Yvette, 'American Protestant Missionary Activity among the Nusayris (Alawis) in Syria in the Nineteenth Century', *Middle Eastern Studies*, 47, 2 (2011), pp. 215–36.

——— 'The Fatwas and the Nusayri/Alawis of Syria', *Middle Eastern Studies*, 46, 2 (2010), pp. 175–94.

BIBLIOGRAPHY

————— 'The Nusayri and Druze Minorities in Syria in the Nineteenth Century: The Revolt against the Egyptian Occupation as a Case Study', *Middle Eastern Studies*, 48, 6 (Nov. 2012), pp. 973–95.

————— 'The Nusayri Leader Isma'il Khayr Bey and the Ottomans (1854–58)', *Middle Eastern Studies*, 44, 6 (Nov. 2008), pp. 895–908.

————— 'The Syrian Muslim Brothers and the Syrian–Iranian Relationship', *Middle East Journal*, 63, 4 (2009).

Tang, Shiping, 'The Security Dilemma and Ethnic Conflict: Toward a Dynamic and Integrative Theory of Ethnic Conflict', *Review of International Studies*, 37 (2011).

Tejel, Jordi, *Syria's Kurds: History Politics and Society*, Oxon: Routledge, 2009.

Telhami, S. and M. Barnett (eds), *Identity and Foreign Policy in The Middle East*, London: Cornell University Press, 2002.

Thomas, David R., 'A General Inductive Approach for Analyzing Qualitative Evaluation Data', *American Journal of Evaluation*, 27, 1 (Mar. 2006).

Thomas, Martin, 'Crisis Management in Colonial States: Intelligence and Counter-Insurgency in Morocco and Syria after the First World War', *Intelligence and National Security*, 21, 5 (2006), pp. 697–716.

————— *Empires of Intelligence: Security Services and Colonial Disorder after 1914*, Berkeley: University of California Press, 2008.

Torrey, Gordon H., 'The Ba'th: Ideology and Practice', *Middle East Journal*, 23, 4 (Autumn 1969), pp. 445–70.

Trentin, Massimiliano, 'Modernization as State Building: The Two Germanies in Syria, 1963–1972', *Diplomatic History*, 33, 3 (June 2009).

Tsugitaka, Sato, *State & Rural Society in Medieval Islam*, Leiden: Brill, 1997.

US State Department, Bureau of Democracy, Human Rights, and Labor, 'International Religious Freedom Report 2009', 26 Oct. 2009.

Van Dam, Nikolaos, *The Struggle for Power in Syria*, New York: St Martin's Press, 1979.

————— *The Struggle for Power in Syria*, 2nd edn, London: I.B Tauris, 1996.

————— *The Struggle for Power in Syria: Politics and Society under Asad and the Ba'th Party*, 4th edn, New York: I.B. Tauris, 2011.

Van Dusen, Michael H., 'Political Integration and Regionalism in Syria', *Middle East Journal*, 26, 2 (Spring 1972), pp. 123–36.

Waines, David, 'The Third Century Internal Crisis of the Abbasids', *Journal of the Economic and Social History of the Orient*, 20, 3 (Oct. 1977), pp. 282–306.

Walpole, Lieutenant F., *The Ansayrii (or Assassins) with Travels in the Further East in 1850–51*, London: Richard Bentley, 1851.

Watenpaugh, Keith, *Being Modern in the Middle East: Revolution, Nationalism, Colonialism and the Arab Middle Class*, Princeton: Princeton University Press, 2006.

————— '"Creating Phantoms": Zaki al-Arzuzi, the Alexandretta Crisis, and the Formation of Modern Arab Nationalism in Syria', *International Journal of Middle East Studies*, 28 (1996).

Wedeen, Lisa, *Ambiguities of Domination: Politics, Rhetoric and Symbols in Contemporary Syria*, Chicago: Chicago University Press, 1999.

BIBLIOGRAPHY

Weinberger, Naomi, *Syrian Intervention in Lebanon*, New York: Oxford University Press, 1986.

Weismann, Itzchak, 'Sa'id Hawwa: The Making of a Radical Muslim Thinker in Modern Syria', *Middle Eastern Studies*, 29, 4 (Oct. 1993), pp. 601–23.

Weulersse, Jacque, *Le pays des Alaouites*, Tours: Arrault & Cie, Maitres imprimeurs, 1940.

Wiederhold, Lutz, 'Blasphemy against the Prophet Muhammad and His Companions (Sabb al-Rasūl, Sabb al-Sahābah): The Introduction of the Topic into Shāfi 'ī Legal Literature and its Relevance for Legal Practice under Mamluk Rule*', *Journal of Semitic Studies*, XLII, 1 (Spring 1997).

Wieland, C., *Syria at Bay: Secularism, Islamism, and Pax Americana*, London: Hurst, 2006.

——— *Syria, a Decade of Lost Chances: Repression and Revolution from Damascus Spring to Arab Spring*, Seattle: Cune Press, 2012.

Wimmer, A., L.E. Cederman and B. Min, 'Ethnic Politics and Armed Conflict: A Configurational Analysis of a New Global Data Set', *American Sociological Review*, 74 (Apr. 2009), pp. 316–37.

Winter, Stefan, 'The Nusayris before the Tanzimat in the Eyes of Ottoman Provincial Administrators 1804–1834', in T. Philip and C. Schumann (eds), *From the Syrian Land to the States of Syria and Lebanon*, Beirut: Orient-Institute, 2004.

——— *The Shiites of Lebanon under Ottoman Rule, 1516–1788*, Cambridge: Cambridge University Press, 2010.

Winckler, Onn, *Arab Political Demography: Population Growth, Labor Migration and Natalist Policies*, 2nd edn, Eastbourne: Sussex Academic Press, 2009.

Winckler, Onn, *Demographic Developments and Population Policies in Ba'thist Syria*, Brighton and Portland: Sussex Academic Press, 1999.

Worren, Torstein Schiøtz, 'Fear and Resistance: The Construction of Alawi Identity in Syria', Master's Thesis, Department of Sociology and Human Geography, University of Oslo, Feb. 2007.

Yaffe, Gitta and Uriel Dann, 'Suleiman al-Murshid: Beginnings of an Alawi Leader', *Middle Eastern Studies*, 29, 4 (Oct. 1993), pp. 624–40.

Yaffe-Schatzmann, Gitta, 'Alawi Separatists and Unionists: The Events of 25 February 1936', *Middle Eastern Studies*, 31, 1 (Jan. 1995), pp. 28–38.

Ziadeh, Radwan, *Power and Policy in Syria: The Intelligence Services, Foreign Relations and Democracy in the Modern Middle East*, London: I.B. Tauris, 2011.

Zisser, Eyal, *Asad's Legacy: Syria in Transition*, London: Hurst, 2001.

——— 'The Syrian Army: Between the Domestic and the External Fronts', *MERIA Journal*, 5, 1 (Mar. 2001).

——— 'Who's Afraid of Syrian Nationalism? National and State Identity in Syria', *Middle Eastern Studies*, 42, 2 (Mar. 2006), pp. 179–98.

Zorob, Anja, 'Trade Liberalization and Adjustment via Regional Integration: The Syrian–European Association Agreement', in R. Hinnebusch (ed.), *Syria and the Euro-Mediterranean Relationship*, Fife: University of St Andrews Centre for Syrian Studies, 2009.

INDEX

INDEX

INDEX